Macroeconomics: An Introduction
to the Non-Walrasian Approach

This is a volume in
ECONOMIC THEORY, ECONOMETRICS, AND MATHEMATICAL
ECONOMICS

A Series of Monographs and Textbooks

Consulting Editor: Karl Shell

A complete listing of titles in this series is available from the Publisher upon request.

Macroeconomics: An Introduction to the Non-Walrasian Approach

Jean-Pascal Benassy

Centre National de la Recherche Scientifique
Centre d'Etudes Prospectives d'Economie Mathématique
Appliquées à la Planification
and
Ecole Normale Supérieure
Paris, France

1986

ACADEMIC PRESS, INC.
Harcourt Brace Jovanovich, Publishers
Orlando   San Diego   New York   Austin
London   Montreal   Sydney   Tokyo   Toronto

ACADEMIC PRESS, INC.
Orlando, Florida 32887

United Kingdom Edition published by
ACADEMIC PRESS INC. (LONDON) LTD.
24–28 Oval Road, London NW1 7DX

Library of Congress Cataloging in Publication Data

Benassy, Jean-Pascal.
    Macroeconomics : an introduction to the non-Walrasian
approach.

    (Economic theory, econometrics, and mathematical
economics)
    Bibliography: p.
    Includes index.
    1. Macroeconomics.   2. Microeconomics.   I. Title.
II. Series.
HB172.5.B45   1986   339   85-20156
ISBN 0–12–086425–8 (hardcover) (alk. paper)
ISBN 0–12–086426–6 (paperback) (alk. paper)

PRINTED IN THE UNITED STATES OF AMERICA

86 87 88 89   9 8 7 6 5 4 3 2 1

To my Parents

Contents

Preface   xiii

Introduction   1

Part I   MICROECONOMIC FOUNDATIONS

Chapter 1   **The Basic Concepts**

1. Walrasian Economics and the Problem of Market Clearing   9
2. The Institutional Framework   14
3. Functioning of Nonclearing Markets and Quantity Signals   16
4. Effective Demand   21
5. Non-Walrasian Equilibrium: An Example   25
6. The Role of Expectations   27
7. The Formation of Prices   29
8. Conclusions   33
   References   34

Chapter 2   **Non-Walrasian Equilibria**

1. Introduction   35
2. Institutional Framework   36
3. Rationing Schemes and Quantity Signals   37
4. Effective Demand   42
5. Fixprice Equilibria   45

6. Expectations and Temporary Equilibrium with Rigid Prices   48
7. K-Equilibrium with Bounded Prices   52
8. K-Equilibrium with Monopolistic Competition   53
9. Conclusions   56
   References   56

Part II CLOSED-ECONOMY MODELS

Chapter 3 Theories of Unemployment

1. Classical and Keynesian Theories of Unemployment   61
2. The Model   64
3. Temporary Walrasian Equilibrium and Situations of Unemployment   66
4. The Three Regimes   68
5. A Global Analysis   73
6. Conclusions   76
   References   77

Chapter 4 Asymmetric Price Flexibility and the Effectiveness of Employment Policies

1. Introduction   78
2. The Three Regimes   79
3. A Dynamic View   86
4. A Graphical Solution   85
5. Conclusions   90
   References   90

Chapter 5 Indexation and Employment Policies

1. Introduction   91
2. The Three Regimes   93
3. A Graphical Solution   96
4. A Particular Case: Rigid Real Wage   99
5. Conclusions   101
   References   102

Chapter 6 The Three Regimes of the IS-LM Model

1. Introduction   103
2. The Model   105
3. The Core Equations and IS-LM   107
4. The Three Regimes   110

5. A Graphical Solution   117
6. The IS-LM Model with a Rigid Real Wage   118
7. Conclusions   119
   References   120

PART III   OPEN-ECONOMY MODELS

Chapter 7   **Economic Policies in an Open Economy**

1. Introduction   123
2. The Model   123
3. International Equilibrium   124
4. Flexible Exchange Rates   126
5. Fixed Exchange Rates   127
6. Conclusions   131
   References   131

Chapter 8   **The Balance of Payments**

1. Introduction   132
2. The Model   132
3. Determination of Incomes and Prices in the Different Regimes   133
4. The Balance of Payments and the Three Traditional Approaches   136
5. The Effects of a Devaluation   137
6. Conclusions   140
   References   141

Part IV   DYNAMIC MODELS

Chapter 9   **Theories of Inflation**

1. Demand and Cost Inflation   145
2. The Model   145
3. Temporary Equilibrium and Dynamics   147
4. Demand Inflation   150
5. Cost Inflation   152
6. Steady States   156
7. Conclusions   161
   References   162

Chapter 10 Phillips Curves, Conflicts, and Expectations

1. Introduction   163
2. The Model   164
3. The Short Run: Equilibrium and the Phillips Curve   166
4. Steady States and the Unemployment–Inflation Dilemma   168
5. Conclusions   171
   References   172

Chapter 11 A Model of the Business Cycle

1. Introduction   173
2. The Model   174
3. Short-Run Equilibrium   176
4. Dynamics and Long-Run Equilibrium   179
5. Stability of the Long-Run Equilibrium   181
6. Existence of Cycles   182
7. Conclusions   184
   References   185

Part V EXPECTATIONS

Chapter 12 The Role of Expectations

1. Introduction   189
2. The Model   190
3. The Structure of Equilibria   191
4. The Effects of Economic Policies and Expectations   192
5. Global Analysis   195
6. Conclusions   197
   References   198

Chapter 13 Non-Walrasian Prices and Perfect Foresight

1. Introduction   199
2. The Model   200
3. The Consumption Function   201
4. The Intertemporal Walrasian Equilibrium   202
5. The Structure of Non-Walrasian Equilibria   203
6. The Effects of Economic Policies   203
7. Expectations of Government Policy   207
8. Conclusions   208
   References   208

Chapter 14 Expectations, Information, and Dynamics

1. Introduction   209
2. The Model   210
3. A Stationary Intertemporal Equilibrium   211
4. A Temporary Deflationary Shock   212
5. An Interpretation   213
6. Conclusions   215
   References   216

APPENDIXES

Appendix A **Existence Theorems**   219

Appendix B **Manipulation**   225

Appendix C **Effective Demand under Uncertainty**   230

Appendix D **The Effects of a Devaluation**   235

Bibliography   237

Index   249

Preface

This book develops a new approach to macroeconomic theory based on the non-Walrasian method. Non-Walrasian theory has developed particularly in recent years in both its microeconomic and macroeconomic aspects. It allows us to describe rigorously states of the economy for which, in the absence of a "Walrasian auctioneer," demand and supply do not match on all markets and thus to give solid microeconomic foundations to numerous elements of macroeconomics involving demand–supply imbalances, such as involuntary unemployment.

The study of the microeconomic concepts of such a theory has been the main object of a previous volume (Benassy, 1982b). The purpose of this book is to show that these concepts can be applied in a simple and relevant manner to the traditional topics of macroeconomic theory. Therefore, after a simple and self-contained presentation of the basic microeconomics, specific models are constructed to deal with various macroeconomic themes such as theories of unemployment, indexation, economic policies in an open economy, balance of payments, inflation, Phillips curves, theory of cycles, expectations, etc. All these themes are treated in a unified framework and in as nontechnical a manner as possible, which thus provides a bridge between traditional macroeconomics and modern non-Walrasian theories.

In writing this book I have incurred a very special debt to Kul Bhatia, Victor Ginsburgh, Daniel Laskar, and Pierre Villa, who read the manuscript at different stages and made most helpful comments. They are responsible for many improvements, but the author alone is responsible for any remaining deficiencies. The Centre National de la Recherche Scientifique and the Centre d'Etudes Prospectives d'Economie Mathématique Appliquées à la Planification provided the financial support that allowed me to carry out the research. Last, but not least, I owe innumerable thanks to Jeanne Picquart at the Laboratoire d'Economie Politique, Ecole Normale Supérieure, for her impeccable typing and everlasting good humor.

Introduction

For a long time, macroeconomics appeared to be a relatively unified field, with a fairly wide consensus around the standard Keynesian paradigm represented by various versions of the IS-LM model. Today, this consensus is broken, and besides the "traditional" Keynesian school, theoretical and applied macroeconomists follow especially two new directions of research.

The first school is that of the "new classical economists," who reject the most fundamental elements of Keynesian analysis. For them all markets, including labor markets, function in a Walrasian manner; i.e., they clear at every point in time through price movements, so that demand and supply always match. There is thus never any involuntary unemployment, since each agent freely chooses his employment level taking into account the (possibly imperfect) information that is available to him. Models of this school can produce fluctuations in activity and employment, but these are voluntary and result from intertemporal tradeoffs chosen by the private agents. Of course with such basic assumptions the results obtained, and notably the policy prescriptions, are often completely opposed to those of traditional Keynesian macroeconomic models.

This new classical school has introduced new and important insights on the economic effects of expectations about prices and government policies. Its strong point is of course the solid microeconomic foundation of demand and supply formation as well as the equilibrium structure, both inherited from Walrasian models. A weak point, nevertheless, is that as in the basic Walrasian model, market clearing is taken as an axiom and not derived from microeconomic analysis of price-making behavior. Of course, there are some real world markets for which the equality between demand and supply is ensured institutionally, for example, the stock market ("la Bourse"), which inspired Walras. For other markets where no auctioneer is present, however, there is, as Arrow (1959) noted, "a logical gap in the usual formulations of the theory of the perfectly competitive economy, namely, that there is no place for a rational decision with respect to prices as there is with respect to quantities," and more precisely, "Each individual participant in the economy is supposed to take prices as given and determine his choices as to purchases and sales accordingly; there is no one left over whose job is to make a decision on price."

In the absence of a satisfactory account of competitive price making for every market, we certainly want to explore the implications of various assumptions about price setting. Because the Walrasian model is so far the only rigorous general description of the functioning of market economies,[1] a worthwhile strategy is, by using methods similar to those of Walrasian economics, to derive rigorously the micro- and macroeconomic consequences of not assuming market clearing at all times. This is the purpose of the second school we mentioned: that of non-Walrasian economics.

Non-Walrasian Economics

One of the most basic insights of non-Walrasian economics is one that also inspired Keynes (1936) in his attack on the then dominant classical economics. Indeed, as Clower (1965) and Leijonhufvud (1968) have shown, one finds behind the Keynesian constructions the idea that in the absence of an "auctioneer," there is very little chance that prices will equate demand and supply in all markets and at all times. An immediate corollary is that in the short run, adjustments will be made through quantities as well as through prices, a central idea in Keynes (1936), where the level of activity appears as an adjustment variable just as much as the interest rate or other price variables.

Starting from this basic insight, the non-Walrasian school has constructed a number of microeconomic concepts that allow the rigorous formalization of the functioning of individual markets and of the whole economy when demand and supply do not balance, and the mixed price–quantity adjustments that result from such situations. These concepts represent a generalization of the traditional Walrasian framework, since, whereas the Walrasian models cover by definition only the case where all markets clear, non-Walrasian models enable the economist to study, both at the microeconomic and macroeconomic levels, the consequences of numerous schemes of price formation, ranging from full rigidity to total flexibility, including various

---

[1] We refer here more specifically to the Arrow–Debreu reformulation of the Walrasian model.

intermediate forms of imperfect competition, and allowing, moreover, different schemes on different markets. We should also emphasize that these models provide a consistent formalization of price making by agents internal to the system, a theory that, as we shall see, bears some resemblance to those of imperfect competition.

Another subject to scrutinize if one wants to assess the generality of the non-Walrasian theory is that of expectations. In the concepts we shall describe, economic agents form expectations based on all information they have accumulated historically. Each agent may have his own expectations scheme, "rational" or not, so that this covers the largest number of specifications. For example, we deal explicitly with the simple cases of perfect foresight and parametric and adaptive expectations, but many other more complex schemes, for example, those incorporating learning procedures, would also be consistent with our general formulation. It should be further noted that in one important respect at least our treatment of expectations generalizes that in market-clearing models: Agents here form expectations not only on price signals, but on quantity signals as well.

The method developed thus yields a large array of non-Walrasian equilibrium concepts that generalize traditional microeconomic concepts in several respects by considering more general price mechanisms, by introducing quantity signals and mixed price–quantity adjustments in the short run, and by studying quantity expectations in addition to price expectations. We should finally note that the non-Walrasian method is not "anti-Walrasian;" on the contrary, it applies the methods that have been so successful in Walrasian theory under more general assumptions.

The generality of the microeconomic method quite naturally results in a similar generality at the macroeconomic level, where the approach developed here appears more general than either the new classical approach, which assumes market clearing, or the traditional Keynesian approach, which considered only excess supply states. Indeed, an important characteristic of non-Walrasian models is that they endogenously generate a multiplicity of subregimes, which makes them an ideal tool to synthesize apparently conflicting theories, to show the limits of each of them, and to actually generalize them by introducing new possibilities. As we shall see in various instances (e.g., in Chapter 6 devoted to IS-LM), some subregimes may have "Keynesian" characteristics and others "new-classical" ones. However, there will also be some subregimes that yield results different from both the Keynesian and new classical models.

All this shows most clearly two things: first, the evident need for making substantial progress, both theoretical and empirical, in understanding how prices and expectations are formed in the real world. Second, until such progress has been made, restricting oneself to any model with particular

assumptions, whether on price formation or expectations, could only lead
to biased results, notably insofar as policy prescriptions are concerned. One
thus needs a general approach, such as the non-Walrasian one, which can
accommodate a variety of realistic price and expectations mechanisms.

Object of the Book

This book belongs without ambiguity to the second school of thought
that we have just described. Its main purpose is to build a number of
macroeconomic models applying the non-Walrasian methodology. The
literature on the subject has grown so rapidly in recent years that it would
be unreasonable to try to give an exhaustive account of all existing models
in the field. We have thus chosen to present here some models that cover
as large a number of questions as possible within a simple and unified
framework. We also wanted to bridge the gap with traditional
macroeconomics while extending the analysis on various points. We shall
therefore study, with the help of some synthetic models, a diverse menu of
topics, such as conflicting views on unemployment and inflation, the IS-LM
model, economic policies in an international framework, the Phillips curve,
business cycles, and the role of expectations. These topics, and a few others,
will be investigated by purposely making each time the simplest possible
assumptions about the formation of the various prices (or, when needed,
expectations) involved. This will allow us to demonstrate in a straightforward manner the synthetic qualities of the theory, both by making a natural
synthesis with traditional macroeconomics, where similar simple assumptions are made, and by treating a large number of topics while using
throughout a very unified macroframework.

Something should also be said about what is outside the scope of this
book. In order to maintain a homogeneous exposition, we have not incorporated in this volume some recent developments emphasizing the game
theoretic and informational problems involved in price formation without
an auctioneer (the theory of contracts for labor markets is a popular
example). These investigations are most interesting and in principle belong
to the non-Walrasian paradigm. But it is clear that they are very far from
having stabilized. Moreover, they have up to now not been developed in
the general equilibrium framework which we have chosen to emphasize in
this volume. For these reasons, only "monopolistic competition" price
making schemes, which have been developed in such a general setting, have
been included here. This principle of selection, while leaving room for a
later and wider synthesis, was clearly the only way to respect the unifying
theme of this book: derive simple, workable, and policy-oriented models
from a full-fledged general equilibrium framework.

Plan of the Book

The contents of this book have been divided into five homogeneous parts.

The first part presents the microeconomic foundations of the models that are constructed in the following four parts. Chapter 1 studies the basic concepts, describing the functioning of nonclearing markets, the formation of quantity signals, the derivation of optimal effective demands and supplies, the role of expectations, and the setting of prices by decentralized agents. Chapter 2 studies various non-Walrasian equilibrium concepts: fixprice equilibria, equilibria with bounded prices, and equilibria with monopolistic competition, while formalizing the role of price–quantity expectations in the agents' behavior.

The second part studies closed-economy macroeconomic models, making various hypotheses on the formation of prices and wages. Chapter 3 compares the classical and Keynesian theories of unemployment in the framework of a model, traditional by now, with three commodities and rigid price and wage. Chapter 4 introduces asymmetric price flexibility into this basic model and examines how it affects the effectiveness of employment policies. Chapter 5 continues in the same direction by introducing some indexation of wages on the price level. Chapter 6 bridges the gap with the IS-LM model by showing how various traditional versions of this model may be synthesized within a model with asymmetric price and wage flexibility.

The third part extends the preceding models to an international framework by considering two-country models. Chapter 7 studies in this framework the comparative effectiveness of classical and Keynesian policies against unemployment. Chapter 8 constructs a model of international trade with many regimes, which allows us to discuss traditional theories of the balance of payments (elasticities, absorption, monetary approach).

The fourth part introduces more explicitly the time dimension by constructing some dynamic models. Chapter 9 sets up a synthetic model of cost and demand inflation. Chapter 10 integrates the theory of short-run non-Walrasian equilibrium and the traditional literature on the Phillips curve, adding to the latter some problems of conflicts over the distribution of income. Chapter 11 shows how the dynamic evolution of a short-run IS-LM model can generate business cycles.

The fifth part introduces expectations in a more explicit manner than in the preceding macroeconomic parts. Chapter 12 incorporates parametric price–quantity expectations into one of the models of the second part and reconsiders in this framework the problem of effectiveness of economic policies as well as the effects of exogenous expectations and expectational errors. Chapter 13 introduces the alternative hypothesis of perfect foresight on prices and quantities and computes the economic multipliers in various subregimes. Chapter 14 presents a dynamic model with explicit expectations, which allows a comparison of the employment effects of various expectations schemes as well as their realism.

A brief section of references at the end of each chapter indicates the origin of that chapter's developments. A more extensive bibliography has been gathered at the end of the book.

PART I

MICROECONOMIC FOUNDATIONS

1

The Basic Concepts

1. Walrasian Economics and the Problem of Market Clearing

Most traditional microeconomic theories are based on the assumption that markets clear by price movements. The basic idea behind these theories is that prices adjust sufficiently fast so that demand and supply are equalized in each market. These prices are thus sufficient signals to guide allocation of resources efficiently in a decentralized economy.

The most elaborate model in this tradition is that of *Walrasian general equilibrium,* which describes how the price mechanism functions in a complex economy with many interrelated markets. This model has been reformulated most elegantly and rigorously in recent decades. Before describing it briefly, we shall first study the simpler but also often used model of partial equilibrium.

Partial Equilibrium

In the partial equilibrium tradition, which is often associated with the name of Marshall, each market is studied separately by assuming that variables pertaining to other markets remain constant. Consider one of these markets in which a particular good is exchanged against a *numéraire* (most usually money) at the price p. In this market there are demanders and suppliers indexed by $i = 1, \ldots, n$. Their demands and supplies can be expressed as functions of the price level p, $d_i(p)$ and $s_i(p)$, respectively.

These functions are constructed under the assumption that each agent can buy or sell as much as he wants at the announced price. These individual demand and supply functions can be summed to derive aggregate demand and supply curves $D(p)$ and $S(p)$:

$$D(p) = \sum_{i=1}^{n} d_i(p)$$

$$S(p) = \sum_{i=1}^{n} s_i(p)$$

The equilibrium price p^* is determined by the condition of equality between aggregate demand and supply (Fig. 1.1). The transactions realized by each agent are equal to quantities demanded and supplied at the equilibrium price, respectively, $d_i(p^*)$ and $s_i(p^*)$.

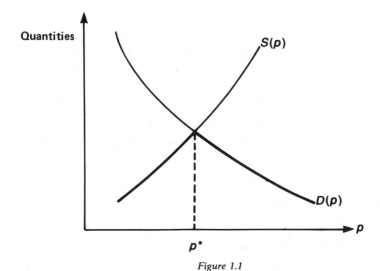

Figure 1.1

Walrasian Equilibrium

Contrary to the partial equilibrium tradition, the Walrasian theory of general equilibrium introduces explicitly an interdependence among markets. Agents determine simultaneously their exchanges for all goods traded as functions of all prices. The offers for exchange by the agents are thus represented by vectors with as many components as the number of goods to be exchanged.

Let us look at an economy where l goods, indexed by $h = 1, \ldots, l$, are exchanged during the period considered. These goods can be traded for each other at relative prices given by a vector p with components p_h, $h = 1, \ldots, l$. The transactions desired by agent i are functions of this price vector p. We thus have *vector* demand and supply functions denoted by $d_i(p)$ and $s_i(p)$. The components $d_{ih}(p)$ and $s_{ih}(p)$ represent, respectively, the quantity of good h demanded or supplied by agent i. These vector functions are constructed individually by maximization of some criterion specific to each agent under the assumption that he can realize the trades he desires for all goods (one example of such functions for a general exchange economy appears in Chapter 2, Section 2). For each agent, they satisfy his budget constraint:[1]

$$\sum_{h=1}^{l} p_h d_{ih}(p) = \sum_{h=1}^{l} p_h s_{ih}(p)$$

Adding the demand and supply functions for the n agents, we obtain the aggregate demand and supply for every good h:

$$D_h(p) = \sum_{i=1}^{n} d_{ih}(p)$$

$$S_h(p) = \sum_{i=1}^{n} s_{ih}(p)$$

A Walrasian equilibrium price vector p^* is such that aggregate demand and supply balance for all goods, i.e.,

$$D_h(p^*) = S_h(p^*) \qquad h = 1, \ldots, l$$

Transactions in good h realized by agent i are equal to $d_{ih}(p^*)$ or $s_{ih}(p^*)$, depending on whether he is a demander or a supplier. These transactions are consistent at both the individual and the market levels, since by construction

$$\sum_{h=1}^{l} p_h^* d_{ih}(p^*) = \sum_{h=1}^{l} p_h^* s_{ih}(p^*) \qquad i = 1, \ldots, n$$

$$\sum_{i=1}^{n} d_{ih}(p^*) = \sum_{i=1}^{n} s_{ih}(p^*) \qquad h = 1, \ldots, l$$

This last set of equalities ensures that at the Walrasian equilibrium, each agent is actually able to exchange as much of every good as he desires. This justifies *ex post* his assumption that he would be able to do so, which was

---

[1]Transfers between agents (for example, distribution of profits by firms) can be added easily, but are omitted here to simplify the exposition.

the basis of the construction of the Walrasian demands and supplies in the first place.

The Relevance of the Market-Clearing Hypothesis

As outlined earlier, the market-clearing assumption applied to all markets allows economists to construct rigorous and consistent models of the functioning of market economies. To assess the relevance of such models, however, we must test the realism of this assumption by examining how real world markets work.

If we consider only their institutional organization, we must first note that very few markets structurally satisfy the market-clearing assumption. Indeed, the supply–demand equality is automatically satisfied only in those markets where a specialized agent—an "auctioneer"—is in charge of finding the market-clearing price and where no transaction takes place until this price has been found. Such are, for example, auction markets and stock markets, but these represent only a very small fraction of existing markets.

Even though market clearing is not "institutionally" ensured, one might be satisfied with it as an approximation of how markets function. This is true of very "competitive" markets, such as markets for some agricultural products or primary materials, but such markets are rare today. In many cases, several forces have come into play that counteract the "law of supply and demand," so that the assumption of competitive market clearing is no longer acceptable, even as an approximation. There are many reasons for this state of affairs.

First, and most evident, some prices are subject to institutional constraints. This is of course particularly relevant in planned economies where many prices are kept fixed for a long time. This also occurs in traditional market economies where prices of certain services are often fixed by professional organizations or by the government, for example, minimum wages or certain professional fees.

Second, the prices of many goods are set nowadays in a framework of imperfect competition, where product differentiation and advertising, *inter alia*, have partially replaced price competition, and oligopolistic tendencies have developed. In such a framework, prices are no longer determined by the equality of supply and demand, and price response to changes in conditions of supply and demand may be substantially modified.

Finally, in considering labor markets it is evident that it would be socially infeasible to adjust workers' pay to every little change in "market conditions." Exchange relations in labor markets are of longer term and are more contractual in nature than in goods markets, so the "spot-market paradigm" does not apply very well. In these markets more than in other markets, the market-clearing assumption therefore cannot be accepted, even as an approximation.

For these reasons it is very necessary to construct a theory of the functioning of market economies in which the assumption of market clearing does not play a pivotal part. Let us now consider to what extent elements of traditional microeconomics can be used for this purpose.

Nonclearing Markets: A First Approach

Let us first place ourselves in the partial equilibrium framework described earlier, and shown in Fig. 1.1. Consider a price p different from the market-clearing price p^*. What will be the transactions made at this price? Although this question is not usually answered in the literature at the microeconomic level, we often find in aggregate models the rule according to which global transactions will settle at the minimum of total supply and demand, an assumption implicit in many Keynesian models and represented in Fig. 1.1, where the bold line represents the level of transactions when the market does not clear. Under this rule, agents on the short side of the market[2] realize their desired transactions, whereas agents on the long side are rationed (how this is done at the microeconomic level is usually not specified). This "short-side rule," or "rule of the minimum," satisfies the two properties of voluntary exchange (nobody is forced to exchange more than he wants) and market efficiency (no extra exchange would be beneficial to both demanders and suppliers), as we shall see later.

If we now go to a multimarket model, we might be tempted to apply the above rule to the *vectors* of Walrasian demands and supplies, taking aggregate transactions for each good as equal to the minimum of total demand and supply. We can, however, easily construct examples showing that such a rule would then lead to inconsistent results.

Consider, for example, a certain firm and assume that the markets for its inputs and outputs are in excess demand. Since there is excess demand on the input market, the firm is rationed and purchases smaller quantities of inputs than its Walrasian demand. However, since there is excess demand on the goods market, the firm can sell its Walrasian supply. The application of the short-side rule would thus imply that the firm produces the Walrasian quantity of output with less inputs than the Walrasian level, which corresponds to a technologically infeasible situation.

---

[2]The "short" side of a market is that where the global volume of desired transactions is the lowest. It is thus the demand side if there is excess supply, the supply side if there is excess demand. The other side is called the "long" side.

Many similar examples could be constructed, and the conclusion is clear: with more than one market, the short-side rule does not work when the traditional Walrasian demands and supplies are used. We shall thus have to construct a new theory of supply and demand that is also valid in situations where markets do not clear. Before that, we must specify the market structure we shall employ and then study the functioning of a nonclearing market and the formation of quantity signals.

2. The Institutional Framework

Money or Barter

Many recent models of Walrasian general equilibrium do not explicitly state the institutional framework of exchange underlying them. In his initial model, Walras himself referred to a barter economy with a market for each pair of goods. Conversely, other authors assume that exchanges are monetary.

To be precise on this point, we must first define what we mean by a barter or a monetary economy. We shall follow here the definition of R. W. Clower (1967) who gives as the basic concept the "exchange relation" of the economy, i.e., the list of pairs of goods that can be exchanged directly one for the other. To each of these pairs corresponds a market. In this framework, the barter economy corresponds to a "maximal" exchange relation: Each good can be exchanged against every other. If there are l goods in the economy, there are then $l(l-1)/2$ markets. On the contrary, in a monetary economy, only one good—money—can be exchanged against all other goods, and these other goods cannot be directly traded among themselves. In a monetary economy there are thus as many markets as there are nonmonetary goods.

As an example, Fig. 1.2 represents the exchange relations corresponding to monetary and barter exchange for a three-good economy: The existence

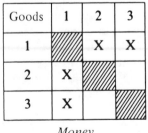
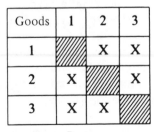

Money   *Barter*

Figure 1.2

of a market for the exchange of two goods is indicated by a crossmark in the corresponding box. Boxes along the diagonal have been suppressed because there obviously exists no market for the exchange of a good against itself.

A Monetary Economy

Nonmonetary exchange is not very common nowadays, and so, for evident reasons of realism, we shall from here on work in the framework of a monetary economy as defined above. Money is thus the only medium of exchange. It also functions as a *numéraire* and a reserve of value. Let there be l active markets during the period considered. In each of these markets a nonmonetary good indexed by $h = 1, \ldots, l$, is exchanged for money at the monetary price p_h.

Consider an agent i in market h. He may make a purchase $d_{ih} > 0$, for which he pays $p_h d_{ih}$ units of money, or a sale $s_{ih} > 0$, for which he receives $p_h s_{ih}$ units of money. Altogether, the net increase in the quantity of money held by agent i and resulting from his transactions on the l markets is equal to

$$\sum_{h=1}^{l} p_h s_{ih} - \sum_{h=1}^{l} p_h d_{ih}$$

Demands and Transactions

After clarifying the nature of the organization of markets, we must now make an important distinction: that between demands and transactions. Transactions, i.e., purchases or sales of goods, are exchanges actually made on a market. They are thus subject to traditional accounting identities. In particular, in each market aggregate purchases must equal aggregate sales. Demands and supplies, on the other hand, are signals transmitted by each agent to the market before exchange takes place and represent as a first approximation the exchanges he wishes to make. Of course, as we shall see, there is no guarantee that he will in fact be able to carry out these desired exchanges.

In order to reinforce the distinction between demands and transactions, we shall use different notations: d_{ih}^* and s_{ih}^*, respectively, are the purchases and sales realized by agent i on market h; $\tilde{d}_{ih}$ and $\tilde{s}_{ih}$ are his demand and supply. If there are n agents in the economy, indexed by $i = 1, \ldots, n$, the identity of total purchases and sales mentioned above can be written as:

$$\sum_{i=1}^{n} d_{ih}^* = \sum_{i=1}^{n} s_{ih}^*$$

No such identity applies to total demand and supply, which may be quite different from each other.

3. Functioning of Nonclearing Markets and Quantity Signals

We shall study in this section the functioning of a market for a particular good h. Since the entire discussion pertains to that market, we shall omit the corresponding subindex h.

Rationing Schemes

Assume first that the price prevailing in this market is not necessarily equal to its market-clearing value. There is no *a priori* reason to assume that demands and supplies balance, and one may have (remember there are n agents),

$$\tilde{D} = \sum_{i=1}^{n} \tilde{d}_i \neq \sum_{i=1}^{n} \tilde{s}_i = \tilde{S}$$

From these inconsistent demands and supplies, the exchange process must generate transactions, i.e., purchases d_i^* and sales s_i^*, which balance globally as an identity:

$$D^* = \sum_{i=1}^{n} d_i^* = \sum_{i=1}^{n} s_i^* = S^*$$

Quite evidently, so long as $\tilde{D} \neq \tilde{S}$, some demands and supplies cannot be satisfied in the exchange process, and some agents must be rationed. The precise determination of transactions naturally depends on the particular organization of exchange in each market. To each particular organization we shall associate a *rationing scheme*, which is the mathematical representation of the exchange process. This rationing scheme gives the transactions level of each agent as a function of the demands and supplies of all agents present in that market. Before studying the properties of these rationing schemes (which are described more formally in Chapter 2), let us give a few examples.

Examples

We shall study here two particular rationing schemes: the proportional rationing scheme, and a system of queue or priority.

In a proportional rationing scheme, agents on the short side realize their demands or supplies. Agents on the long side realize a transaction proportional to their demand or supply, the rationing coefficient being the same for all agents on the long side. This rule can thus be written as follows:

$$d_i^* = \tilde{d}_i \times \min\left(1, \frac{\tilde{S}}{\tilde{D}}\right)$$

$$s_i^* = \tilde{s}_i \times \min\left(1, \frac{\tilde{D}}{\tilde{S}}\right)$$

where

$$\tilde{D} = \sum_{j=1}^{n} \tilde{d}_j \qquad \tilde{S} = \sum_{j=1}^{n} \tilde{s}_j$$

In a queueing system, the demanders (or the suppliers) are ranked in a predetermined order and served according to that order. Let there be $n - 1$ demanders ranked in the order $i = 1, \ldots, n - 1$, each having a demand $\tilde{d}_i$, and a supplier indexed by n who supplies $\tilde{s}_n$. When the turn of demander i comes, the maximum quantity he can obtain is that which demanders before him, i.e., agents $j < i$, have not taken, i.e.,

$$\tilde{s}_n - \sum_{j<i} d_j^* = \max\left(0, \tilde{s}_n - \sum_{j<i} \tilde{d}_j\right)$$

The level of his purchase is simply the minimum of this quantity and his demand:

$$d_i^* = \min\left[\tilde{d}_i, \max\left(0, \tilde{s}_n - \sum_{j<i} \tilde{d}_j\right)\right]$$

As for the supplier, he sells the minimum of his supply and of total demand:

$$s_n^* = \min\left(\tilde{s}_n, \sum_{j=1}^{n-1} \tilde{d}_j\right)$$

Voluntary Exchange, Market Efficiency, and the Short-Side Rule

We shall study here two important properties that rationing schemes may satisfy: voluntary exchange and market efficiency.

There is *voluntary exchange* when no agent is forced either to purchase more than he demands or to sell more than he supplies, which can be written as

$$d_i^* \leqslant \tilde{d}_i \qquad s_i^* \leqslant \tilde{s}_i \qquad \text{for all} \quad i$$

Most markets in reality meet this condition (except perhaps some labor markets), and we shall henceforth assume that it is always satisfied. In the market considered, we can therefore divide the agents into two categories: rationed agents, for whom $d_i^* < \tilde{d}_i$ or $s_i^* < \tilde{s}_i$, and unrationed agents, whose transaction is equal to their demand or supply. We may remark that under voluntary exchange, the total volume of transactions is less than both global demand and supply, so that

$$D^* = S^* \leqslant \min(\tilde{D}, \tilde{S})$$

The second property we shall focus on is that of market efficiency, or absence of friction, which corresponds to the idea of exhaustion of all mutually advantageous exchanges. To give *a contrario* an example of inefficiency, consider a market in which there would be a rationed demander i and a rationed supplier j at the same time:

$$d_i^* < \tilde{d}_i \qquad s_j^* < \tilde{s}_j$$

Obviously, the corresponding organization would be inefficient, since an additional exchange between i and j would be beneficial to both. We shall thus say *a contrario* that a rationing scheme is *efficient* or *frictionless* if one never finds rationed demanders and rationed suppliers simultaneously in the market. An immediate implication of this property (still assuming, of course, voluntary exchange) is the short-side rule according to which all agents on the short side realize their supplies and demands,

$$\tilde{D} \geqslant \tilde{S} \Rightarrow s_i^* = \tilde{s}_i \qquad \text{for all} \quad i$$
$$\tilde{S} \geqslant \tilde{D} \Rightarrow d_i^* = \tilde{d}_i \qquad \text{for all} \quad i$$

and which yields a total volume of transactions equal to the minimum of global supply and demand,

$$D^* = S^* = \min(\tilde{D}, \tilde{S})$$

If indeed one agent on the short side does not realize his desired transaction, and the global volume of transactions is thus below that given by the previous formula, there would be at least one rationed demander and one rationed supplier, which is contrary to the property of efficiency of the rationing scheme. The short-side rule is thus a direct consequence of the two assumptions of voluntary exchange and market efficiency.

Realism of the Market Efficiency Hypothesis

The efficiency assumption is quite acceptable when we consider a centralized market (as in the proportional rationing system) or a small decentralized market, where each demander meets each supplier (like the queue described earlier). It becomes less acceptable when we consider a fairly wide and decentralized market because some buyers and sellers might not meet, whereas all demanders must be connected with all suppliers for the efficiency property to be valid in all circumstances. One may note in particular that the efficiency property is usually lost by aggregation of submarkets (whereas, on the contrary, the voluntary exchange property remains intact in this aggregation process). Let us consider indeed a number of submarkets labeled by k, each functioning efficiently so that

$$d_k^* = s_k^* = \min(\tilde{d}_k, \tilde{s}_k)$$

Now, aggregate these submarkets and define aggregate demand, supply, purchases, and sales by

$$\tilde{D} = \sum_k \tilde{d}_k \qquad \tilde{S} = \sum_k \tilde{s}_k$$

$$D^* = \sum_k d_k^* \qquad S^* = \sum_k s_k^*$$

It is easy to see that as soon as only two markets have excess demands of opposite signs, the efficiency assumption is contradicted for the aggregate market because

$$D^* = S^* < \min(\tilde{D}, \tilde{S})$$

The market efficiency assumption will be very useful in constructing simple macroeconomic models, but we must keep in mind that it may not always hold. Fortunately, this hypothesis is not necessary for the microeconomic concepts presented in this chapter and in Chapter 2.

Manipulable and Nonmanipulable Schemes

We shall now introduce a distinction that will be useful later: that between manipulable and nonmanipulable rationing schemes. The difference between them is most easily seen graphically: In Fig. 1.3 we show the level of purchase d_i^* of an agent i as a function of his demand $\tilde{d}_i$, the demands and supplies of the other agents being assumed given.

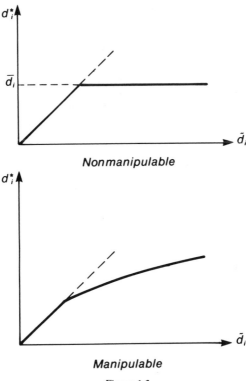

Nonmanipulable

Manipulable

Figure 1.3

In the manipulable case the agent can, even when rationed, increase his transactions by announcing higher demands, thus "manipulating" the exchange process. Conversely, in the nonmanipulable case, the agent is faced with bounds on his transactions that depend only on the demands and supplies of the other agents and that he thus cannot manipulate. We shall denote respectively by $\bar{d}_i$ and $\bar{s}_i$ these limits on his purchases and sales. A nonmanipulable rationing scheme can thus be written

$$d_i^* = \min(\tilde{d}_i, \bar{d}_i)$$
$$s_i^* = \min(\tilde{s}_i, \bar{s}_i)$$

The queueing system described earlier is nonmanipulable and can be written in this form, with

$$\bar{d}_i = \max\left(0, \tilde{s}_n - \sum_{j<i} \tilde{d}_j\right) \qquad 1 \leq i \leq n-1$$
$$\bar{s}_n = \sum_{j=1}^{n-1} \tilde{d}_j$$

Quantity Signals and Perceived Constraints

We have seen in this section how transactions are formed in a market where demands and supplies do not balance. In the same exchange process, the agents receive *quantity signals* in addition to the traditional price signals. The nature of these signals varies according to the particular form of the rationing scheme. For example, in a proportional rationing scheme the quantity signal is a rationing coefficient, the same for all agents.

If the rationing scheme is nonmanipulable, a category that we shall study often in this book, the quantity signal received always has the form of an upper bound on purchases or sales. We have denoted these bounds by $\bar{d}_i$ or $\bar{s}_i$, and we shall hereinafter refer to them as the *perceived constraints*. In the preceding subsection, we gave an example of these perceived constraints in the case of a queueing system. One may note in general that the perceived constraint is always equal to the realized transaction when the agent is rationed.

In all cases we should expect that quantity signals, as well as price signals, will influence the level of supplies and demands. This is what we shall study next.

4. Effective Demand

We saw in Section 3 how transactions and quantity signals were formed in a market where supplies and demands had been expressed. We shall now discuss how these supplies and demands themselves are generated when some markets do not clear. We noted earlier that in such situations one could not use Walrasian demands and supplies, which are only functions of price signals. We shall thus now study how *effective* demands and supplies are determined, which will be functions of price *and* quantity signals. A particularly noticeable feature will be the apparition of spillover effects, which reflect the repercussions of imbalances in one market on the other markets.

Let us say that there is a *spillover effect* when an agent who is constrained to exchange less than he wants in a market because of rationing modifies his demands or supplies in the other markets. The existence of such spillover effects is quite intuitive: It is easy to see that constraints on labor income will affect household consumption, whereas difficulties in selling output will reduce labor demand by firms. These spillover effects are actually central to Keynesian theory, where consumption is a function of realized income and the level of employment is determined by the volume of sales on the output market.

We shall now give a definition of effective demand, which results from rational maximization behavior and takes into account these spillover effects. We shall then examine a few traditional examples.

Effective Demand: A Definition

Before going to a precise definition, let us first briefly describe the framework of the analysis: We consider a multimarket monetary economy. In each of these markets the price may be different from its market-clearing value, and transactions are determined through a rationing scheme specific to the market. We can see in Appendix B that if the rationing scheme is manipulable, demands and supplies have no relation with the true desires for exchange of the agents, and no stable situation can be reached. We shall thus assume nonmanipulable rationing schemes in all markets. As a consequence, the agents receive in each market quantity signals that have the form of maximum bounds on their trades—the perceived constraints— which we have denoted by $\bar{d}_i$ and $\bar{s}_i$ in Section 3 and which we shall denote by a bar above the corresponding symbol. We can now move to a more precise definition, separating for ease of exposition consumers and firms, since they have rather different objective functions.

The effective demand of a household on a market is determined by maximizing its utility function subject to the budget constraint and taking into account the perceived constraints on the *other* markets. Similarly, the effective demand of a firm on a market is obtained by maximizing profit (or any other decision criterion of the firm) subject to the technological constraints and the perceived constraints on the *other* markets.

This definition is formalized and rigorously justified in Chapter 2, where it is also shown that it leads each agent to optimum transactions, given all prices and perceived quantity constraints. It integrates in a simple and natural manner the spillover effects, because effective demand in a particular market is influenced by perceived constraints on the other markets.

It is also worth noting that in this definition, an agent does not take into account the perceived constraint on the market where he expresses his effective demand. If the agent is rationed, this demand can thus be greater than the perceived constraint and the transaction, which is a signal to the market that he is constrained and would like to exchange more. It appears intuitively that it is very important to transmit such signals and that constrained agents do not limit their demands and supplies to what the market lets them exchange because otherwise they could miss out on profitable exchange opportunities. For example, an unemployed worker who would limit his labor supply to what he succeeds in selling would not supply any labor at all and might thus remain unemployed forever.

We shall now study two traditional examples of this effective demand.

The Employment Function

We shall describe here the employment demand function of a firm that may be constrained on the output market. Consider a firm with a production function $F(l)$, where l is the amount of labor employed, and let y be the level of its sales. The firm maximizes profits $py - wl$, where p is the price level and w the wage. Its Walrasian demand for labor is thus the solution in l of the following program:

$$\text{Maximize } py - wl \quad \text{s.t.}$$

$$y \leq F(l)$$

which immediately yields the traditional neoclassical demand $F'^{-1}(w/p)$. Suppose now that the firm perceives a constraint $\bar{y}$ on its sales of output. The effective demand for labor $\tilde{l}^d$ is solution in l of the program

$$\text{Maximize } py - wl \quad \text{s.t.}$$

$$y \leq F(l)$$

$$y \leq \bar{y}$$

which yields

$$\tilde{l}^d = \min\{F'^{-1}(w/p), F^{-1}(\bar{y})\}$$

One thus sees that there are two possible cases. If the constraint $\bar{y}$ is not binding, we find the Walrasian labor demand $F'^{-1}(w/p)$. If, however, the constraint is binding, we find a more "Keynesian" form $F^{-1}(\bar{y})$, which is the quantity of labor necessary to produce $\bar{y}$.

The Consumption Function

We shall now show how to obtain a consumption function of the Keynesian type by integrating in the consumer's program some constraints on labor sales. Consider a household endowed with a quantity of labor l_0 and an initial quantity of money $\bar{m}$. It receives an amount δ of distributed profits. The household's budget constraint is written:

$$pc + m = wl + \delta + \bar{m}$$

where c is the consumption level, l the quantity of labor actually sold, and m the final money holdings. Assume that the household has a utility function

$$U(c, l, m/p) = \alpha \log c + (1 - \alpha) \log(m/p)$$

The household's Walrasian labor supply and consumption demand are given by the following program:

Maximize $\alpha \log c + (1 - \alpha) \log(m/p)$ s.t.

$$pc + m = wl + \delta + \bar{m}$$

$$l \leq l_0$$

which immediately yields a labor supply l_0 and a Walrasian consumption demand equal to

$$\alpha(\bar{m} + \delta + wl_0)/p$$

Consider now the possibility of an imbalance on the labor market. The agent perceives a constraint $\bar{l}$ that limits his employment possibilities to $l \leq \bar{l}$. The effective demand for consumption is the solution in c of the following program:

Maximize $\alpha \log c + (1 - \alpha) \log(m/p)$ s.t.

$$pc + m = wl + \delta + \bar{m}$$

$$l \leq l_0$$

$$l \leq \bar{l}$$

If the constraint $\bar{l}$ is not binding, i.e., if $\bar{l} \geq l_0$, we obtain the Walrasian demand for consumption. If, however, $\bar{l} < l_0$, the constraint is binding, and the consumption demand is equal to

$$\alpha(\bar{m} + \delta + w\bar{l})/p$$

The general formula for effective demand is thus

$$\tilde{c} = \min\left\{ \alpha\left(\frac{\bar{m} + \delta + wl_0}{p}\right), \quad \alpha\left(\frac{\bar{m} + \delta + w\bar{l}}{p}\right) \right\}$$

$$= \alpha\left[\frac{\bar{m} + \delta + w \min(l_0, \bar{l})}{p}\right]$$

We see that effective consumption demand depends on a quantity signal $\bar{l}$, contrary to the Walrasian demand, which depends only on initial endowments and price signals. We may bring the above formula still closer to Keynesian formulations by noting that $\min(l_0, \bar{l})$ is equal to l^*, the household's transaction on the labor market. Therefore the consumption demand is equal to

$$\tilde{c} = \alpha \left(\frac{\bar{m}}{p} + \rho \right) \quad \text{with} \quad \rho = \frac{\delta + wl^*}{p}$$

where we recognize a very Keynesian form of the consumption function, since ρ is the household's real income. If all profits are distributed, which we shall assume in what follows, then,

$$\delta = py - wl$$

and the formula becomes

$$\tilde{c} = \alpha \left(\frac{\bar{m}}{p} + y \right)$$

an even more familiar Keynesian consumption function.

5. Non-Walrasian Equilibrium: An Example

We saw in Section 3 how transactions and quantity signals were determined as functions of effective demands and supplies on a nonclearing market. Then we saw in Section 4 how these effective demands and supplies themselves were formed as functions of price and quantity signals. We can now put these elements together and give a first example of non-Walrasian equilibrium, a fixprice equilibrium. This equilibrium will be characterized by a set of mutually consistent effective demands and supplies, transactions, and perceived constraints.

Continuing with the examples of Section 4, we shall consider a particularly simple economy with two markets (output and labor) and two agents (a household and a firm). Price p and wage w are assumed given, and transactions on the two markets y and l are assumed to be given by the minimum of demand and supply. The two agents are, as in Section 4, a firm with a production function $F(l)$ and a household with a supply of labor l_0 and a utility function

$$\alpha \log c + (1 - \alpha) \log(m/p)$$

We shall, moreover, assume that all profits are distributed; i.e., $\delta = py - wl$. It is easily seen that the form of equations defining a fixprice equilibrium fundamentally depends on the sign of excess demand in each of the markets. As an example, we shall show here how to compute such an equilibrium for the case, traditional in Keynesian theory, of excess supply in both the output and labor markets.

Since there is excess supply in the two markets, in each of them the transaction is determined by the demand

$$y^* = \tilde{c} \qquad l^* = \tilde{l}^d$$

Since there is excess supply on the output market, the effective demand for labor has the "Keynesian" form seen above,

$$\tilde{l}^d = F^{-1}(\bar{y})$$

where $\bar{y}$, the constraint perceived by the firm on the output market is equal to consumption demand

$$\bar{y} = \tilde{c}$$

Since there is excess supply of labor, as we saw in Section 4, the effective demand for consumption is equal to

$$\tilde{c} = \alpha(\bar{m} + \delta + w\bar{l})/p$$

the constraint $\bar{l}$ perceived by the household on the labor market being of course equal to the demand coming from the firm:

$$\bar{l} = \tilde{l}^d$$

Combining these equations and using the equality $\delta = py^* - wl^*$, we easily compute the equilibrium levels of transactions:

$$y^* = \frac{\alpha}{1 - \alpha} \cdot \frac{\bar{m}}{p} \qquad l^* = F^{-1}\left(\frac{\alpha}{1 - \alpha} \cdot \frac{\bar{m}}{p}\right)$$

Note that as an example we gave here complete computations showing the relations among effective demands, transactions, and perceived constraints but that we could have directly obtained the level of equilibrium transactions by using the form of the consumption function seen above,

$$\tilde{c} = \alpha\left(\frac{\bar{m}}{p} + y\right)$$

and by noting that at equilibrium, y is equal to $\tilde{c}$ (since there is excess supply) and is thus determined by the equation

$$y = \alpha\left(\frac{\bar{m}}{p} + y\right)$$

which immediately yields the previously computed value

$$y^* = \frac{\alpha}{1 - \alpha} \cdot \frac{\bar{m}}{p}$$

This equation is a well-known Keynesian multiplier formula, where $1/(1 - \alpha)$ is the multiplier and $\alpha(\bar{m}/p)$ is the "autonomous spending" as it appears in the consumption function.

We should note further that transactions are determined by the above formulas only for a subset of possible values of p and w, those for which there is actually excess supply in the two markets. How these subsets are determined is taken up in Chapter 3, where a more general model is studied for all possible configurations of excess demands and supplies.

6. The Role of Expectations

So far expectations have not played any explicit role in our discussions, whereas, they are a fundamental element in Keynesian theory, where they appear at least implicitly in the marginal efficiency of capital schedule and in the money demand function. We shall now show that expectations are actually present in our theory and how they can be integrated explicitly. As in Keynesian theory, this integration of expectations goes through an evaluation of the utility of stocks, which are the physical links between present and future. The construction of such indirect utilities allows one to convert expectations on future exchanges into effective demands and supplies for current goods.

As an example we shall show how to construct an indirect utility function for money, such as that used earlier in Sections 4 and 5. We had indeed a utility function of the form

$$\alpha \log c + (1 - \alpha) \log(m/p)$$

We have to show how money, which has no intrinsic utility, yields indirect utility in its role as a reserve of value. We shall also see that this indirect utility depends fundamentally on expectations and that the above utility function corresponds to particular assumptions about these expectations.

Consider an agent living two periods: present and future. All variables in the future period will have an index e, since they correspond to expectations. The agent is endowed with quantities of labor l_0 and l_0^e and has a direct utility function for present and future consumption:

$$U = \alpha \log c + (1 - \alpha) \log c^e$$

Let p^e and w^e be the expected price and wage, $\bar{c}^e$ and $\bar{l}^e$ the expected constraints on the goods and labor market, respectively, and δ^e the expected profit distribution for the second period. Assume that the agent has consumed a quantity c in the first period and saved a quantity of money m. His optimal second-period consumption, as expected from the first period, is that which maximizes the utility function subject to all prices and quantity constraints expected for the second period (this is seen in a more formal way in Chapter 2). It is thus the solution in c^e of the following program:

Maximize $\alpha \log c + (1 + \alpha) \log c^e$ s.t.

$$p^e c^e \leqslant w^e l^e + \delta^e + m$$

$$l^e \leqslant l_0^e$$

$$l^e \leqslant \bar{l}^e$$

$$c^e \leqslant \bar{c}^e$$

Since there is no disutility from labor, the optimum consumption is the highest that can be attained, taking into account the second-period constraints; that is,

$$c^e = \min\left\{ \bar{c}^e, \frac{m + \delta^e + w^e \min(l_0^e, \bar{l}^e)}{p^e} \right\}$$

and the corresponding expected utility is

$$\alpha \log c + (1 - \alpha) \log\left[\min\left\{ \bar{c}^e, \frac{m + \delta^e + w^e \min(l_0^e, \bar{l}^e)}{p^e} \right\} \right]$$

One thus sees that the indirect utility of money depends not only on the usual "Walrasian" expectations p^e, w^e, δ^e but also on the expected quantity signals $\bar{c}^e$ and $\bar{l}^e$. Note that the "marginal utility" of money is a decreasing function of $\bar{l}^e$: It thus increases when employment prospects become less favorable, an intuitive result. Noting that

$$\delta^e + w^e \min(l_0^e, l^e) = p^e y^e$$

where y^e is real expected income for the future period, we see that the indirect utility function can be written in the form

$$\alpha \log c + (1 - \alpha) \log[\min \{\bar{c}^e, (m/p^e) + y^e\}]$$

The utility function used in Section 4 thus corresponds to the following particular assumptions on expectations:

$$p^e = p \qquad \bar{c}^e = +\infty \qquad y^e = 0$$

The agent's consumption function is obtained by maximizing this indirect utility function under the budget constraint:

$$pc + m = py + \bar{m} \qquad m \geqslant 0$$

Assuming that $\bar{c}^e = +\infty$ and that the constraint $m \geqslant 0$ is not binding, one obtains

$$\tilde{c} = \alpha \left(\frac{\bar{m}}{p} + y + \frac{p^e y^e}{p} \right)$$

In Chapter 12 we shall study a complete macroeconomic model incorporating expectations and a consumption function similar to those just described.

7. The Formation of Prices

In the previous sections we showed how effective demands and supplies, transactions, and quantity signals were determined, the prices being taken as exogenous. As we shall see in later chapters, all this is consistent with many price-determination schemes, ranging from full rigidity to complete flexibility. We shall show in this section how we can formalize price determination by agents internal to the system. Two modes of decentralized price formation are generally observed in reality: Either the agents on one side of the market (most often the sellers) announce prices, and transactions occur at these announced prices, or the prices are the object of a bargaining process between sellers and buyers. The formalization of bargaining would lead us almost immediately into unsolved game theory problems, so we shall limit ourselves to a formal treatment of the first mode of price fixation. As we shall see, we obtain a theory close to that of monopolistic competition.

Framework of Analysis

We shall thus have price makers on one side of the market and price takers on the other side. Note first that if in a particular market there were many price makers, we would have a problem of definition of that market, for there is no reason for independent agents to announce the same price, even if the goods sold are physically identical. However, until now we have always studied markets characterized by a unique price. We shall thus assume in what follows that goods are differentiated not only by their physical characteristics, but also by the agent who decides on the price, so that the price of a good will be fixed by a single agent. Although this agent appears in a purely formal manner as a monopoly, this does not imply any real monopoly power, since other agents can buy or sell in other markets goods that are identical or close substitutes and that will compete with the goods he is selling.

Consider thus a particular market (the index of which is omitted to simplify notation) where the price p is fixed by an agent i. After this price p is announced, agent i like anyone else emits an effective demand or supply $\tilde{d}_i$ or $\tilde{s}_i$, realizes transactions d_i^* or s_i^*, and perceives constraints $\bar{d}_i$ or $\bar{s}_i$.

Perceived Demand and Supply Curves

It is with respect to the formation of expected constraints that agent i differs from the other agents who do not control prices. Indeed, the other agents take the price and the expected constraints as parametric data that they cannot influence. Agent i on the contrary decides on the price and by so doing he can modify his constraint via price changes. The relation between the expected constraint and the price fixed by pricemaker i is the well-known "perceived demand curve," which gives the maximal quantity of controlled good that the pricemaker expects to sell (or purchase if he is a demander) as a function of the price he will announce. It would be evidently unrealistic to assume that pricemaker i knows the "true" demand curve. The perceived demand curve is an estimate of the true curve, and it is denoted

$$\bar{S}_i(p, \eta_i)$$

where η_i is a vector of parameters estimated using all observations available to agent i (we shall see below what conditions these estimated parameters must satisfy). It is assumed that the function $\bar{S}_i$ is nonincreasing in p. We note that the perceived demand curve is denoted as a constraint on sales, which is natural since the total demand of other agents on the market indeed represents a constraint on the sales of agent i.

Symmetrically, if the pricemaker i is a buyer on the market, he has a perceived supply curve, giving the maximum quantity he expects to be able to buy as a function of the price p he will set. This perceived supply curve is denoted

$$\bar{D}_i(p, \eta_i)$$

and is assumed nondecreasing in p. Note again that the perceived supply curve is denoted as a constraint on i's purchases, since the total supply of the other agents is actually a constraint on his purchases.

Price Making

Assume for the moment that the parameters η_i of the perceived demand curve are known. The choice of the price p will then proceed along lines that are traditional in the theories of monopoly or monopolistic competition: In maximizing his objective function, the pricemaker takes into account parametric prices and quantity constraints on the markets where he does not set prices. In the markets where he decides on prices, however, sales must be less than or equal to the level given by the perceived demand curve, or, if he is a demander, purchases must be less than or equal to the level given by the perceived supply curve.

Consider as an example a firm with a cost function $C_i(y_i)$, where y_i is the level of output sold (there are no inventories). The firm chooses the price p so as to maximize profits, taking into account the maximum sales level given by the perceived demand curve $\bar{S}_i(p, \eta_i)$. The price p is thus a solution of the following program:

$$\text{Maximize } py_i - C_i(y_i) \quad \text{s.t.}$$

$$y_i \leqslant \bar{S}_i(p, \eta_i)$$

It is worth pointing out that the pricemaker always chooses his price p (and expected sales y_i) so as to be "on" the perceived demand curve, i.e., so that

$$y_i = \bar{S}_i(p, \eta_i)$$

Indeed, assume *a contrario* that the corresponding constraint is not binding, i.e., that

$$y_i < \bar{S}_i(p, \eta_i)$$

Agent i could, while maintaining the same production–sales plan y_i, increase slightly his price without violating the constraint of the perceived demand curve, which would obviously increase profits, and that would contradict the profit maximization hypothesis. Thus, *ex ante* the pricemaker will always be on the perceived demand curve, i.e., he plans to satisfy all demand forthcoming at the price he sets. Of course in an equilibrium situation, such as is considered in later chapters, the pricemaker does actually satisfy all demands addressed to him.

The price chosen satisfies a condition of the type "marginal cost equals marginal revenue." This price is of course a function of the parameters η_i of the perceived demand curve. We now turn to the process of estimating these parameters.

Estimation of the Perceived Demand Curve

In order to estimate the vector η_i, which determines the perceived demand curve, one should in reality estimate a very large number of parameters. Indeed, to compute the exact effect of a variation in p on the demand facing agent i, one must not only know the original demand curve, taking into account the price p and the prices of substitutes sold by competitors, but also correctly forecast the price reactions of these competitors to variations in p, and so on. For each of these elements, distortions with respect to the true demand curve may come in. In Chapter 2 we shall study a non-Walrasian equilibrium concept with endogenous price making, where a minimal degree of consistency with observations is required. Let us define here these minimal consistency conditions.

Consider a particular period where agent i has announced a price $\bar{p}$ and observed a perceived constraint $\bar{s}_i$ (which actually corresponds to the demand of the other agents). The pair of observations ($\bar{p}, \bar{s}_i$) corresponds to a point on the true demand curve, and the perceived demand curve can be consistent with observations only if it goes through that point. Call $\bar{\eta}_i$ the vector of estimated parameters. The consistency defined earlier can be expressed mathematically by the following condition on $\bar{\eta}_i$:

$$\bar{s}_i = \bar{S}_i(\bar{p}, \bar{\eta}_i)$$

This condition is shown in Fig. 1.4, where we immediately see that it does not determine completely the parameters of $\bar{S}_i$. Indeed, although the "position" of the curve is determined at the observed point, its elasticity is not, and thus a multiplicity of perceived demand curves are consistent with the period's observations. The problem is still more acute if, as in some situations of oligopoly, kinked demand curves are considered.

In order to determine the perceived demand curve, we thus need an estimation procedure using other data; for example, the set of all past observations or any *a priori* information about the market and competitors' behavior. Even with such extra data, however, it is difficult to assume that the agent knows the true demand curve.

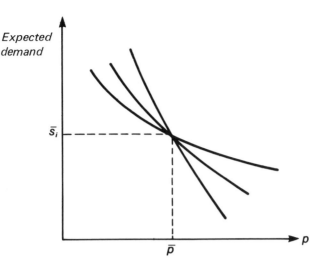

Figure 1.4

8. Conclusions

In this chapter we have developed in a simple manner the elements of a microeconomic theory that applies to cases in which markets do not clear. After characterizing the institutional framework of exchange, we have seen how transactions are formed on a nonclearing market through rationing schemes and how agents receive in this process quantity signals in addition to the traditional price signals. These quantity signals naturally influence demands and supplies, and we saw how effective demands and supplies incorporating quantity constraints could be constructed. As an example we saw that the Keynesian consumption and employment functions could be reinterpreted rigorously in this way. Since not only current signals but also expectations influence current agents' behavior, we have incorporated these expectations into the analysis. Furthermore, quantity signals also play a role in the process of price formation, and we have considered this process in a decentralized economy.

In Section 5, we gave a first example of non-Walrasian equilibrium related to traditional Keynesian equilibria with excess supply in labor and output markets. In Chapter 2 we shall continue in the same direction and study a number of non-Walrasian equilibrium concepts that are used in later macroeconomic applications.

References

This chapter is based on Benassy (1976c, 1982b). The starting point of many works on effective demand is found in the article by Clower (1965), where he showed how to reinterpret the Keynesian consumption function in a framework of nonclearing markets, and in the book by Leijonhufvud (1968). Early elements of theory in the same direction are found in Hansen (1951), Patinkin (1956), who studied an employment function outside Walrasian equilibrium, and Hicks (1965). The consumption and employment functions have been combined in the first macroeconomic non-Walrasian equilibrium model by Barro and Grossman (1971, 1976).

The formation of quantity signals and a general definition of effective demand have been studied in Benassy (1975a, 1977b, 1982b) and Drèze (1975). Arrow (1959) had noticed that price formation on nonclearing markets was related to problems of monopolistic competition (Chamberlin, 1933; Robinson, 1933). The perceived demand curve was developed in Bushaw and Clower (1957) and Negishi (1961), and the relation with the above non-Walrasian theories in Benassy (1973, 1976b, 1977a, 1982b).

2

Non-Walrasian Equilibria

1. Introduction

We saw in Chapter 1 the basic components of a microeconomic theory, which applies when supply and demand are not equal on all markets. We shall now put these elements together and construct a number of non-Walrasian equilibrium concepts, which we shall denote by the generic name of K-equilibria. A main characteristic of these equilibria is that in the adjustment process quantity signals play as important a role as price signals. As for prices, even when they are flexible, they do not necessarily adjust to equate supply and demand on all markets. We shall thus have a class of equilibria rather more general than Walrasian equilibria, where only price signals are considered and all markets clear.

We may furthermore note that we shall deal with concepts of short-run equilibrium, where the agents' actions are made consistent with each other in the current period. Agents' future plans are the subject of their expectations, but nothing guarantees that these expectations will be mutually consistent.[1] The equilibria to be studied here will thus have a structure of temporary non-Walrasian equilibria. We may remark that this structure is that of traditional Keynesian models, where agents' current plans have adjusted to each other through income movements but where their future plans (reflected, for example, in the investment and savings functions) are independent of each other and thus in general mutually inconsistent.

---

[1]Although the particular case where they are consistent can be treated as well; see, for example, the model of Chapter 13.

In what follows we shall successively study a few non-Walrasian equilibrium concepts: We shall start with a concept of fixprice equilibrium, which is the simplest and somehow the polar case of the concept of Walrasian general equilibrium. We shall then discuss the role of expectations in the behavior of agents and in the formation of a temporary equilibrium. We shall then study two concepts of non-Walrasian equilibrium with flexible prices: one where prices can vary between bounds given *a priori*, and the other where they are fixed in a framework of monopolistic competition. Before describing these concepts in detail, we shall indicate the common institutional framework of all these models.

2. Institutional Framework

A Monetary Economy

In all that follows we shall work in a monetary exchange economy where money has at the same time the roles of *numéraire*, medium of exchange, and reserve of value. Assume that there are l active markets in the period considered. On each of these markets one of the l nonmonetary goods, indexed by $h = 1, \ldots, l$, is exchanged against money. We shall denote by p_h the monetary price of good h, and by $p \in R_+^l$ the vector of these prices. (Money being the numéraire, its price is implicitly equal to 1.)

Agents in this economy are indexed by $i = 1, \ldots, n$. At the beginning of the period agent i has a quantity of money $\bar{m}_i \geq 0$ and holdings of nonmonetary goods represented by a vector $\omega_i \in R_+^l$, with components $\omega_{ih} \geq 0$ for each good. After carrying out exchanges in the various markets, the agent holds a quantity of money $m_i \geq 0$, which is saved for future periods, and a quantity of goods represented by a vector $x_i \in R_+^l$ with components $x_{ih} \geq 0$. Quantities x_{ih} are assumed to be consumed, and we shall thus generally call x_i the consumption vector.

We shall call z_{ih} the net volume of transactions of good h against money, the elementary transaction being the exchange of one unit of good h against p_h units of money. With the notation of Chapter 1, z_{ih} is defined as

$$z_{ih} = d_{ih} - s_{ih}$$

Reciprocally d_{ih} and s_{ih} are determined from z_{ih} by the formulas:

$$d_{ih} = \max(z_{ih}, 0)$$

$$s_{ih} = -\min(z_{ih}, 0)$$

and z_{ih} is thus positive in case of a purchase and negative in case of a sale. We call $z_i \in R^l$ the vector of these net transactions for agent i. Final holdings of money and goods, m_i and x_i, are related to z_i and p by the following relations:

$$x_i = \omega_i + z_i$$

$$m_i = \bar{m}_i - pz_i$$

Note that the last equation, which describes the evolution of money holdings, is simply the conventional budget constraint.

Walrasian Equilibrium

Let us briefly describe here the Walrasian demands and equilibrium in such a monetary economy in order to highlight the differences between them and the concepts that follow. Assume that each agent i has a utility function $U_i(x_i, m_i)$, which depends on its consumption vector x_i and final money holdings m_i,[2] which we shall assume to be strictly concave in its arguments. His Walrasian net demand function $z_i(p)$ is the solution in z_i of the following program:

Maximize $U_i(x_i, m_i)$ s.t.

$$x_i = \omega_i + z_i \geqslant 0$$

$$m_i = \bar{m}_i - pz_i \geqslant 0$$

There is no "demand for money" since there is no such thing as a "market for money." A Walrasian short-run equilibrium price vector is given by the condition that net excess demands be zero on all markets:

$$\sum_{i=1}^{n} z_{ih}(p) = 0 \qquad h = 1, \ldots, l$$

3. Rationing Schemes and Quantity Signals

If the situation is not one of Walrasian equilibrium, we must carefully distinguish between demands and transactions, as we saw in Chapter 1. We

[2]We shall see later in Section 6 how such a utility function incorporating money can be constructed from an intertemporal problem.

shall denote by z_{ih}^* the net transaction of agent i on market h. In the notation of Chapter 1:

$$z_{ih}^* = d_{ih}^* - s_{ih}^*$$

Net transactions must identically balance on each market:

$$\sum_{i=1}^{n} z_{ih}^* \equiv 0 \quad \text{for all} \quad h$$

Now we shall denote by $\tilde{z}_{ih}$ the net effective demand of agent i on market h:

$$\tilde{z}_{ih} = \tilde{d}_{ih} - \tilde{s}_{ih}$$

There is no reason, however, why these effective demands should always balance, so we shall often have

$$\sum_{i=1}^{n} \tilde{z}_{ih} \neq 0$$

Each market h has a particular organization, which allows it to transform inconsistent demands and supplies into a set of consistent transactions. We shall represent the organization of each market h by a *rationing scheme*, i.e., by a set of n functions:

$$z_{ih}^* = F_{ih}(\tilde{z}_{1h}, \ldots, \tilde{z}_{nh}) \qquad i = 1, \ldots, n$$

such that

$$\sum_{i=1}^{n} F_{ih}(\tilde{z}_{1h}, \ldots, \tilde{z}_{nh}) = 0 \quad \text{for all} \quad \tilde{z}_{1h}, \ldots, \tilde{z}_{nh}$$

Each transaction is thus a function of all agents' net effective demands on the market, and the sum of net transactions is equal to zero. The particular form of the rationing functions depends on the exchange mechanism prevailing in each market, and we saw some examples (queue, proportional rationing) and various possible properties of rationing schemes in Chapter 1. We shall in general assume that F_{ih} is continuous in its arguments and nondecreasing in $\tilde{z}_{ih}$.

A property we had insisted on in Chapter 1 is that of *voluntary exchange*, according to which no agent can be forced to exchange more than he wants or to change the sign of his transaction. This property can be expressed algebraically as:

$$|z_{ih}^*| \leq |\tilde{z}_{ih}| \qquad z_{ih}^* \cdot \tilde{z}_{ih} \geq 0$$

and we shall assume that it always holds. Another property we shall often use in macroeconomic applications is that of efficient, or frictionless markets, according to which one can never simultaneously find a rationed demander and a rationed supplier on the same market. Together with the voluntary exchange assumption, this property implies the short-side rule, according to which agents on the short side of a market can realize their desired transactions, which is expressed mathematically by

$$\left(\sum_{j=1}^{n} \tilde{z}_{jh} \right) \cdot \tilde{z}_{ih} \leq 0 \Rightarrow z_{ih}^* = \tilde{z}_{ih}$$

As we saw, this rule also implies that the level of transactions on a market settles at the minimum of aggregate demand and supply, which yields particularly simple calculations in macroeconomic applications. We remarked in Chapter 1, however, that this efficiency property does not always hold. It is thus important to note that, as will appear later, this property is absolutely not necessary for most developments of this chapter.

Manipulation and Quantity Signals

We have already insisted in Chapter 1 on the important distinction between manipulable and nonmanipulable rationing schemes. Intuitively, a scheme is manipulable if the agent can, even when rationed, increase his transaction by increasing his demand. A scheme is nonmanipulable if the agent is faced with lower and upper bounds on his net trades that he cannot manipulate. More precisely, as we have indicated, a rationing scheme is nonmanipulable if it can be written in the form

$$d_{ih}^* = \min(\tilde{d}_{ih}, \bar{d}_{ih})$$
$$s_{ih}^* = \min(\tilde{s}_{ih}, \bar{s}_{ih})$$

or in algebraic notations as

$$z_{ih}^* = \begin{cases} \min(\tilde{z}_{ih}, \bar{d}_{ih}) & \tilde{z}_{ih} \geq 0 \\ \max(\tilde{z}_{ih}, -\bar{s}_{ih}) & \tilde{z}_{ih} \leq 0 \end{cases}$$

where the bounds $\bar{d}_{ih}$ and $\bar{s}_{ih}$ depend only on the net demands of the other agents (and are thus independent of $\tilde{z}_{ih}$). In order to show this property of the rationing schemes in a more formalized way, it is convenient to separate $\tilde{z}_{ih}$ from the other net demands and thus to write down rationing schemes in the form

$$z_{ih}^* = F_{ih}(\tilde{z}_{ih}, \tilde{Z}_{ih})$$

with

$$\tilde{Z}_{ih} = \{\tilde{z}_{1h}, \ldots, \tilde{z}_{i-1,h}, \tilde{z}_{i+1,h}, \ldots, \tilde{z}_{nh}\}$$

where $\tilde{Z}_{ih}$ is the set of net demands of all agents on market h, except for agent i's demand. One can then represent the relation between the net transaction of an agent z_{ih}^* and his net demand $\tilde{z}_{ih}$ (Fig. 2.1).

One can immediately see in Fig. 2.1 that in the nonmanipulable case, the bounds $\bar{d}_{ih}$ and $\bar{s}_{ih}$ are respectively equal to the maximum demand and supply of agent i, which could be exactly satisfied by the market, taking into account the other agents' effective demands on market h, i.e., $\tilde{Z}_{ih}$. Let

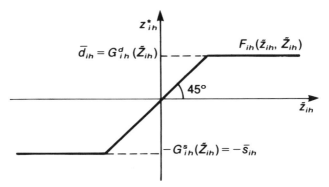

Nonmanipulable

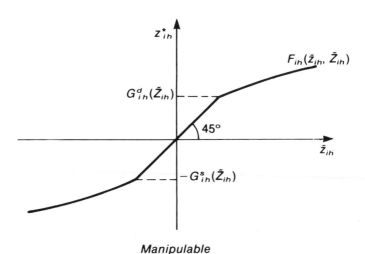

Manipulable

Figure 2.1

us define algebraically these maximum demands and supplies (cf. Fig. 2.1 for their graphical representation):

$$G_{ih}^d(\tilde{Z}_{ih}) = \max\{\tilde{z}_{ih} | F_{ih}(\tilde{z}_{ih}, \tilde{Z}_{ih}) = \tilde{z}_{ih}\}$$

$$G_{ih}^s(\tilde{Z}_{ih}) = -\min\{\tilde{z}_{ih} | F_{ih}(\tilde{z}_{ih}, \tilde{Z}_{ih}) = \tilde{z}_{ih}\}$$

Because of voluntary exchange, $F_{ih}(0, \tilde{Z}_{ih}) = 0$, and thus,

$$G_{ih}^d(\tilde{Z}_{ih}) \geq 0 \qquad G_{ih}^s(\tilde{Z}_{ih}) \geq 0$$

We shall say that the rationing scheme on market h is nonmanipulable if one can write for every agent $i = 1, \ldots, n$,

$$F_{ih}(\tilde{z}_{ih}, \tilde{Z}_{ih}) = \begin{cases} \min[\tilde{z}_{ih}, G_{ih}^d(\tilde{Z}_{ih})] & \text{if} \quad \tilde{z}_{ih} \geq 0 \\ \max[\tilde{z}_{ih}, -G_{ih}^s(\tilde{Z}_{ih})] & \text{if} \quad \tilde{z}_{ih} \leq 0 \end{cases}$$

otherwise the scheme is manipulable.

Perceived Constraints

As already noted in Chapter 1, it is shown in Appendix B how manipulable rationing schemes lead to an explosive phenomenon of overbidding, which may prevent existence of an equilibrium. In what follows we shall thus concentrate on nonmanipulable rationing schemes, which may be represented by

$$z_{ih}^* = \begin{cases} \min(\tilde{z}_{ih}, \bar{d}_{ih}) & \tilde{z}_{ih} \geq 0 \\ \max(\tilde{z}_{ih}, -\bar{s}_{ih}) & \tilde{z}_{ih} \leq 0 \end{cases}$$

or in a more compact manner by

$$z_{ih}^* = \min\{\bar{d}_{ih}, \max(\tilde{z}_{ih}, -\bar{s}_{ih})\}$$

with

$$\bar{d}_{ih} = G_{ih}^d(\tilde{Z}_{ih}) \qquad \bar{s}_{ih} = G_{ih}^s(\tilde{Z}_{ih})$$

As in Chapter 1, $\bar{d}_{ih}$ and $\bar{s}_{ih}$ are called *perceived constraints*.

Summary

We shall thus consider in what follows various non-Walrasian equilibrium concepts concerning current markets indexed by $h = 1, \ldots, l$. As we said, we shall deal only with nonmanipulable rationing schemes on these markets.

On a market h, agent i realizes a transaction z_{ih}^*, given as a function of all demands expressed by the rationing scheme

$$Z_{ih}^* = F_{ih}(\tilde{z}_{ih}, \tilde{Z}_{ih})$$

Furthermore, since these rationing schemes are nonmanipulable, each agent receives quantity signals, the perceived constraints

$$\bar{d}_{ih} = G_{ih}^d(\tilde{Z}_{ih}) \geqslant 0$$
$$\bar{s}_{ih} = G_{ih}^s(\tilde{Z}_{ih}) \geqslant 0$$

In order to simplify notation, we shall represent the rationing functions and perceived constraints concerning an agent i as vector functions

$$z_i^* = F_i(\tilde{z}_i, \tilde{Z}_i)$$
$$\bar{d}_i = G_i^d(\tilde{Z}_i)$$
$$\bar{s}_i = G_i^s(\tilde{Z}_i)$$

Before going on to the specific study of the various concepts, we shall investigate the determination of effective demands.

4. Effective Demand

We saw above (Section 2) how the Walrasian demands of an agent facing a price system p are determined. We shall now consider an agent i faced with a price vector p *and* vectors of perceived constraints $\bar{s}_i$ and $\bar{d}_i$, and we shall see how he can choose a vector of effective demands $\tilde{z}_i$, which leads him to the best possible transaction. Before that let us describe agent i a little more.

As at the beginning of this chapter, we assume that agent i holds initially quantities of goods and money ω_i and $\bar{m}_i$ and that transactions z_i lead him to final quantities x_i and m_i given by

$$x_i = \omega_i + z_i \geqslant 0$$
$$m_i = \bar{m}_i - pz_i \geqslant 0$$

Agent i has a utility function $U_i(x_i, m_i)$ that depends on the consumption vector x_i and on the quantity of money saved m_i. We shall assume the function U_i to be continuous and concave in its arguments, with strict concavity in x_i. We shall now see how this agent chooses his effective demand z_i to maximize the utility of the resulting transaction.

Optimal Transaction and Demand

Let us consider first the best transaction that the agent can reach. Agent i knows that on every market h his transactions are limited to the interval

$$-\bar{s}_{ih} \le z_{ih} \le \bar{d}_{ih}$$

The best transaction he can obtain, which we denote by $\zeta_i^*(p, \bar{d}_i, \bar{s}_i)$, is thus the solution in z_i of the following program:

$$\text{Maximize } U_i(x_i, m_i) \qquad \text{s.t.}$$

$$x_i = \omega_i + z_i \ge 0$$

$$m_i = \bar{m}_i - pz_i \ge 0 \tag{A}$$

$$-\bar{s}_{ih} \le z_{ih} \le \bar{d}_{ih} \qquad h = 1, \ldots, l$$

Since the function U_i is strictly concave in x_i, the solution of this program is unique, and ζ_i^* is thus a function. However, in our system an agent cannot choose directly the level of his transactions, which are determined on each market from the effective demands announced by agents. Each agent will thus try to find a vector of effective demands $\tilde{z}_i$ leading to the optimal transaction vector $\zeta_i^*(p, \bar{d}_i, \bar{s}_i)$. If agent i expresses a demand $\tilde{z}_{ih}$ on market h, the resulting transaction is

$$z_{ih}^* = \begin{cases} \min(\tilde{z}_{ih}, \bar{d}_{ih}) & \text{if} \quad \tilde{z}_{ih} \ge 0 \\ \max(\tilde{z}_{ih}, -\bar{s}_{ih}) & \text{if} \quad \tilde{z}_{ih} \le 0 \end{cases}$$

or more compactly,

$$z_{ih}^* = \min[\bar{d}_{ih}, \max(\tilde{z}_{ih}, -\bar{s}_{ih})]$$

If $\tilde{z}_{ih}$ is the effective demand of agent i on market h, we must thus have in order to obtain the optimal transaction ζ_i^*:

$$\min[\bar{d}_{ih}, \max(\tilde{z}_{ih}, -\bar{s}_{ih})] = \zeta_{ih}^*(p, \bar{d}_i, \bar{s}_i)$$

This equation has a unique solution if ζ_{ih}^* is interior to the segment $[-\bar{s}_{ih}, \bar{d}_{ih}]$ but has an infinity of solutions if ζ_{ih}^* is equal to $\bar{d}_{ih}$ or $-\bar{s}_{ih}$. In what follows we shall make a selection from the set of solutions and define an effective demand *function* that has the two properties of leading to the optimal transaction and revealing when an agent is constrained on markets.

The Effective Demand Function

We shall define formally the effective demand of agent i on market h, denoted by $\tilde{\zeta}_{ih}(p, \bar{d}_i, \bar{s}_i)$, as the solution in z_{ih} of the following program:

$$\text{Maximize } U_i(x_i, m_i) \qquad \text{s.t.}$$

$$x_i = \omega_i + z_i \geqslant 0$$

$$m_i = \bar{m}_i - pz_i \geqslant 0 \qquad \qquad (B_h)$$

$$-\bar{s}_{ik} \leqslant z_{ik} \leqslant \bar{d}_{ik} \qquad k \neq h$$

In other words, the effective demand on a market h corresponds to the exchange that maximizes utility, taking into account the constraints on the *other* markets. This definition, which we saw in Chapter 1, Section 4, integrates the spillover effects from the other markets. The solution of the program just given is unique, and we thus obtain a function. Repeating this program for all markets $h = 1, \ldots, l$, we obtain a vector of effective demands $\tilde{\zeta}_i(p, \bar{d}_i, \bar{s}_i)$. We must immediately verify that this effective demand function leads to the optimal transaction, which results from the following proposition, proved in Appendix A:

Proposition. *Assume that U_i is strictly concave in x_i, then*

$$\min\{\bar{d}_i, \max[-\bar{s}_i, \tilde{\zeta}_i(p, \bar{d}_i, \bar{s}_i)]\} = \zeta_i^*(p, \bar{d}_i, \bar{s}_i)$$

We may note, moreover, that this effective demand function has the property of revealing when an agent is constrained on a market. More precisely, we shall say that agent i is constrained in his demand for good h if the utility of his optimal transaction, as computed earlier in program (A), can be increased by suppressing the constraint $\bar{d}_{ih}$ (in other words, the constraint $\bar{d}_{ih}$ is binding in this program). The definition is symmetrical for the supply side and the constraint $\bar{s}_{ih}$. One sees intuitively that agent i would like to purchase more than $\bar{d}_{ih}$ when he is demand-constrained, to sell more than $\bar{s}_{ih}$ when he is supply-constrained. The effective demand function $\tilde{\zeta}_i$ reveals when an agent is constrained, since, as is easily verified,

Agent i is constrained in his demand for good $h \Leftrightarrow \tilde{\zeta}_{ih}(p, \bar{d}_i, \bar{s}_i) > \bar{d}_{ih}$
Agent i is constrained in his supply of good $h \Leftrightarrow \tilde{\zeta}_{ih}(p, \bar{d}_i, \bar{s}_i) < -\bar{s}_{ih}$

So, while announcing a demand that ensures the best possible transaction, the agent transmits to the markets where he is constrained his desire to exchange more, which is a signal of market imbalance.

5. Fixprice Equilibria

We shall now study the first non-Walrasian equilibrium concept by assuming that the price vector p is exogenously given, and we shall see how quantities adjust on all markets. The fixprice equilibrium concept involves three types of quantities for each agent: his vectors of effective demands ($\tilde{z}_i$), of transactions (z_i^*), and of perceived constraints ($\bar{d}_i$ and $\bar{s}_i$). We saw in Section 3 how transactions and quantity signals are formed in each market as functions of effective demands, and in Section 4 we showed how effective demands are determined as a function of price and quantity signals. We thus naturally obtain the following definition of a fixprice equilibrium, where "exogenous" data are the price system and the rationing schemes in all markets, F_i, $i = 1, \ldots, n$.

Definition. *A K-equilibrium associated with a price system p and rationing schemes represented by functions F_i, $i = 1, \ldots, n$, is a set of effective demands $\tilde{z}_i$, transactions z_i^*, and perceived constraints $\bar{d}_i$ and $\bar{s}_i$ such that*

$$\tilde{z}_i = \tilde{\zeta}_i(p, \bar{d}_i, \bar{s}_i) \qquad i = 1, \ldots, n \tag{1}$$

$$z_i^* = F_i(\tilde{z}_i, \tilde{Z}_i) \qquad i = 1, \ldots, n \tag{2}$$

$$\bar{d}_i = G_i^d(\tilde{Z}_i) \qquad i = 1, \ldots, n \tag{3}$$

$$\bar{s}_i = G_i^s(\tilde{Z}_i) \qquad i = 1, \ldots, n$$

We see that in a fixprice K-equilibrium, the quantity constraints $\bar{d}_i$ and $\bar{s}_i$, from which the agents construct their effective demands [(Eq. (1)], are those that will be generated by the exchange process [Eq. (3)]. At equilibrium the agents thus have a correct perception of these quantity constraints. One may note that such a condition is implicit in traditional Keynesian short-run equilibrium models.

Intuitively, we may consider a fixprice K-equilibrium as a fixed point of a "quantity tatonnement", where agents would announce effective demands on the basis of some perceived constraints [Eq. (1)]. From these effective demands the "market" would send to agents new perceived constraints [Eq. (3)] on the basis of which they would announce new effective demands [Eq. (1)], and so on. A fixprice equilibrium would be attained if effective demands and perceived constraints were reproduced identically over time. Transactions could then take place [Eq. (2)]. We shall consider later the properties of these equilibrium transactions.

A fixprice K-equilibrium exists under the usual concavity and continuity conditions for the utility functions and if the rationing schemes are continuous. An existence theorem can be found in Appendix A.

An Example

Consider the traditional Edgeworth box example (Fig. 2.2), which represents a single market where agents A and B exchange a good (measured horizontally) against money (measured vertically). Point O corresponds to initial endowments; DC is the budget line of the two agents at price p, and points A and B are the tangency points of the indifference curves with this budget line.

Measuring the level of exchanges along the line OC, we see that A demands a quantity OA, and B supplies a quantity OB. They exchange the minimum of these two quantities, i.e., OA, and agent B is rationed. Perceived constraints are respectively OA for agent B and OB for agent A. Agent B is constrained on his supply, whereas A is not constrained.

The Structure of Fixprice Equilibria

The conditions seen above in the definition of a fixprice equilibrium yield a consistent set of effective demands, transactions, and quantity signals. We shall now briefly indicate a few properties of the transactions obtained that will throw some light on the structure of these equilibria.

If we first consider a particular market h, the transactions of the various agents are by construction mutually consistent, since they result from

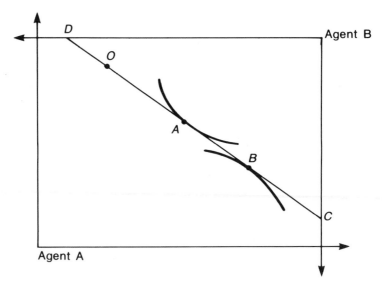

Figure 2.2

rationing schemes:

$$\sum_{i=1}^{n} z_{ih}^* = 0$$

However, in a fixprice equilibrium one may have inconsistent demands and supplies, i.e.,

$$\sum_{i=1}^{n} \tilde{z}_{ih} \neq 0$$

On a particular market one may thus have three different categories of agents:

(a)   Unrationed agents such that

$$z_{ih}^* = \tilde{z}_{ih} \quad \text{with} \quad -\bar{s}_{ih} \leqslant z_{ih}^* \leqslant \bar{d}_{ih}$$

(b)   Rationed demanders such that

$$\tilde{z}_{ih} > z_{ih}^* = \bar{d}_{ih}$$

(c)   Rationed suppliers such that

$$\tilde{z}_{ih} < z_{ih}^* = -\bar{s}_{ih}$$

Note that since our concept permits inefficient rationing schemes, we may have both rationed demanders and rationed suppliers on the same market. If, however, the rationing scheme on the market considered is frictionless, one side of that market at most is rationed.

If we now consider the point of view of a particular agent i, we see by using the proposition in Section 6 that his transactions vector z_i^* is the best, taking into account the perceived constraints on all markets. Mathematically, z_i^* is the solution in z_i of the following program (cf. Program A):

$$\text{Maximize } U_i(x_i, m_i) \quad \text{s.t.}$$

$$x_i = \omega_i + z_i \geqslant 0$$

$$m_i = \bar{m}_i - pz_i \geqslant 0$$

$$-\bar{s}_{ih} \leqslant z_{ih} \leqslant \bar{d}_{ih} \quad h = 1, \dots, l$$

In this program, the constraint $\bar{d}_{ih}$ is binding if i is rationed in his demand for good h,[3] and the constraint $\bar{s}_{ih}$ is binding if i is rationed in his supply of good h. Assuming that the above program has an interior solution, the Kuhn–Tucker conditions allow us to characterize the three situations in

---

[3]Note indeed that at a fixprice equilibrium there is an identity between agents rationed on a market and agents constrained on this market. This results from the fact that the effective demand function has the property seen above of "revealing" constrained agents.

which an agent can find himself in terms of marginal utilities:

$$\frac{1}{p_h}\frac{\partial U_i}{\partial x_{ih}} = \frac{\partial U_i}{\partial m_i} \qquad \text{if} \quad i \text{ is not rationed in market } h \qquad\qquad (a)$$

$$\frac{1}{p_h}\frac{\partial U_i}{\partial x_{ih}} > \frac{\partial U_i}{\partial m_i} \qquad \text{if} \quad i \text{ is rationed in his demand of good } h \qquad (b)$$

$$\frac{1}{p_h}\frac{\partial U_i}{\partial x_{ih}} < \frac{\partial U_i}{\partial m_i} \qquad \text{if} \quad i \text{ is rationed in his supply of good } h \qquad (c)$$

Note that the last two inequalities express in a very intuitive manner the desire of rationed agents to exchange more at the market price.

Fixprice Equilibria and Inefficiency

The preceding conditions allow us to show in a very simple manner some inefficiency properties of fixprice equilibria, obviously a very important theme if corrective policies are contemplated.

Consider, for example, the case, traditional in Keynesian theory, of an excess supply in several markets and consider two markets h and k in excess supply. We shall assume that these two markets are frictionless. Consider two agents i and j; i is a rationed supplier in k and unrationed demander in h; j is a rationed supplier in h and an unrationed demander in k. Then, the preceding conditions immediately lead to

$$\frac{1}{p_h}\frac{\partial U_i}{\partial x_{ih}} = \frac{\partial U_i}{\partial m_i} > \frac{1}{p_k}\frac{\partial U_i}{\partial x_{ik}}$$

$$\frac{1}{p_k}\frac{\partial U_j}{\partial x_{jk}} = \frac{\partial U_j}{\partial m_j} > \frac{1}{p_h}\frac{\partial U_j}{\partial x_{jh}}$$

One thus sees that i and j would both be interested in exchanging goods h and k directly against each other at the prices p_h and p_k, but this exchange is not realized even though each market taken individually functions efficiently. The existence of such unrealized exchange possibilities suggests that in such cases government intervention may improve the situation of other agents even without price changes, as we shall see in Chapter 3.

6. Expectations and Temporary Equilibrium with Rigid Prices

The K-equilibrium concept developed in Section 5 does not explicitly involve expectations about future periods. In this section we shall continue to develop the concept by incorporating expectations in a fully explicit manner. The method, already sketched in Chapter 1, consists of making explicit the role of expectations in the agents' indirect utility functions and redefining accordingly the concept of K-equilibrium with rigid prices.

We have assumed in Section 5 that agents derived utility not only from their current consumptions x_i, but also from the quantity of money held at the end of the period m_i, although this money has no intrinsic utility. We shall now see how such a utility function can be constructed from an intertemporal optimization program, taking into account expectations of future prices and quantities, and where only current and future consumptions yield direct utility. The utility of money, which is of course indirect, derives from the utility of future exchanges, which it makes possible as a store of value.[4] It thus also naturally depends on price–quantity expectations, which will appear in the indirect function through a vector of current price–quantity signals σ_i. We shall also study in this framework the concept of fixprice K-equilibrium, which will then incorporate expectations explicitly.

Markets and Agents

We shall consider here an exchange economy with n agents and l markets, as in Section 5. Each agent now has a two-period horizon;[5] he thus makes plans for the current period and the future period. We shall denote the variables relative to the future period by a superindex e (for expected). Agent i has vectors of initial endowments ω_i and ω_i^e for the first and second periods. His consumption vectors are x_i and x_i^e. They are related to the net exchange vectors z_i and z_i^e by the following relations:

$$x_i = \omega_i + z_i \geq 0$$

$$x_i^e = \omega_i^e + z_i^e \geq 0$$

At the beginning of the current period, the agent holds an initial quantity of money $\bar{m}_i$. He transfers to the second period a quantity m_i equal to

$$m_i = \bar{m}_i - pz_i \geq 0$$

[4]The same method could thus also apply to any other reserve of value.

[5]Note that the method would extend without difficulty to any finite number of periods. Furthermore, even if each agent makes plans for a finite number of periods only, the economy considered may have an infinite horizon since "new" agents, whose horizon will extend further, will be born after the current period, as in overlapping generations models "à la Samuelson," an example of which is seen in Chapter 14.

The expected transactions in the second period must satisfy

$$p^e z_i^e \leq m_i$$

We assume that each agent has a utility function bearing on his current and future consumptions, which we shall denote by $V_i(x_i, x_i^e)$ and which we shall assume to be strictly concave in its arguments.

Current and Expected Signals

Each agent must form expectations about the prices and quantity constraints he will face in the future period, because these signals will determine his exchange possibilities in the second period. We shall denote by σ_i^e the set of these expected signals,

$$\sigma_i^e = \{ p^e, \bar{d}_i^e, \bar{s}_i^e \}$$

and we shall denote by σ_i the corresponding set of signals for the current period,

$$\sigma_i = \{ p, \bar{d}_i, \bar{s}_i \}$$

We shall assume that expectations are formed from current signals σ_i and past signals, which are a datum in the current period. We shall thus write the expectations formation scheme as

$$\sigma_i^e = \psi_i(\sigma_i)$$

The Indirect Utility Function

Assume that agent i has consumed x_i in the first period and transfers a quantity of money m_i to the second period. Given some expectations $\sigma_i^e = \{ p^e, \bar{d}_i^e, \bar{s}_i^e \}$, his expected second-period transactions are those which maximize his utility under the budget constraint while taking all quantity signals into account. Thus, z_i^e and x_i^e are solution of the following program:

$$\text{Maximize } V_i(x_i, x_i^e) \qquad \text{s.t.}$$

$$x_i^e = \omega_i^e + z_i^e \geq 0$$

$$p^e z_i^e \leq m_i$$

$$-\bar{s}_i^e \leq z_i^e \leq \bar{d}_i^e$$

We shall denote functionally the vector x_i^e, which is the solution of this program, as

$$X_i^e(x_i, m_i, p^e, \bar{d}_i^e, \bar{s}_i^e) = X_i^e(x_i, m_i, \sigma_i^e)$$

One can then write the level of utility expected in the first period as

$$U_i^e(x_i, m_i, \sigma_i^e) = V_i[x_i, X_i^e(x_i, m_i, \sigma_i^e)]$$

Under this form, the indirect utility function depends explicitly on expectations of future signals σ_i^e. We saw above that these were functions of current signals σ_i via ψ_i. Inserting this into the function U_i^e, we then obtain the indirect utility function as

$$U_i(x_i, m_i, \sigma_i) = U_i^e[x_i, m_i, \psi_i(\sigma_i)]$$

This indirect utility function now has as arguments first-period variables only: consumption x_i, the quantity of money saved m_i, and current price-quantity signals σ_i.

Effective Demand and Fixprice K-Equilibrium

From the indirect utility function just constructed, we can define the effective demand function in the same way as in Section 5: The component h of the effective demands vector $\tilde{\zeta}_{ih}(p, \bar{d}_i, \bar{s}_i)$ is the solution in z_{ih} of the following program:

$$\text{Maximize } U_i(x_i, m_i, \sigma_i) \quad \text{s.t.}$$

$$x_i = \omega_i + z_i \geq 0$$

$$m_i = \bar{m}_i - pz_i \geq 0$$

$$-\bar{s}_{ik} \leq z_{ik} \leq \bar{d}_{ik} \quad k \neq h$$

We may note that through the expectations imbedded in the indirect utility function, expected constraints produce spillover effects just as well as current constraints.

As in Section 5, a fixprice K-equilibrium is defined by a set of vectors $\tilde{z}_i, z_i^*, \bar{d}_i, \bar{s}_i$ such that

$$\tilde{z}_i = \tilde{\zeta}_i(p, \bar{d}_i, \bar{s}_i) \qquad i = 1, \ldots, n \tag{1}$$

$$z_i^* = F_i(\tilde{z}_i, \tilde{Z}_i) \qquad i = 1, \ldots, n \tag{2}$$

$$\bar{d}_i = G_i^d(\tilde{Z}_i) \qquad i = 1, \ldots, n \tag{3}$$

$$\bar{s}_i = G_i^s(\tilde{Z}_i) \qquad i = 1, \ldots, n$$

Such an equilibrium exists under standard assumptions of concavity of utility functions and continuity of expectations. A precise existence theorem is in Appendix A.

7. K-Equilibrium with Bounded Prices

The concepts described in Sections 5 and 6 assumed a completely rigid price system. We shall now introduce some price flexibility but without reverting to full flexibility and the Walrasian equilibrium. In this section we shall study a non-Walrasian equilibrium concept where each price is flexible between two predetermined bounds. As long as the price remains between these bounds, it reacts "competitively" to excess effective demand on the market. The price may, however, hit one of these two bounds, in which case there may remain excess demands or supplies.

Markets

We shall thus assume that in each market h the price p_h must remain between two bounds

$$\bar{p}_h \le p_h \le \bar{\bar{p}}_h$$

or, in terms of price vectors,

$$\bar{p} \le p \le \bar{\bar{p}}$$

Let us furthermore define total excess demand on each market:

$$\tilde{z}_h = \sum_{i=1}^{n} \tilde{z}_{ih}$$

We shall assume that the price p_h has a tendency to decrease if there is excess supply, to increase if there is excess demand. It must, however, remain between the above bounds. One may thus have at equilibrium three types of situations: (1) supply and demand are equal on the market; (2) the market is in excess supply, and the price is at the minimum bound; and (3) the market is in excess demand, and the price is at the maximum bound. Mathematically these three situations are respectively written

$$\tilde{z}_h = 0 \qquad \bar{p}_h \le p_h \le \bar{\bar{p}}_h$$

$$\tilde{z}_h < 0 \qquad p_h = \bar{p}_h$$

$$\tilde{z}_h > 0 \qquad p_h = \bar{\bar{p}}_h$$

We shall now characterize a non-Walrasian equilibrium corresponding to this mode of functioning of markets.

K-Equilibrium with Bounded Prices: Definition

We have considered in previous sections the conditions of consistency between the various quantity variables for a given price vector. In order to obtain a concept of equilibrium with bounded prices, all we need is to add to these consistency conditions the conditions relating prices and effective demands that we have just described. We thus obtain the following definition:

Definition: *A K-equilibrium with bounded prices corresponding to bounds $\bar{p}$ and $\bar{\bar{p}}$ is a set of vectors z_i, z_i^*, $\bar{d}_i$, $\bar{s}_i$ and a price vector p^* such that*

(1) $(z_i), (z_i^*), (\bar{d}_i, \bar{s}_i)$ *form a K-equilibrium for the price p^**

(2) $\bar{p} \leqslant p^* \leqslant \bar{\bar{p}}$

(3) $\tilde{z}_h < 0 \Rightarrow p_h^* = \bar{p}_h$ $\forall h$

$\tilde{z}_h > 0 \Rightarrow p_h^* = \bar{\bar{p}}_h$ $\forall h$

The existence of such equilibria can be proved under the usual conditions of concavity of the utility functions so long as the vectors $\bar{p}$ and $\bar{\bar{p}}$ have no components equal to zero or infinity (cf. Appendix A).

8. K-Equilibrium with Monopolistic Competition

We shall now study another non-Walrasian equilibrium concept with flexible prices where the agents themselves determine prices. As we saw in Chapter 1, Section 7, one arrives at a formulation fairly close to the literature on monopolistic competition. An agent who makes the price on a market perceives a relation between his maximal transactions and the price he decides. He will change his price so as to "manipulate" his quantity constraints, and an equilibrium is attained when he is satisfied with the price–quantity combination obtained.

Institutional Framework

We shall assume that each agent i controls the prices of a subset of goods $h \in H_i$, with

$$H_i \cap H_j = \{\varnothing\}$$

The price of each good is thus determined by at most one agent. There may be a subset of goods H_0, whose prices are exogenously fixed in the period considered. We shall denote by p_i the subvector of dimension H_i of the prices controlled by agent i, i.e.

$$p_i = \{ p_h \,|\, h \in H_i \}$$

Perceived Demand and Supply Curves

Consider a pricemaker i who must determine the price p_h of a good $h \in H_i$, which he sells. As we saw in Chapter 1, for this purpose he will use a perceived demand curve, which is an estimate of the "true" demand curve. The corresponding function depends on the vector of prices announced by agent i, p_i, and on a set of parameters η_i, which are themselves estimated on the basis of price–quantity signals, as we shall see later. We can thus denote the perceived demand curve as

$$\bar{S}_{ih}(p_i, \eta_i)$$

and we shall assume that it is nonincreasing in p_h. As explained in Chapter 1, the perceived demand curve is denoted as a constraint on the sales of agent i, since the total demand of the other agents represents the maximum quantity that agent i can sell. Symmetrically, the perceived supply curve of an agent i, who determines the price of a good h that he buys, will be denoted as

$$\bar{D}_{ih}(p_i, \eta_i)$$

and we shall assume that it is nondecreasing in p_h. Note that with this formulation we can take into account an interdependency among the various goods controlled by agent i, for each perceived demand and supply curve is a function of the vector p_i of all prices announced by agent i. Such an interdependency will occur, for example, if the agent practices some product differentiation.

Estimation of the Perceived Curves

Before determining his prices, agent i must estimate the parameters η_i. The estimation procedure generally uses past and present price and quantity signals. Since the past is already given, we shall make explicit in this estimation procedure only the dependence with respect to current signals σ_i, so we shall write

$$\eta_i = \eta(\sigma_i)$$

The estimation procedure obviously depends on the parametrization of the perceived curve. However, because we are going to examine an equilibrium concept for the current period, this estimation procedure must be such that perceived demand and supply curves be consistent with current observations, as we saw in Chapter 1, Section 7. This means that whatever the estimation procedure, if agent i has observed a signal $\sigma_i = \{\bar{p}, \bar{d}_i, \bar{s}_i\}$, one must have

$$\bar{D}_{ih}[p_i, \eta_i(\bar{p}, \bar{d}_i, \bar{s}_i)] = \bar{d}_{ih} \qquad \text{for} \quad p_i = \bar{p}_i$$

$$\bar{S}_{ih}[p_i, \eta_i(\bar{p}, \bar{d}_i, \bar{s}_i)] = \bar{s}_{ih} \qquad \text{for} \quad p_i = \bar{p}_i$$

i.e., the perceived curves must "go through" the observed point.

Price Formation

Once the parameters of the perceived demand and supply curves are known, the pricemaker i chooses a price vector p_i so as to maximize his utility, taking into account the exchanges that he perceives are possible. We assume that the agent receives price-quantity signals $\sigma_i = \{\bar{p}, \bar{d}_i, \bar{s}_i\}$. He chooses his price vector as the solution in p_i of the following program:

$$\text{Maximize } U_i(x_i, m_i, \sigma_i) \qquad \text{s.t.}$$

$$x_i = \omega_i + z_i \geq 0$$

$$m_i = \bar{m}_i - pz_i \geq 0$$

$$p_h = \bar{p}_h \qquad -\bar{s}_{ih} \leq z_{ih} \leq \bar{d}_{ih} \qquad\qquad h \notin H_i$$

$$-\bar{S}_{ih}[p_i, \eta_i(\sigma_i)] \leq z_{ih} \leq \bar{D}_{ih}[p_i, \eta_i(\sigma_i)] \qquad h \in H_i^6$$

We shall denote this optimal price vector by

$$\mathcal{P}_i^*(\sigma_i) = p_i^*(\bar{p}, \bar{d}_i, \bar{s}_i)$$

K-Equilibrium with Monopolistic Competition

An equilibrium is intuitively defined as a K-equilibrium where no agent has an interest in modifying the prices he controls. More precisely, we have the following definition:

Definition. *A K-equilibrium with monopolistic competition is defined by a price vector p^*, effective demands $\tilde{z}_i$, transactions z_i^*, and quantity signals $\bar{s}_i$*

---

[6] Actually in each market $h \in H_i$ only one of the curves $\bar{S}_{ih}$ or $\bar{D}_{ih}$ is used, since the pricemaker is on a given side of the market.

and $\bar{d}_i$ such that

(1) $(\tilde{z}_i)$, (z_i^*), $(\bar{d}_i, \bar{s}_i)$ *form a K-equilibrium for the price vector p^*.*

(2) $p_i^* = \mathscr{P}_i^*(p_i^*, \bar{d}_i, \bar{s}_i)$ *for all i.*

Obviously, the equilibrium so obtained depends on the prices given *a priori*, i.e., on the prices of goods $h \in H_0$. Existence of such equilibria can be proved if one makes supplementary assumptions on the function $\mathscr{P}_i^*$ which ensure that equilibrium prices are finite.

9. Conclusions

We have constructed in this chapter the various non-Walrasian equilibrium concepts that will be used in what follows. First, we rigorously described the rationing schemes in each market and showed how quantity signals, the perceived constraints, were formed. Then we gave a general definition of the effective demand function through which a rational agent faced with both a price system and quantity constraints can achieve optimal transactions, given the set of these signals.

We then moved on to the study of the concepts themselves, the K-equilibria, starting with the basic concept of fixprice equilibrium whose properties were studied. We then explicitly introduced price–quantity expectations into this basic scheme, obtaining in that way a temporary equilibrium structure.

The hypothesis of fixed prices, although a useful step in building other concepts, is of course an extreme assumption, so we studied other concepts incorporating some price flexibility: first, a concept of K-equilibrium with bounded prices where prices must remain within predetermined bounds but react competitively between these bounds; then, a concept of K-equilibrium with monopolistic competition where agents internal to the system themselves determine the prices.

We now have at our disposal a wide range of non-Walrasian equilibrium concepts, including modes of price formation going from full rigidity to total flexibility, with intermediate forms of imperfect competition. In the following chapters, we shall use these concepts to study various problems in macroeconomic theory.

References

The concepts developed in this chapter are drawn from Benassy (1975a, 1976b, 1977b, 1982b) and Drèze (1975). A more complete exposition with further developments is found in Benassy (1982b).

The concept of fixprice equilibrium described in this chapter is taken from Benassy (1975a, 1977b), where a more "subjective" approach of perceived constraints was adopted. An alternative concept of fixprice equilibrium is found in Drèze (1975); see also Younès (1975), Böhm and Levine (1979), and Heller and Starr (1979). The introduction of expectations in non-Walrasian equilibrium models was made in Benassy (1973, 1975a). An extension to nonmonetary economies can be found in Benassy (1975b).

The concept of equilibrium with bounded prices has been developed by Drèze (1975). The concept we describe here synthesizes his approach and the K-equilibrium notion. The concept of K-equilibrium with monopolistic competition has been developed in Benassy (1973, 1976a, 1977a, 1982b). Before that, Negishi (1961, 1972) had developed a concept of general equilibrium with monopolistic competition based on perceived demand curves.

PART II

CLOSED-ECONOMY MODELS

CHAPTER

3

Theories of Unemployment

1. Classical and Keynesian Theories of Unemployment

One often finds two conflicting theories of unemployment in the literature dealing with problems of economic policy: For the "classicals," unemployment is due to too high real wages, whereas for "Keynesians," the cause is insufficient effective demand. Policies prescribed by the two schools are just as different: For the classicals, the real wage should be reduced, which may be done by letting the "laws of market" drive it down or by appropriate income policies. Keynesians, on the contrary, recommend an increase in public spending, tax reductions, or other measures inducing increases in consumption or investment.

These two theories can be illustrated graphically quite simply: Let l be the level of employment and $F(l)$ a production function representing the economy's technological possibilities. In order to keep the analysis as simple as possible, let us also assume an inelastic supply of labor l_0, and thus a full employment production level $F(l_0)$.

For the classicals, the cause of unemployment lies fundamentally in the labor market. They must compute the demand for labor emanating from firms, and they generally assume that firms choose the employment and production levels which maximize profits, taking the price p and the wage w as given. If y is the level of sales on the output market, short-run profit is equal to $py - wl$. The "classical" demand for labor l_c and the corresponding supply of goods y_c are thus the solutions in l and y of the following

61

program:

$$\text{Maximize } py - wl \qquad \text{s.t.}$$

$$y \leqslant F(l)$$

which yields immediately,

$$l_c = F'^{-1}(w/p)$$

$$y_c = F[F'^{-1}(w/p)]$$

The labor supply l_0 and the classical demand for labor $F'^{-1}(w/p)$ are shown in Fig. 3.1. It can be seen that in this framework there is unemployment if and only if the real wage is above its Walrasian equilibrium value $F'(l_0)$.

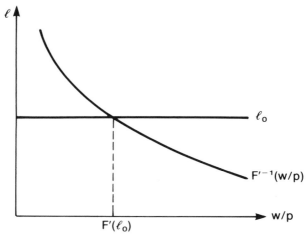

Figure 3.1

In Keynesian theory, where spillover effects from one market to the other play a prominent role, effective demand in the goods market appears as the principal determinant of the ·production level, employment, and income. This aggregate effective demand is defined as the sum of the consumption, investment, and government demands. All these elements are assumed to be functions of real income, which itself depends on y, and of other variables (including, notably, expectations) considered as given in the short run. One may thus represent this aggregate effective demand as a function of y (Fig. 3.2). The "equilibrium" level of y, which we denote by y_k, is given by the intersection of the effective demand curve with the 45° line. The employment level is that necessary to produce y_k, given by $F^{-1}(y_k)$. Clearly, in this framework unemployment is due to insufficient effective demand, which

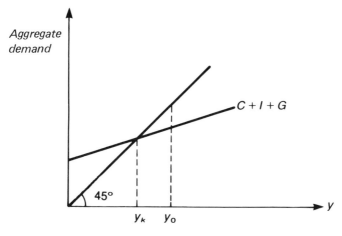

Figure 3.2

means a value of y_k lower than $y_0 = F(l_0)$. This may be remedied by public spending, tax reductions, or other "Keynesian" measures aimed at stimulating demand.

From the two descriptions just given and Figs. 3.1 and 3.2, it should be apparent that each of the two theories ignores a fundamental point which the other takes into account: The classicals ignore the fact that outside Walrasian equilibrium, firms may not succeed in selling as much output as they would want, which would of course change their demand for labor. Keynesians, on the other hand, forget that effective demand may be higher than the firms' Walrasian supply y_c, in which case it is output supply and not output demand that determines the level of sales. These simple remarks show that there is not much point in looking for *the* better theory. Rather we should attempt a synthesis that can show in which circumstances each of the two approaches might be applied.

A Fixprice Model

Quite obviously, a model aimed at comparing classical and Keynesian theories of unemployment must introduce some degree of rigidity in wages and prices: Indeed, traditional Keynesian models are often constructed under the assumption of rigid prices and wages (or at least the latter), whereas the classical model usually implies a rigid real wage. In order to obtain a particularly simple synthetic model, we shall push these rigidities to the extreme and study in this chapter a model of fixprice equilibrium similar to those described in Chapters 1 and 2. In order to remain close to the macroeconomic models sketched earlier, this model is treated at a very aggregated level.

2. The Model

We shall consider here an aggregate monetary economy with three representative agents (a household, a firm, and the government), and three types of goods (a consumption good (output), labor, and money). There are thus two markets in the period considered: one where output is exchanged against money at the price p, the other where labor is exchanged against money at the wage w. As indicated before, p and w are assumed to be rigid in the current period. Each of these two markets is assumed to function without frictions, so that realized transactions are equal to the minimum of demand and supply.

In what follows we shall be interested in the equilibrium levels of employment l^* and output sales y^* for various values of p and w.[1] Before that we shall describe each of the agents and his behavior in more detail.

The Firm

The representative firm has a short-run production function $F(l)$ with the traditional properties

$$F(0) = 0 \qquad F'(l) > 0 \qquad F''(l) < 0$$

It is assumed that there are no inventories. Under these conditions, at equilibrium, output sales y are equal to production $F(l)$. The firm's objective is to maximize profits $py - wl$. These profits are entirely distributed to the household, whose real income (before taxes) is thus equal to y.

The Household

The representative household consumes a quantity c, sells l units of labor, and saves a quantity of money m. It is endowed with an initial quantity of money $\bar{m}$ and a quantity of labor l_0. His labor sales cannot exceed this

---

[1]Thus, in general we shall not compute the complete system, including, besides transactions, the effective demands and perceived constraints. For an example of such a computation, see Chapter 1, Section 5.

quantity: $l \leq l_0$. Denote the level of taxes in real terms by τ. The household's budget constraint is written

$$pc + m = \bar{m} + p(y - \tau)$$

We shall assume that the household has no utility for leisure so that his labor supply is constant and equal to l_0. His effective demand for output $\tilde{c}$ is described by a consumption function that depends on real income (here equal to y), the price level p, and taxes τ:

$$\tilde{c} = C(y, p, \tau)$$

This function obviously also depends on the intial quantity of money $\bar{m}$, but we shall omit it as an argument in the function because it is given in this period. We saw in Chapter 1 an example of construction of such a function. More generally it can be derived from an intertemporal utility maximization program under budget constraints similar to the one seen previously for each future period and where expected real incomes, prices, and taxes depend on the current values of these variables (the general method of treating such programs has been studied in Chapter 2). We shall assume[2]

$$0 \leq C_y \leq \delta < 1 \qquad C_p < 0 \qquad C_\tau < 0$$

In order to have an explicit example, in what follows we shall sometimes use a linear consumption function:

$$\tilde{c} = \alpha(y - \tau) + \beta \frac{\bar{m}}{p}$$

with

$$0 < \alpha < 1 \qquad 0 < \beta < 1$$

The Government

The government collects taxes τ in real terms and has an effective demand for goods $\tilde{g}$. Purchases actually realized are denoted by g^*. Any budget deficit is financed through the creation of money.

---

[2]Here and in all that follows, a subindex attached to a function denotes a partial derivative, for example, $C_y = \partial C / \partial y$.

3. Temporary Walrasian Equilibrium and Situations of Unemployment

In this section we shall compute as a reference point the parameters of the temporary Walrasian equilibrium in this model. We shall then consider potential unemployment situations, and we shall see how our model allows us to show the classical and Keynesian diagnoses.

Temporary Walrasian Equilibrium

The Walrasian price and wage levels, p_0 and w_0, respectively, are determined by the conditions of market clearing for labor and output. Labor market clearing implies

$$F'^{-1}\left(\frac{w_0}{p_0}\right) = l_0$$

or

$$\frac{w_0}{p_0} = F'(l_0)$$

In other words, the Walrasian real wage is equal to the marginal productivity of labor at full employment. Output market clearing implies that full employment production is equal to the sum of consumption (evaluated at full employment income) and government spending, which yields the second equation:

$$C(y_0, p_0, \tau) + \tilde{g} = y_0$$

It is assumed in what follows that the consumption function and the values of the various parameters are such that this equation has a solution. This second equation allows us to study directly the crowding-out effects of government spending. Recall that there is *crowding out* when an increase in public spending "displaces," partially or totally, private spending. We can see from the second equation that at the temporary Walrasian equilibrium, there is full crowding out of consumption by government spending because the sum of the two is equal to y_0, the full-employment production. This full crowding-out effect occurs here through the price increases that accompany an increase in government demand.

The characteristics of temporary Walrasian equilibrium, however, are not the main subject of interest in this chapter. We want to know those values of the exogenous parameters p, w, $\tilde{g}$, τ for which unemployment has classical or Keynesian characteristics. Before that we shall recast both theories in the framework of our model.

Classical and Keynesian Diagnoses

It is indeed possible to express both the classical and the Keynesian diagnoses in this very simple model. Faced with a situation of unemployment, classicals would simply say that this is due to the real wage being above the Walrasian value, i.e.,

$$\frac{w}{p} > F'(l_0)$$

Keynesians, conversely, would compute the "equilibrium" level y_k as the solution in y of the following equation (cf. Fig. 3.3):

$$C(y, p, \tau) + \tilde{g} = y$$

Because we assumed a propensity to consume smaller than 1, this equation has a unique solution in y that we shall denote functionally,

$$y_k = K(p, \tilde{g}, \tau)$$

As an example, for the linear consumption function seen earlier we simply get a traditional multiplier formula:

$$y_k = \frac{1}{1 - \alpha}\left[\frac{\beta\bar{m}}{p} + \tilde{g} - \alpha\tau\right]$$

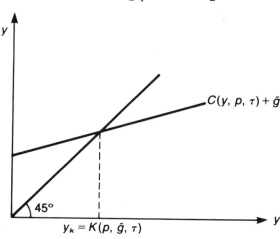

$C(y, p, \tau) + \tilde{g}$

$45°$

$y_k = K(p, \tilde{g}, \tau)$

Figure 3.3

For the Keynesians, there is unemployment because $F^{-1}(y_k) < l_0$, or, equivalently, because $y_k < y_0$. In order to determine which parameter changes would allow an increase in y_k, it is sufficient to compute the partial derivatives of the function $K(p, \tilde{g}, \tau)$:

$$K_g = \frac{1}{1 - C_y} > 1 \qquad K_\tau = \frac{C_\tau}{1 - C_y} < 0$$

We see that $y_k = K(p, \tilde{g}, \tau)$ increases when $\tilde{g}$ increases or τ decreases; We thus obtain the traditional Keynesian results.

4. The Three Regimes

As in all fixprice equilibrium models, the determination of transactions on the labor and output markets is quite different, depending on the sign of excess demand in each market. With two markets, one might *a priori* expect four possible cases since each market could be in excess supply or in excess demand. However—and anticipating a little the discussion to follow—we shall see that there are in this simple model only three types of equilibria:[3]

Keynesian unemployment, with excess supply of labor and output.
Classical unemployment, with excess supply of labor and excess demand for goods.
Repressed inflation, with excess demand for goods and labor.

Since there are no inventories, the fourth regime (excess supply of goods, excess demand for labor) degenerates into a limiting case between the zones of Keynesian unemployment and repressed inflation, as we shall see later. We shall now determine the level of employment l^* and sales y^* in each of these cases, examine the effectiveness of various policies, and see which values of the parameters lead to what regime.

Keynesian Unemployment

This case corresponds to the traditional Keynesian situation of excess supply on the markets for output and labor. Transactions are thus demand

---

[3]The terminology used here is not the best, since it rigidly associates excess supply of goods and Keynesian unemployment on the one hand, and excess demand for goods and classical unemployment on the other. However, such an association is not valid in general, notably when inventories are introduced. Since this is the only chapter where we use it, we shall retain this terminology, which has by now become fairly common.

determined. On the goods market, sales are equal to total effective demand, i.e.,

$$y = C(y, p, \tau) + \tilde{g}$$

We have already denoted $y_k = K(p, \tilde{g}, \tau)$ the solution in y of this equation. We thus have

$$y^* = y_k = K(p, \tilde{g}, \tau)$$

The employment level is determined by the demand for labor. Since there is excess supply of goods, this demand for labor has the "Keynesian" form (cf. Chapter 1); i.e., it is equal to the volume of labor just necessary to produce the quantity of goods demanded y_k:

$$l^* = F^{-1}(y_k) = F^{-1}[K(p, \tilde{g}, \tau)]$$

We can immediately verify that in this region we obtain the Keynesian economic policy results. Indeed, we find

$$\frac{\partial y^*}{\partial \tilde{g}} = \frac{1}{1 - C_y} > 1$$

$$\frac{\partial y^*}{\partial \tau} = \frac{C_\tau}{1 - C_y} < 0$$

These are traditional "multiplier" formulas that show that an increase in public spending $\tilde{g}$ or a reduction in taxes τ has a positive effect on production and employment. We can also compute the effects of an identical increase in $\tilde{g}$ and τ. We then find the "balanced-budget multiplier"

$$\frac{\partial y^*}{\partial \tilde{g}} = \frac{1 + C_\tau}{1 - C_y}$$

If we assume, as is usually done in traditional expositions, that $C_\tau = -C_y$ (which happens in particular when consumption is function of real disposable income $y - \tau$), we find the traditional balanced-budget multiplier equal to 1. Moreover, we see that a price decrease has a favorable effect on employment, whereas a variation in the wage level has no effect. This last result is of course due to the fact that in the formulation we considered the propensity to consume is identical for wage income and profit income, and total consumption thus does not depend on the distribution of real income y between wages and profits. If the marginal propensity to consume is higher for wage income than for profit income (which would happen, for example, if the firm distributed only part of the period's profits), then the consumption function C depends positively on w, and an increase in wages increases the level of employment.

We can now consider the equilibrium level of consumption c^*, which is equal to $y_k - \tilde{g}$. A particularly interesting result is that c^* is an increasing function of the level of public spending:

$$\frac{\partial c^*}{\partial \tilde{g}} = \frac{\partial y^*}{\partial \tilde{g}} - 1 = \frac{C_y}{1 - C_y} > 0$$

There is thus no crowding-out effect in the Keynesian region, since an increase in $\tilde{g}$ is not made at the expense of private consumption as in the Walrasian case; rather, it allows this consumption to increase. This remarkable result shows the inefficiency of the Keynesian situation, which we shall reexamine later in Section 5.

We now have to determine the values of the parameters for which this Keynesian regime will occur. We must thus verify that the values of y^* and l^* found before indeed correspond to an excess supply in the two markets. For excess supply to prevail in the labor market, we must have

$$l^* \leq l_0$$

i.e., with the value of l^* found previously,

$$K(p, \tilde{g}, \tau) \leq y_0$$

For excess supply of goods to prevail in the goods market, y^* must be below what the firm would supply in the absence of a constraint on the output market, i.e., the solution of the program

$$\text{Maximize } py - wl \qquad \text{s.t.}$$

$$y \leq F(l)$$

$$l \leq l_0$$

which yields

$$y^* \leq \min\{y_0, F[F'^{-1}(w/p)]\}$$

or, with the value of y^* found above,

$$K(p, \tilde{g}, \tau) \leq \min\{y_0, F[F'^{-1}(w/p)]\}$$

Combining the above conditions, we see that the region of excess supply on both markets corresponds to the subset of parameters defined by

$$K(p, \tilde{g}, \tau) \leq y_0$$
$$K(p, \tilde{g}, \tau) \leq F[F'^{-1}(w/p)]$$

We shall see later a graphical representation of this region in the parameter space.

Classical Unemployment

In this case, as we indicated before, there is excess supply of labor and excess demand for goods. The household is thus constrained on the two markets, whereas the firm experiences no binding quantity constraint. It can thus carry out its Walrasian employment and sales plan. The corresponding values for l^* and y^* are thus,

$$l^* = l_c = F'^{-1}(w/p)$$
$$y^* = y_c = F[F'^{-1}(w/p)]$$

We immediately see in these formulas that all "classical" results apply in this case: Only a reduction in the real wage can increase production and employment. Keynesian measures (increase in $\tilde{g}$ or decrease in τ) would only increase excess demand on the output market. The distribution of production y_c between the private sector and the public sector depends on the rationing scheme prevalent in the output market. If we assume that government has priority over the private sector, then the levels of government purchases and private consumption are given by

$$g^* = \min(\tilde{g}, y_c)$$
$$c^* = y_c - \min(\tilde{g}, y_c)$$

We see that an increase in $\tilde{g}$ reduces consumption by the same amount. In this case there is thus full crowding out of private consumption by public consumption, through direct quantity rationing and not through prices as in the Walrasian case.

We must now determine for which values of the parameters we shall be in this regime. We should first verify that there is excess supply in the labor market, i.e., $l^* \le l_0$, or

$$F'^{-1}(w/p) \le l_0$$

Furthermore, the level of income must be such that there is excess demand in the output market, i.e.,

$$C(y_c, p, \tau) + \tilde{g} \ge y_c$$

an equation which is equivalent to (cf. Fig. 3.3)

$$y_c \le y_k$$

or

$$F[F'^{-1}(w/p)] \le K(p, \tilde{g}, \tau)$$

Repressed Inflation

Here we are in a situation of excess demand in the two markets. In the labor market the employment level is thus determined by the inelastic supply l_0. Production is equal to $y_0 = F(l_0)$, and since there is excess demand in ·the output market, sales of goods are determined by the level of production. One thus has

$$l^* = l_0 \qquad y^* = y_0$$

Continuing with the example in which the government has priority in the output market, we find that the consumption level is equal to

$$c^* = y_0 - \min(\tilde{g}, y_0)$$

As long as we remain in this repressed inflation region, the various economic policies have no effect on employment. However, an increase in public spending will crowd out private consumption and increase the excess demand for goods.

For this regime to obtain, parameters must lead to an excess demand for goods,

$$C(y_0, p, \tau) + \tilde{g} \geq y_0$$

or, equivalently,

$$K(p, \tilde{g}, \tau) \geq y_0$$

Moreover, there must be excess demand for labor, which implies

$$F'^{-1}(w/p) \geq l_0$$

The Fourth Regime

As we said earlier, this regime would correspond to an excess supply of goods and an excess demand for labor. With an excess supply of goods, transactions are demand determined,

$$y = C(y, p, \tau) + \tilde{g}$$

or

$$y^* = K(p, \tilde{g}, \tau) = y_k$$

whereas with an excess demand for labor, employment is supply determined,

$$l^* = l_0$$

For this regime to obtain, we should be in a situation where the two values y^* and l^* found earlier constrain the firm in the two markets. More precisely, consider the program giving the firm's transactions;

$$\text{Maximize } py - wl \quad \text{s.t.}$$

$$y \le F(l)$$

$$y \le y_k$$

$$l \le l_0$$

Both the constraints l_0 and y_k must be binding, which can only happen in the degenerate case, where

$$w/p \le F'(l_0) \quad \text{and} \quad y_k = F(l_0) = y_0$$

We may remark that the degeneracy of this region is not surprising: Indeed, in the absence of inventories, why would a firm demand more labor to produce goods it cannot sell?

5. Global Analysis

Delimitation of the Regimes

We saw in Section 4 how the levels of employment l^* and sales y^* are determined in each regime, as well as the values of the parameters leading to each case. Let us summarize briefly the results obtained above.

In the Keynesian unemployment regime,

$$y^* = K(p, \tilde{g}, \tau) \quad l^* = F^{-1}[K(p, \tilde{g}, \tau)]$$

$$K(p, \tilde{g}, \tau) \le y_0$$

$$K(p, \tilde{g}, \tau) \le F[F'^{-1}(w/p)]$$

In the classical unemployment regime,

$$y^* = F[F'^{-1}(w/p)] \quad l^* = F'^{-1}(w/p)$$

$$F[F'^{-1}(w/p)] \le y_0$$

$$F[F'^{-1}(w/p)] \le K(p, \tilde{g}, \tau)$$

In the repressed inflation regime,

$$y^* = y_0 \quad l^* = l_0$$

$$y_0 \le K(p, \tilde{g}, \tau)$$

$$y_0 \le F[F'^{-1}(w/p)]$$

These conditions allow us to determine the values of l^* and y^* and the nature of the regime as a function of the exogenous parameters p, w, $\tilde{g}$, and

τ. As it turns out, all the equalities and inequalities above are actually functions of only two fundamental parameters: the real wage w/p and the "Keynesian" level of sales $y_k = K(p, \tilde{g}, \tau)$. This has nice consequences for representation of results: First, employment and sales are given by a simple and unique formula,

$$y^* = \min\{K(p, \tilde{g}, \tau), F[F'^{-1}(w/p)], y_0\}$$
$$l^* = F^{-1}(y^*)$$

Second, since the inequalities listed above, showing for which range of parameters each regime obtains, also depend only on w/p and y_k (they actually simply tell us which of the three quantities in the above formula is lowest), one may represent the three regimes in a two-dimensional diagram (Fig. 3.4), which has the advantage of being invariant with respect to changes in the four original parameters. The values of w/p and y_k corresponding to the Walrasian equilibrium are, respectively, $F'(l_0)$ and y_0. The Keynesian region is denoted by the letter K, the classical region by the letter C, and the repressed inflation region by the letter I. The fourth regime, for which the parameters must satisfy the condition

$$w/p \leq F'(l_0) \qquad y_k = y_0$$

corresponds to the boundary between the zone of Keynesian unemployment and the zone of repressed inflation.

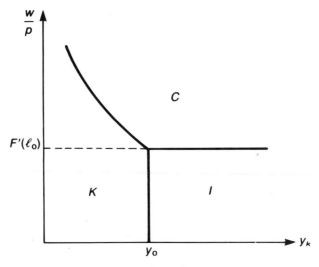

Figure 3.4

Using the same formulas, we can also represent these three regimes in the subspace of parameters p and w, assuming $\tilde{g}$ and τ to be constant (Fig. 3.5). The corresponding Walrasian price and wage are p_0 and w_0. We must note that unlike the previous invariant diagram, the representation in (p, w) space is modified if $\tilde{g}$ or τ changes.

We can finally remark that the distinction between classical and Keynesian unemployment is only locally valid. For example, in the subregion of Fig. 3.4 characterized by $y_k < y_0$ and $w/p > F'(l_0)$, one should both increase y_k and reduce w/p in order to eliminate unemployment; i.e., both classical and Keynesian measures should be applied together.

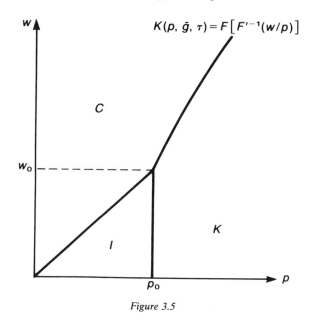

Figure 3.5

Efficiency Problems

We indicated in Chapter 2, Section 5 that in some fixprice equilibria, a remarkable form of inefficiency may be observed because although each market taken individually functions efficiently, we can find additional exchanges that would improve the situation of all agents without changing prices.

One may first remark that in our very simple model such possibilities do not exist in the zones of classical unemployment or repressed inflation: Indeed, in the zone of classical unemployment the firm realizes the employment and sales levels l_c and y_c, which maximize its profits, and these cannot be increased without a change in price or wage. Similarly, in the repressed inflation zone the household sells all its available labor l_0 and consumes the corresponding production y_0 minus government purchases. Its situation thus cannot be improved.[4]

If we now place ourselves in the interior of the Keynesian unemployment region, i.e., in a situation of excess supply in the two markets similar to the situation considered in Chapter 2, we shall see that there exist additional exchanges that are beneficial to both the household and the firm. Imagine, indeed, that a central authority would impose an employment level equal to $\min(l_0, l_c)$ and force the household to purchase all production not taken by the government, i.e., $F[\min(l_0, l_c)] - \tilde{g}$. It is easy to verify that the firm's profits would increase, as well as the household's consumption (and thus its utility). Nevertheless, this situation, which is superior from every point of view, cannot be attained in a decentralized way in our monetary economy since employment settles at the level $F^{-1}(y_k) < \min(l_0, l_c)$ and production at the level y_k. From this comes the possibility for the government to improve simultaneously employment, profits, and private consumption in this region without even touching the price system.

6. Conclusions

This chapter has shown that classical and Keynesian theories of unemployment can be synthesized in a single model. For that we constructed a simple macroeconomic model with rigid price and wage where the classical and Keynesian cases appear as subregimes of the same model. We can distinguish these subregimes both by the factors determining employment and by economic policy measures allowing a reduction of unemployment.

In the classical case, the level of employment depends only on the real wage, which determines the profitable level of production for the firms. Thus, only a reduction of this real wage can bring an improvement in employment. Traditional Keynesian measures would have very undesirable effects, since a decrease in taxes or an increase in public spending would lead only to an increased excess demand.

On the contrary, in the Keynesian case an increase in public spending or a tax reduction diminishes unemployment and even increases private consumption. A wage reduction has at best no effect, whereas a price reduction can reduce unemployment by stimulating consumption.

---

[4]Note, however, that we would obtain a different result if the labor supply were elastic. In that case, rationing in the output market would lead the household to supply less labor, and the inefficiency mentioned here would appear within the repressed inflation zone.

The model studied in this chapter made the simple but unrealistic assumption of complete rigidity of price and wage, which allowed a particularly easy characterization of the various regimes. In the following chapters, we shall study some models with more realistic assumptions incorporating partial flexibility of wages and prices.

References

The initial model from which this chapter is derived is due to Barro and Grossman (1971, 1976). Elements of it can also be found in the works of Solow and Stiglitz (1968) and Younès (1970).

Numerous adaptations of this model have been made by Benassy (1976a; 1977a; 1982a, b), Malinvaud (1977), K. Hildenbrand and W. Hildenbrand (1978), Muellbauer and Portes (1978), and Grandmont (1982). The classical unemployment-Keynesian unemployment distinction is due to Malinvaud (1977). Most of the discussion of this chapter is adapted from Benassy (1982b).

4

Asymmetric Price Flexibility and the Effectiveness of Employment Policies

1. Introduction

In Chapter 3, two traditionally opposed theories of unemployment were synthesized within a single model. That model, however, had a few unrealistic features: for example, in two of three regimes there was excess demand in the goods market and thus consumer rationing. However, except for the case where prices are fixed for a long time, as in some planned economies, such rationing is rarely observed in market economies, for even if prices display some downward rigidity, it is widely believed that in the case of excess demand they will increase until that excess demand has disappeared. To deal with such situations we shall modify the model of Chapter 3, assuming now that the price of goods is flexible only upward, so that excess demand and consumer rationing will never appear on the goods market. We first study this asymmetric flexibility in a short-run equilibrium framework: We shall see that the model still has multiple regimes and compute for each of them the effects of economic policies. We shall then study a dynamic version of this asymmetric flexibility, which will enable us to show the asymmetric effects of some economic shocks.

The Model

We shall study here an economy very similar to that of Chapter 3. It is a monetary economy with two markets (goods and labor) and three agents: A firm with a production function $F(l)$; a household with labor supply l_0 and a consumption function $C(y, p, \tau)$; a government that levies taxes τ and expresses an effective demand for goods $\tilde{g}$. Because the price is flexible upward, the government's purchases g^* are always equal to its demand $\tilde{g}$, and we shall denote both of them by g.

The Walrasian equilibrium in this model is again determined by the two equations

$$w_0/p_0 = F'(l_0)$$

$$C(y_0, p_0, \tau) + g = y_0$$

and we shall assume that it exists.

The departure from the previous model of course comes in the determination of prices. We still assume that the nominal wage w is given. The price of goods p, however, is assumed to be flexible upward but rigid downward with a minimum value $\bar{p}$ so that

$$p \geq \bar{p}$$

For the moment, we shall take $\bar{p}$ as a given parameter. In a more dynamic version of this downward rigidity (Section 4) $\bar{p}$ is the level attained in the preceding period.

We shall now study the various regimes of this model and investigate for each case the effectiveness of economic policies. Following the usage implicit in Chapter 3, we shall hereafter refer to policies aimed at increasing effective demand as "Keynesian" and to policies aimed at reducing the real cost of labor as "classical" (not "new classical"). As an example, in the simple models we shall be considering an increase in government spending or a decrease in household taxes is termed a Keynesian policy, whereas an incomes policy aimed at reducing wages is a classical policy.

2. The Three Regimes

As we shall see, this model displays three regimes:

Excess supply in the two markets (regime A)
Excess supply of labor, goods market cleared (regime B)
Excess demand for labor, goods market cleared (regime C)

A fourth potential regime, with excess demand for labor and excess supply of goods, turns out to be a degenerate one, as in Chapter 3. In what follows we shall determine the equilibrium values p^*, y^*, l^* as functions of the "exogenous" parameters w, $\bar{p}$, g, τ and study the policy measures that might remedy a situation of unemployment. Note first that there is one equation that remains valid in *all* regimes: Indeed, the sales of goods are always equal to demand because the price of good is flexible upward. We shall thus have in every regime

$$y = C(y, p, \tau) + g$$

or

$$y = K(p, g, \tau)$$

We shall now study the other equations in each of the three regimes.

Regime A: Excess Supply in Both Markets

Since there is excess supply in the goods market, the price is blocked at its minimum level:

$$p = \bar{p}$$

Because of excess supply in the labor market, the level of employment is equal to the demand for labor, but since there is excess supply in the goods market, this demand for labor has the "Keynesian" form, i.e.,

$$l = F^{-1}(y)$$

Adding the two previous equations to the "demand-side" equation, we obtain the following system in y^*, l^* and p^*,

$$y^* = C(y^*, p^*, \tau) + g$$
$$p^* = \bar{p}$$
$$l^* = F^{-1}(y^*)$$

which yields

$$y^* = K(\bar{p}, g, \tau)$$
$$l^* = F^{-1}[K(\bar{p}, g, \tau)]$$

We see that in this regime we obtain all the traditional Keynesian effects already discussed before in Chapter 3: An increase in public spending g or a reduction in taxes τ increases production and sales and reduces unemployment:

$$\frac{\partial y^*}{\partial g} = \frac{1}{1 - C_y} > 1$$

$$\frac{\partial y^*}{\partial \tau} = \frac{C_\tau}{1 - C_y} < 0$$

Here it is worth noting that private consumption is also an increasing function of g:

$$\frac{\partial c^*}{\partial g} = \frac{C_y}{1 - C_y} > 0$$

In contrast to these Keynesian measures, a classical policy of reducing the nominal wage w has no effect on production and employment. A reduction in the minimum price $\bar{p}$, however, has a positive effect on employment and production:

$$\frac{\partial y^*}{\partial \bar{p}} = \frac{C_p}{1 - C_y} < 0$$

For regime A to obtain, the values of l^*, y^*, and p^* found here must actually correspond to an excess supply in both markets, which yields (cf. Chapter 3),

$$l^* \leq l_0$$

$$y^* \leq F[F'^{-1}(w^*/p^*)]$$

Inserting the values of l^* and y^* found earlier yields the following conditions on the parameters:

$$K(\bar{p}, g, \tau) \leq y_0$$

$$K(\bar{p}, g, \tau) \leq F[F'^{-1}(w/\bar{p})]$$

These conditions can be represented graphically in the subspace of parameters $(\bar{p}, w)$, holding g and τ constant (Fig. 4.1). The corresponding region has been marked A.

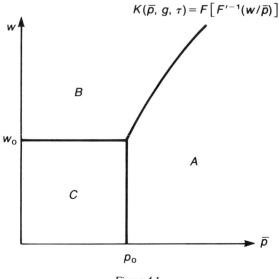

Figure 4.1

Regime B: Excess Supply of Labor, Goods Market Cleared

Since the goods market is cleared and the labor market is in excess supply, the firm can realize its "neoclassical" plan for employment and sales of goods. Therefore,

$$l = F'^{-1}(w/p)$$

$$y = F[F'^{-1}(w/p)]$$

Combining these two equations with the demand-side equation of the goods market, we obtain the following system for the equilibrium values l^*, y^*, and p^*:

$$y^* = C(y^*, p^*, \tau) + g$$

$$y^* = F[F'^{-1}(w/p^*)]$$

$$l^* = F'^{-1}(w/p^*)$$

It is easy to see that the minimum price $\bar{p}$ no longer has any effect, a predictable result because the goods market is cleared. In order to compute the multipliers associated with other policies, let us define

$$S(p, w) = F[F'^{-1}(w/p)] \qquad S_p > 0 \quad S_w < 0$$

The multipliers corresponding to Keynesian policies are

$$\frac{\partial y^*}{\partial g} = \frac{1}{1 - C_y - C_p/S_p} > 0$$

$$\frac{\partial y^*}{\partial \tau} = \frac{C_\tau}{1 - C_y - C_p/S_p} < 0$$

We see that these policies are still effective but that the multipliers are smaller than those in regime A. This is due to the fact that by increasing demand, these Keynesian policies induce some price increases, which reduce consumption and thus the multiplier effects:

$$\frac{\partial p^*}{\partial g} = \frac{1}{S_p(1 - C_y) - C_p} > 0$$

$$\frac{\partial p^*}{\partial \tau} = \frac{C_\tau}{S_p(1 - C_y) - C_p} < 0$$

We may remark that these price effects may be sufficient to diminish private consumption in case of an increase in public spending. We find, indeed,

$$\frac{\partial c^*}{\partial g} = \frac{C_y + C_p/S_p}{1 - C_y - C_p/S_p}$$

The denominator of this expression is always positive, but the numerator may be positive or negative. In this last case there is a partial crowding out.

If we now study classical measures of reducing the nominal wage, we see that they become effective in this regime; indeed,

$$\frac{\partial y^*}{\partial w} = \frac{-S_w C_p}{S_p(1 - C_y) - C_p} < 0$$

Note also that as opposed to Keynesian measures, a wage-reduction policy reduces the price level:

$$\frac{\partial p^*}{\partial w} = \frac{-S_w(1 - C_y)}{S_p(1 - C_y) - C_p} > 0$$

For regime B to obtain, the parameters must be such that the equilibrium price p^* is higher than its minimum value $\bar{p}$ and that there is an excess supply of labor, i.e.,

$$p^* \geq \bar{p} \qquad l^* \leq l_0$$

From the graphical representation of the solution (Section 3 and Fig. 4.2 below), we see that these two conditions are, respectively, equivalent to the two inequalities

$$K(\bar{p}, g, \tau) \geq F[F'^{-1}(w/\bar{p})]$$

$$K[w/F'(l_0), g, \tau] \leq y_0$$

The corresponding region in the subspace of parameters $(\bar{p}, w)$ is marked B in Fig. 4.1.

Regime C: Excess Demand for Labor, Goods Market Cleared

Since there is excess demand in the labor market, the level of employment is determined by the supply

$$l = l_0$$

In the goods market, transactions equal both demand and supply. Because the quantity of labor available to the firm is limited to l_0, the supply of goods is blocked at $F(l_0) = y_0$, and thus,

$$y = y_0$$

The equilibrium values are thus determined by the following system:

$$y^* = C(y^*, p^*, \tau) + g$$
$$y^* = y_0$$
$$l^* = l_0$$

We immediately see that neither Keynesian nor classical policies will have any effect on the level of employment, for it is already at its maximum level l_0. Keynesian policies, however, lead to price increases:

$$\frac{\partial p^*}{\partial g} = -\frac{1}{C_p} > 0$$

$$\frac{\partial p^*}{\partial \tau} = -\frac{C_\tau}{C_p} < 0$$

Note that in this regime there is complete crowding out since

$$c^* = y_0 - g$$

Price increases induced by an increase in g are sufficient to diminish private consumption by the same amount. The crowding-out mechanism works through prices and is thus here the same as in Walrasian equilibrium.

For regime C to obtain, the parameters must be such that the equilibrium price is higher than the minimum price and such that there is excess demand in the labor market, i.e.,

$$p^* \geq \bar{p}$$
$$l^* \leq F'^{-1}(w/p^*)$$

These conditions are respectively equivalent to (cf. Fig. 4.2),

$$K(\bar{p}, g, \tau) \geq y_0$$
$$K[w/F'(l_0), g, \tau] \geq y_0$$

The corresponding subset of parameters is represented by region C in the $(\bar{p}, w)$ space (Fig. 4.1).

3. A Graphical Solution

If we look at the systems of equations giving the equilibrium values p^* and y^* in each of the three regimes, as well as the inequalities they must satisfy, we see that p^* and y^* can be determined as the intersection point in (p, y) space of a "demand curve" and a "supply curve," which we shall denote respectively as

$$y = \hat{D}(p) \qquad \text{and} \qquad y = \hat{S}(p)$$

The employment level l^* can then be deduced from y^* by means of the inverse production function, $l^* = F^{-1}(y^*)$. The demand curve is simply the Keynesian aggregate demand curve

$$\hat{D}(p) = K(p, g, \tau)$$

which represents, as we saw earlier, the solution in y to the equation

$$y = C(y, p, \tau) + g$$

an equation which is satisfied in all regimes.

The supply curve consists of three parts (Fig. 4.2):

(1) a vertical part (section A) of equations:

$$p = \bar{p} \qquad y \leq y_0 \qquad y \leq F[F'^{-1}(w/p)]$$

(2) an upward sloping part (section B) of equations

$$y = F[F'^{-1}(w/p)] \qquad y \leq y_0 \qquad p \geq \bar{p}$$

(3) a horizontal part (section C) of equations:

$$y = y_0 \qquad p \geq \bar{p} \qquad y \leq F[F'^{-1}(w/p)]$$

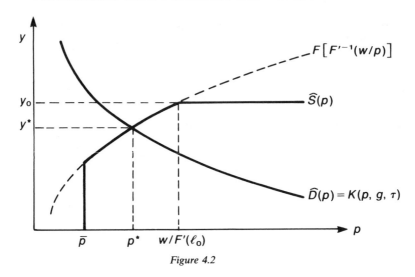

Figure 4.2

Note that the upward sloping part of the supply curve may not exist if $\dot{w}/\bar{p} \leq F'(l_0)$. We immediately see that the resulting equilibrium will be of type A if the two curves intersect in the vertical part of the supply curve, of type B if they intersect in the upward sloping part, and of type C if they intersect in the horizontal part. Indeed, consider for example case B, which has been represented in Fig. 4.2. We saw in Section 2 that an equilibrium of type B was defined by the following equations and inequalities:

$$y^* = C(y^*, p^*, \tau) + g$$
$$y^* = F[F'^{-1}(w/p)]$$
$$p^* \geq \bar{p}$$
$$y^* \leq y_0$$

The first equation is equivalent to the demand curve, and the other three relations correspond exactly to the definition of section B of the supply curve. The same exercise can be performed for cases A and C.

Note that an equilibrium might not exist if the curve $K(p, g, \tau)$ is above the line y_0 for all prices, but in such a case, a Walrasian equilibrium would not exist either, an event that we excluded before by assumption.

4. A Dynamic View

In Sections 2 and 3 we have considered a static view of downward rigidity of prices, the minimal price level being given as a parameter. When people speak of downward rigidity, however, they often have in mind a dynamic version of this phenomenon: The main idea behind it is that if prices have historically attained some level, they will not fall below it, although they might increase beyond it if market circumstances are favorable. Such a dynamic downward rigidity of the price level is rather easy to model using the preceding developments: All we need is to set the minimum price $\bar{p}$ in one period equal to the price realized in the preceding period, i.e.,

$$\bar{p}(t) = p(t-1)$$

We shall now show, using mostly our simple graphical representation, that this asymmetry in dynamic adjustments may give rise to various phenomena. First, we shall see that this asymmetric flexibility of prices may imply that multipliers are themselves asymmetric—in some cases multipliers "upward" are smaller than multipliers "downward". Second, transitory shocks to the economy may have permanent consequences because of the ratchet effects induced by the asymmetric flexibility. For example, purely transient modifications of the private sector's demand or "stop-go" government policies may have stagflationary effects, as we shall see later.

A Graphical Approach

We shall simply use here the graphical representation of Section 3, indexing now the variables by the time index t (Fig. 4.3) and taking $\bar{p}(t) = p(t-1)$. We have also shown in dashed lines on Fig. 4.3 the demand curve in period $t-1$ and the "initial point" with coordinates $p(t-1)$ and $y(t-1)$.

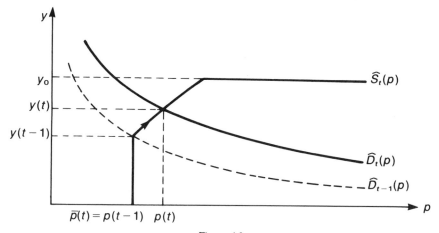

Figure 4.3

Note that from Fig. 4.3 we can directly find the unemployment rate $u(t) = l_0 - F^{-1}[y(t)]$ and the inflation rate $\pi(t)$ by

$$1 + \pi(t) = p(t)/p(t-1) = p(t)/\bar{p}(t)$$

Also note that if the equilibrium in period t is of type A, there is unemployment without inflation. If it is of type B, there is unemployment and inflation. If it is of type C, there is inflation and full employment.

Asymmetric Multipliers

Figure 4.3 enables us to see that in numerous cases we will naturally have asymmetric multipliers, even for infinitesimal variations in g or τ. Indeed, the starting point is always on the line $p = \bar{p}(t)$. One thus obtains the three possible cases represented in Fig. 4.4.

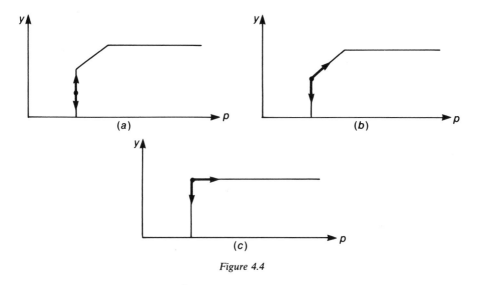

Figure 4.4

Let us call respectively ρ_A, ρ_B, and ρ_C the three public-spending multipliers[1] computed for regimes A, B, C in Section 2. Let us recall that

$$\rho_A > \rho_B > \rho_C = 0$$

If the starting point in $t-1$ is in regime A, the multiplier is equal to ρ_A in both directions (Fig. 4.4.a). If the starting point is in regime B, the

[1]The same reasoning would apply to the multipliers relative to variations in taxes.

multiplier is equal to ρ_B "upward" (i.e., for public-spending increases) but to ρ_A "downward" (i.e., for public-spending decreases. Fig. 4.4.b). Finally, if the starting point is in regime C, the multiplier is ρ_A downward and $\rho_C = 0$ upward (Fig. 4.4.c). Moreover, in cases B and C, a movement upward is accompanied by a price increase.

Transitory Shocks and Stagflation

Because of these asymmetric multipliers, it is easy to understand that transitory shocks will have stagflationary "ratchet" effects. Let us look at the case illustrated in Fig. 4.5. Consider a transitory shock on demand, such that the "demand curve" moves from $\hat{D}_{t-1}(p)$ to a higher position $\hat{D}_t(p)$ and then goes back in $t + 1$ to the initial position; i.e.,

$$\hat{D}_{t+1}(p) = \hat{D}_{t-1}(p)$$

Assume that, as in Fig. 4.5, the starting point in period $t - 1$ was in regime B. We see that the shift of the demand curve in t provokes both a decrease in unemployment and an increase in price. When the demand curve goes back in $t + 1$ to its initial position, the price level remains at the level $p(t) > p(t - 1)$, and unemployment rises to a level higher than in $t - 1$. Over the two periods there has been a rise in both unemployment and price, i.e., stagflation. This stagflationary effect is due to the asymmetric flexibility of the price of goods. Similar effects would also appear if we consider asymmetric wage flexibility.

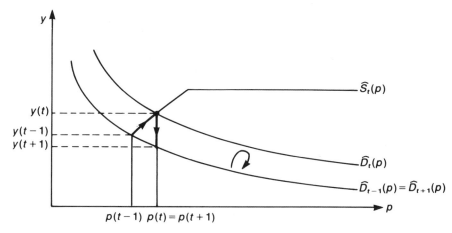

Figure 4.5

5. Conclusions

In this chapter we dropped an unsatisfactory feature of the Chapter 3 model by assuming that prices were flexible upward, thus eliminating any demand rationing, which appeared in two of three regimes in the preceding model. Although the demand for goods is satisfied under all circumstances in this model, there are still three regimes in the short run, denoted by A, B, and C, and the effectiveness of employment policies depends on the prevailing regime. In regime A we obtain the traditional results of Keynesian fixprice models; i.e., demand policies are fully effective. In regime C, by contrast, demand policies yield only price increases, just as in full-employment neoclassical models. Finally, in regime B Keynesian demand policies both reduce unemployment and increase the price level; classical policies of wage reductions, on the other hand, have a beneficial effect on both employment and the price level.

Moving then to a more dynamic version of downward price rigidity, we saw that this asymmetric flexibility leads to multipliers which are themselves asymmetric, notably lower for increases than for decreases in regimes B and C. An important consequence is that temporary shocks may have durable stagflationary effects on employment and price level.

In this chapter, as also in Chapter 3, we have assumed a rigid nominal wage. We shall now abandon this assumption by studying the consequences of partial or total indexation of wages on prices.

References

This chapter is derived from Benassy (1984b, 1985).

5

Indexation and Employment Policies

1. Introduction

In Chapter 4, as in most usual Keynesian models, we have assumed a rigid nominal wage in the short run. However, one observes more and more that wage earners try to defend not the nominal value, but the real value of their salary. This is often attained by implicit or explicit wage indexation with respect to prices. We shall now study the effects that such an indexation may have on the effectiveness of economic policies within the framework of a model very similar to that of Chapter 4.

The Wage Equation

We shall thus assume that the wage w, instead of being rigid, is related to the price level by the following relation:

$$w = \gamma \xi(p) \qquad \xi' > 0$$

The degree of wage indexation with respect to prices depends on the elasticity of the function ξ, which we shall denote by ϵ:

$$\epsilon = \frac{p\xi'(p)}{\xi(p)}$$

We shall assume that this elasticity is always between 0 and 1. The extreme values correspond respectively to a rigid nominal wage ($\epsilon = 0$) and a rigid real wage ($\epsilon = 1$). The parameter γ can be modified through incomes policies, and we shall refer to it as the "classical" economic policy variable. Note that γ has the dimension of a nominal wage if $\epsilon = 0$ and of a real wage if $\epsilon = 1$.

The Rest of the Model

Except for this hypothesis of wage indexation, our model is the same as that of Chapter 4. We thus have two markets, for output and labor. The price of output is flexible upwards, with a minimal value $\bar{p}$, whereas the nominal wage is determined by the previous indexation formula. Here also we have three agents: A firm with a production function $F(l)$, a household with a labor supply l_0 and a consumption function $C(y, p, \tau)$, and a government that collects taxes τ and has a demand for output equal to g.[1] The Walrasian equilibrium of this model is again given by the equations

$$C(y_0, p_0, \tau) + g = y_0$$

$$w_0/p_0 = F'(l_0)$$

The parameter γ_0 corresponding to the Walrasian equilibrium is thus

$$\gamma_0 = \frac{p_0}{\xi(p_0)} F'(l_0)$$

The Aggregate Demand Function

In what follows we shall once more use the aggregate demand function $K(p, g, \tau)$, which is the solution in y of the equation

$$y = C(y, p, \tau) + g$$

Recall that the partial derivatives of this function are

$$K_g = \frac{1}{1 - C_y} > 1 \qquad K_p = \frac{C_p}{1 - C_y} < 0 \qquad K_\tau = \frac{C_\tau}{1 - C_y} < 0$$

---

[1]Let us recall that, as in Chapter 4, g denotes both the transaction and the demand for goods of the government, since this demand is always satisfied because of the upward flexibility of price.

2. The Three Regimes

As in Chapter 4, this model has three regimes:

Excess supply on both markets (regime A)
Excess supply of labor, goods market cleared (regime B)
Excess demand for labor, goods market cleared (regime C)

We shall describe in detail these three regimes. In each case we shall compute the values p^*, w^*, y^*, and l^* associated with the basic parameters $\bar{p}$, γ, g and τ, and we shall assess the effects of the various economic policies. Before that we may note that two equations will remain the same in all the three regimes. The first is the wage equation seen before,

$$w = \gamma\xi(p)$$

and the second, as in Chapter 4, states that output sales are always equal to total demand, due to upward price flexibility,

$$y = C(y, p, \tau) + g$$

This equation can also be written as the aggregate demand curve

$$y = K(p, g, \tau)$$

and this is the form we shall mostly employ. We shall now study the other equations in each of the three regimes and draw economic policy implications.

Regime A: Excess Supply in Both Markets

With an excess supply of goods, the price is blocked at its minimum level:

$$p = \bar{p}$$

Employment is equal to the demand for labor, which has itself the "Keynesian" form since there is excess supply of goods:

$$l = F^{-1}(y)$$

Equilibrium values p^*, w^*, y^*, and l^* are thus given by the following system:

$$p^* = \bar{p}$$

$$w^* = \gamma \xi(p^*)$$

$$y^* = K(p^*, g, \tau)$$

$$l^* = F^{-1}(y^*)$$

Since the price and wage are fixed in this regime, the results are the same as those in regime A of Chapter 4. In particular, an incomes policy (a decrease in γ) has no effect, whereas Keynesian demand policies are effective:

$$\frac{\partial y^*}{\partial g} = K_g = \frac{1}{1 - C_y} > 0$$

$$\frac{\partial y^*}{\partial \tau} = K_\tau = \frac{C_\tau}{1 - C_y} < 0$$

For regime A to obtain, the parameters must be such that there is actually excess supply in both markets, which yields

$$l^* \leqslant l_0$$

$$y^* \leqslant F[F'^{-1}(w^*/p^*)]$$

We shall see later to which subregion of the parameter space this corresponds.

Regime B: Excess Supply of Labor, Goods Market Cleared

In this case the firm is not constrained in either of the two markets, it therefore realizes its neoclassical plan of sales and employment:

$$l = F'^{-1}(w/p)$$

$$y = F[F'^{-1}(w/p)]$$

Combining these two equations with the two invariant ones, we obtain the following system in p^*, w^*, y^*, l^*:

$$y^* = K(p^*, g, \tau)$$
$$y^* = F[F'^{-1}(w^*/p^*)]$$
$$w^* = \gamma\xi(p^*)$$
$$l^* = F'^{-1}(w^*/p^*)$$

To study the effects of the economic policy variables, let us define the following elasticities:

σ: Elasticity of the neoclassical output supply function $F[F'^{-1}(w/p)]$ with respect to w/p (in absolute value).

κ: Partial elasticity of $K(p, g, \tau)$ with respect to p (in absolute value).

Resolution of the above system first yields the effects of Keynesian policies:

$$\frac{\partial y^*}{\partial g} = \frac{\sigma(1 - \epsilon)}{\sigma(1 - \epsilon) + \kappa} \cdot K_g = \frac{\sigma(1 - \epsilon)}{\sigma(1 - \epsilon) + \kappa} \cdot \frac{1}{1 - C_y} \geq 0$$

$$\frac{\partial y^*}{\partial \tau} = \frac{\sigma(1 - \epsilon)}{\sigma(1 - \epsilon) + \kappa} \cdot K_\tau = \frac{\sigma(1 - \epsilon)}{\sigma(1 - \epsilon) + \kappa} \cdot \frac{C_\tau}{1 - C_y} \leq 0$$

We see that Keynesian policies, even without indexation ($\epsilon = 0$), are less effective than in regime A, a result already seen in Chapter 4. Moreover, the effectiveness of such policies decreases strictly with the degree of indexation ϵ. If there is complete indexation ($\epsilon = 1$), Keynesian policies become totally ineffective against unemployment. The degree of indexation is thus quite crucial in evaluating the effectiveness of Keynesian policies in this region.

By contrast, incomes policies are very effective in this regime. Indeed, if we compute the effects of variations in γ we obtain

$$\frac{\partial y^*/y^*}{\partial \gamma/\gamma} = -\frac{\sigma\kappa}{\sigma(1 - \epsilon) + \kappa} < 0$$

We see that for a given relative variation of γ, the effect on output and employment is higher, the higher the degree of indexation ϵ. This result is quite intuitive since in that case a variation in γ is reflected more directly in the real wage, and we are on the neoclassical supply curve in this regime.

For regime B to obtain, the parameters must be such that the equilibrium price is higher than its minimum value and that there is an excess supply of labor:

$$p^* \geq \bar{p} \qquad l^* \leq l_0$$

We shall see later the corresponding parameter subregion.

Regime C: Excess Demand in the Labor Market, Goods Market Cleared

Since there is excess demand in the labor market, employment is supply determined:

$$l = l_0$$

With the supply of labor available to the firm limited to l_0, its supply of output is fixed at $y_0 = F(l_0)$, and since the goods market clears, transactions on that market are equal to supply:

$$y = y_0$$

Equilibrium values w^*, p^*, y^*, l^* are thus given by the system

$$y^* = K(p^*, g, \tau)$$
$$y^* = y_0$$
$$l^* = l_0$$
$$w^* = \gamma \xi(p^*)$$

Since employment is already at its maximal value l_0, demand or incomes policies affect only the price and wage according to the following equations:

$$y_0 = K(p^*, g, \tau)$$
$$w^* = \gamma \xi(p^*)$$

Moreover, government spending g completely crowds out private consumption since

$$c^* = y_0 - g$$

For regime C to obtain, the equilibrium price must be higher than the minimum price level, and there must be excess demand on the labor market, which yields

$$p^* \geq \bar{p}$$
$$l^* \leq F'^{-1}(w^*/p^*)$$

3. A Graphical Solution

As in Chapter 4, the equilibrium values p^* and y^* can be found graphically at the intersection of a demand curve $\hat{D}(p)$ and a supply curve $\hat{S}(p)$ in

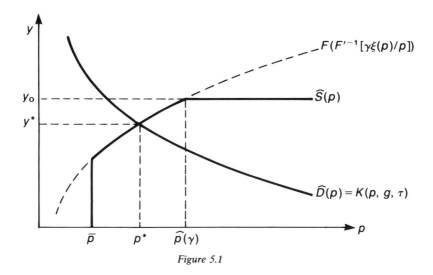

Figure 5.1

(p, y) space (Fig. 5.1). The demand curve is the Keynesian aggregate demand

$$\hat{D}(p) = K(p, g, \tau)$$

The supply curve $\hat{S}(p)$ has again three parts: a vertical part (section A) with equation $p = \bar{p}$, a horizontal part (section C) with equation $y = y_0$, and an upward sloping part (section B) with equation

$$y = F(F'^{-1}[\gamma\xi(p)/p])$$

We may note that this section B becomes horizontal if there is full indexation ($\epsilon = 1$). Moreover, it is actually a part of the supply curve only if

$$\gamma\xi(\bar{p})/\bar{p} > F'(l_0)$$

In Section 2 for each regime we derived the equilibrium values of all the variables and the inequalities they must satisfy. Using these we can see that the equilibrium is of type A, B, or C if the demand and supply curves intersect respectively in the sections A, B, or C of the supply curve. Case B has been represented in Fig. 5.1; the other cases can be similarly depicted.

Delimitation of the Regimes

To determine the subset of parameters for which each of the three regimes obtains, all we have to do is to find in which section the curves will intersect.

Using Fig. 5.1 and the corresponding figures for cases A and C, one obtains
the following conditions:

for regime A,

$$K(\bar{p}, g, \tau) \leqslant F(F'^{-1}[\gamma\xi(\bar{p})/\bar{p}])$$

$$K(\bar{p}, g, \tau) \leqslant y_0$$

for regime B,

$$K(\bar{p}, g, \tau) \geqslant F(F'^{-1}[\gamma\xi(\bar{p})/\bar{p}])$$

$$K[\hat{p}(\gamma), g, \tau] \leqslant y_0$$

and for regime C,

$$K(\bar{p}, g, \tau) \geqslant y_0$$

$$K[\hat{p}(\gamma), g, \tau)] \geqslant y_0$$

where $\hat{p}(\gamma)$ is defined by (cf. fig. 5.1),

$$F(F'^{-1}[\gamma\xi(\hat{p})/\hat{p}]) = y_0$$

or

$$\gamma\xi(\hat{p})/\hat{p} = F'(l_0)$$

The three corresponding regions have been represented in $(\gamma, \bar{p})$ space,
the parameters g and τ being assumed given (Fig. 5.2). The condition

$$K[\hat{p}(\gamma), g, \tau] = y_0$$

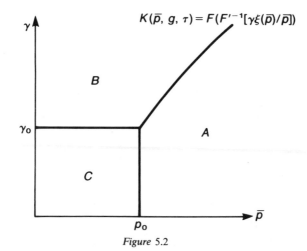

Figure 5.2

is then equivalent to $\hat{p}(\gamma) = p_0$, and thus,

$$\gamma = \gamma_0 = \frac{p_0}{\xi(p_0)} F'(l_0)$$

We must note that the interpretation of Fig. 5.2 depends on the degree of indexation since the parameter γ has a different dimension: As noted in the beginning of this chapter, if there is no indexation ($\epsilon = 0$), γ has the dimension of a nominal wage, whereas if there is full indexation ($\epsilon = 1$), γ has the dimension of a real wage.

4. A Particular Case: Rigid Real Wage

We shall briefly study here a useful special case of the model developed in this chapter: that where the real wage is rigid, which corresponds to the situation where ϵ is equal to 1 (full indexation). We shall see that the results on employment policies will be very similar to those in Chapter 3, but there will be no more problems of interpretation related to the existence of consumer rationing in the goods market.

We shall thus assume that the nominal wage is given by

$$w = \omega p$$

where ω is the fixed real wage. We continue to assume that the price of goods is flexible upward but rigid downward with a minimum value $\bar{p}$.

The Three Regimes

We shall compute here the equilibrium values y^*, p^*, w^* in the three regimes. The employment level l^* is deduced directly from y^* by $l^* = F^{-1}(y^*)$.

In regime A, the equilibrium values are given by

$$p^* = \bar{p}$$

$$w^* = \omega\bar{p}$$

$$y^* = K(\bar{p}, g, \tau)$$

We obtain here the traditional Keynesian results fully discussed earlier, and about which we shall not comment further.

In regime B, the equilibrium values are given by

$$y^* = F[F'^{-1}(\omega)]$$
$$y^* = K(p^*, g, \tau)$$
$$w^* = \omega p^*$$

We see that in this regime only a fall in the real wage ω can increase employment, as in the classical zone of Chapter 3. Moreover, a reduction in ω decreases the output price and the nominal wage. If we now consider Keynesian measures (an increase in g or a decrease in τ), they have no effect on production and employment but lead to an increase in price and nominal wage. Furthermore, an increase in g, because of these price increases, leads to full crowding out, reducing private consumption by the same amount.

Finally, in regime C the equations are

$$y^* = y_0$$
$$y_0 = K(p^*, g, \tau)$$
$$w^* = \omega p^*$$

where we see that neither Keynesian measures nor decreases in ω have any effect on employment, which is at its maximum. Keynesian measures lead to price and wage increases, whereas a reduction in ω leads to a decrease of the nominal wage.

Delimitation of the Regimes

If we look at Fig. 5.1 again, we see that with fixed real wage it reduces to a simpler figure (Fig. 5.3), for both portions B and C of the "supply

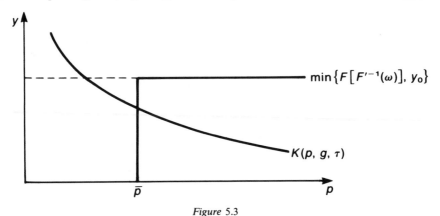

Figure 5.3

curve" become a single horizontal branch of equation

$$y = \min\{F[F'^{-1}(\omega)], y_0\}$$

It appears immediately in Fig. 5.3 that the level of y^* is given by

$$y^* = \min\{K(\bar{p}, g, \tau), F[F'^{-1}(\omega)], y_0\}$$

a formula very similar to that seen in Chapter 3. One can also divide the parameter space $(\omega, \bar{p})$ into subregions corresponding to each regime (Fig. 5.4). We obtain then a diagram where the separating lines among the three regimes A, B, C have exactly the same equations as those seen in Chapter 3. This diagram, however, differs a little from the corresponding diagram in Chapter 3 (Fig. 3.5), which was drawn in (p, w) space, whereas Fig. 5.4 is drawn in $(\bar{p}, \omega)$ space.

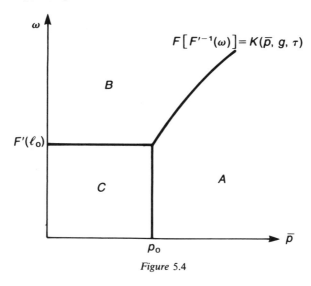

Figure 5.4

5. Conclusions

We have seen in this chapter that indexation can considerably modify the relative effectiveness of various policies against unemployment. We saw in particular that in regime B, Keynesian demand policies decrease in effectiveness as the degree of indexation increases, becoming even completely ineffective if the nominal wage is completely indexed on prices, whereas in the same circumstances, incomes policies keep their full effectiveness. This result is especially noteworthy since it is obtained in a regime with involuntary unemployment and where transactions in the goods market are always equal to demand. We thus find again the polar cases of Chapter 3, insofar as effectiveness of economic policies goes, but we avoid any demand rationing, which makes the model more realistic and brings it closer to more conventional macroeconomic modes.

References

The model of this chapter is adapted from Benassy (1984b, 1985). Models studying the effectiveness of Keynesian policies with indexed wages can be found, for example, in Modigliani and Padoa-Schioppa (1978) and in Branson and Rotemberg (1980).

CHAPTER

6

The Three Regimes of the IS-LM Model

1. Introduction

We shall show in this chapter that it is possible to achieve a synthesis between the analyses of the previous chapters and traditional Keynesian models of the IS-LM type. More precisely, we shall construct a model of non-Walrasian equilibrium similar to those already seen and show that each of its three subregimes corresponds to one of the three specifications of the IS-LM model usually found in the literature.

We may indeed observe that one does not find in the various expositions a unique version of the IS-LM model. On the contrary, the two basic IS-LM equations (which are described later) are generally used in conjunction with three sets of assumptions on wage and price formation and thus on the state of excess demands or supplies on the goods and labor markets. One version assumes fixed wage and price, with excess supply on the two corresponding markets. In a second version, the wage is rigid, whereas the price level adjusts to clear the goods market, so that excess supply appears on the labor market only. Finally, in a third version, it is assumed that both markets clear. The fiscal and monetary policy multipliers, as well as the conclusions that can be drawn about economic policy, are evidently quite different in these three cases.

We shall develop in this chapter a synthetic model that will admit these three versions as particular subregimes of a single non-Walrasian model of

103

a monetary economy with three markets (output, labor, and bonds). In order to obtain the Keynesian models listed above we shall have to make appropriate assumptions about relative price flexibility for the three markets. We shall assume that the price of bonds (and thus the interest rate) is fully flexible and clears the bonds market. On the output and labor markets, however, we shall assume an *asymmetric* flexibility, both price and wage being rigid downward but flexible upward. Such an hypothesis corresponds rather well with the assumptions implicit in Keynesian analysis. Before studying the various regimes of the corresponding model, let us briefly review the traditional IS-LM equations.

The IS-LM Equations

We shall give here slightly more general forms than those commonly found in the literature, which allows us to cover a number of specifications. The IS equation has the form

$$y = C(y, r, p) + I(y, r, p) + g$$

where r is the interest rate, $C(y, r, p)$ the consumption function, and $I(y, r, p)$ the investment function. We shall most often write in what follows the IS equation in the form

$$y = Z(y, r, p) + g$$

where $Z(y, r, p)$ is the total effective demand coming from the private sector. It is usually assumed that

$$0 < Z_y < 1 \qquad Z_r < 0 \qquad Z_p < 0$$

The LM equation, meant to represent money market equilibrium, is of the form

$$L(y, r, p) = m$$

where $L(y, r, p)$ is the money demand function and m the total quantity of money in the economy. It is usually assumed that

$$L_y > 0 \qquad L_r < 0 \qquad L_p > 0$$

Taxes have been omitted in this basic model because their treatment varies widely (taxes determined in real terms, in nominal terms, proportional to income, etc.). Any particular specification can be easily included, as in the preceding chapters.

2. The Model

As indicated earlier, we shall consider here a model with three markets: output against money at the price p, labor against money at the wage w, and bonds against money at the price $1/r$. The interest rate is flexible, and the bonds market clears. On the output and labor markets, the price and wage have lower bounds:

$$p \geq \bar{p} \qquad w \geq \bar{w}$$

The Agents

We shall have here, as in the models of the preceding chapters, three aggregated agents: firm, household, and government. A few modifications are necessary, however, with respect to these chapters: All three agents will be active in the bonds markets, which was not considered previously. The firm will have investment activities, and we shall introduce a self-financing behavior. Let us now describe the agents in more detail.

The firm has a production function $F(l)$. It does not accumulate any inventories and maximizes short-run profits $py - wl$. Furthermore, it invests a quantity i. Its budget constraint is written as[1]

$$pi + \frac{b_f}{r} + m_f = \bar{m}_f + a$$

where b_f is the net *flow* of bonds purchases by the firm, $\bar{m}_f$ its initial quantity of money, m_f the final quantity of money, and a the amount of undistributed profits (these are retained by the firm for the purpose of investment self-financing). Profits distributed to the household are thus

$$py - wl - a \qquad \text{with} \qquad a \leq py - wl$$

The household has a labor supply l_0. It actually sells a quantity l and receives a total money income equal to $py - a$, where wl is wage income and $py - wl - a$ comes from profits. The household's budget constraint is thus

$$pc + \frac{b_h}{r} + m_h = \bar{m}_h + py - a$$

---

[1] In order to simplify notation we shall omit from all budget constraints the interest payments on outstanding bonds. These payments are assumed to be made at the beginning of the period, and thus included in initial money holdings, $\bar{m}_f$ for the firm and $\bar{m}_h$ for the household.

where c is the flow of consumption, b_h net flow purchases of bonds by the household, $\bar{m}_h$ his initial money holdings, and m_h his final money holdings.

Government purchases a quantity of goods g (equal to its demand), sells a net quantity of bonds b, and creates a net quantity of money $m - \bar{m}$, where $\bar{m}$ is the total quantity of money in the economy at the outset of the period. These quantities are related via the government's budget constraint, which is written

$$m - \bar{m} = pg - \frac{b}{r}$$

We finally have the two definitional identities:

$$m = m_h + m_f \qquad \bar{m} = \bar{m}_h + \bar{m}_f$$

Signals and Behavioral Equations

We shall now briefly describe some effective demand and supply functions for the household and the firm. They differ from what we saw in the preceding chapters because of the introduction of bonds, investment, and undistributed profits. We shall mainly study the consumption, investment, and net bond demand functions, the determination of which involves some intertemporal choices. It is not necessary to make these intertemporal programs explicit here, because we shall be interested mainly in the nature of quantity signals that may appear in the corresponding functions.

The firm's net effective demands for investment and bonds should naturally be functions of the three "price signals" p, r, and w. As for quantity signals, the firm is never constrained in the bonds market (which always clears) or in the labor market (where the firm is a demander and where the wage is flexible upward). The firm may, however, be constrained in the goods market, where the quantity it exchanges y may be a constraint. We shall thus denote the investment and bond demands of the firm as

$$I(y, r, p, w) \qquad \text{and} \qquad B_f(y, r, p, w)$$

Of course, these functions should have as arguments the initial quantities of money, bonds, and investment goods held by the firm. We shall omit them, however, since these quantities are a datum in the period considered. In order to completely describe the firm's behavior, we must also describe its profit-distribution behavior. We shall assume that a is a function of the same signals as investment and bond demands; so, we shall write

$$a = A(y, r, p, w)$$

Consider now the household. It is never constrained in the bonds market (which always clears) nor on the output market (where the price is flexible upward, and the household is a demander). It may be constrained, however, in the labor market, in which case its realized income may be lower than full-employment income. We shall assume that the consumption and bond demands of the household are functions of this realized income and of the price signals p, r, and w. Because the household's realized income is $py - A(y, r, p, w)$, the two functions can be written as

$$C(y, r, p, w) \quad \text{and} \quad B_h(y, r, p, w)$$

These functions, of course, also depend on the initial holdings of money and bonds of the household, but we shall omit them since they are given in the period considered.

3. The Core Equations and IS-LM

In the various regimes of the model that we shall now study, some equations change, whereas others do not. Let us begin with the invariant equations and relate them to the IS-LM equations. The first is the equilibrium condition for the bonds market. Let us call

$$B(y, r, p, w) = B_f(y, r, p, w) + B_h(y, r, p, w)$$

the private sector's net demand for bonds function. The equilibrium condition is

$$B(y, r, p, w) = b$$

which, using the government's budget constraint, can also be written as

$$B(y, r, p, w) = r(pg - m + \bar{m})$$

The second equation, which concerns the output market, is not a supply-demand equilibrium equation, since the output market may be in a state of excess supply. However, because the price is flexible upward, the quantity exchanged on the goods market is always equal to total demand, which we shall write

$$y = C(y, r, p, w) + I(y, r, p, w) + g$$

Relation with IS-LM

We shall now rewrite the previous two core equations, making particular assumptions that allow us to obtain from these the IS-LM system described in the introduction to this chapter. First, as in most usual Keynesian models, we shall ignore the wage variable w in all equations. We thus obtain the new system

$$y = C(y, r, p) + I(y, r, p) + g = Z(y, r, p) + g$$

$$B(y, r, p) = b = r(pg - m + \bar{m})$$

The first equation is now identical to the IS equation, which thus expresses the fact that transactions on the goods market are equal to effective demand for output.

In order to obtain the LM equation we have to transform the system a little more, since in our model there is no such thing as a "money market." By adding the firm's and household's budget constraints we obtain

$$m = \bar{m} + py - pi - pc - \frac{b_h}{r} - \frac{b_f}{r}$$

We can replace c, i, b_h, and b_f by the corresponding effective demands (which are always satisfied) and thus,

$$m = \bar{m} + py - pZ(y, r, p) - \frac{1}{r}B(y, r, p)$$

We can take this as a "demand for money" and identify it with the Keynesian demand for money $L(y, r, p)$. Reciprocally, we obtain the IS-LM system if in our model we take the following particular form for the net bonds demand:

$$B(y, r, p) = r[\bar{m} - L(y, r, p) + py - pZ(y, r, p)]$$

which we shall assume in all that follows.

The Core Equations

In the following sections we shall study the various regimes of the model whose core equations are

$$y = Z(y, r, p) + g$$

$$B(y, r, p) = b = r(pg - m + \bar{m})$$

with the particular form of the bonds demand function seen earlier. This system is thus equivalent to the IS-LM system:

$$y = Z(y, r, p) + g$$
$$L(y, r, p) = m$$

and we shall make the assumptions already seen at the beginning of this chapter, namely,

$$0 < Z_y < 1 \qquad Z_p < 0 \qquad Z_r < 0$$
$$L_y > 0 \qquad L_p > 0 \qquad L_r < 0$$

The Aggregate Demand Curve

For the computations that follow, it is useful to compute the solution in y to the previous two equations, which we shall denote by $K(p, m, g)$. Note that this function is very similar to the aggregate demand function of traditional Keynesian IS-LM models. Partial derivatives of this function are computed as

$$K_g = \frac{L_r}{(1 - Z_y)L_r + Z_r L_y} > 0$$

$$K_m = \frac{Z_r}{(1 - Z_y)L_r + Z_r L_y} > 0$$

$$K_p = \frac{Z_p L_r - Z_r L_p}{(1 - Z_y)L_r + Z_r L_y} < 0$$

Walrasian Equilibrium

For later use, it is also useful to compute the values of the Walrasian equilibrium price and wage p_0 and w_0 associated with given values of m and g.

Labor market clearing implies that the neoclassical labor demand $F'^{-1}(w/p)$ is equal to labor supply l_0, which yields

$$\frac{w_0}{p_0} = F'(l_0)$$

Output market clearing implies that the total demand for goods is equal to full-employment production y_0. Combining this condition and the bond market equilibrium condition, we obtain

$$K(p_0, m, g) = y_0$$

We may note that this equation need not be satisfied for a finite price level. A necessary (though not sufficient) condition for the existence of Walrasian equilibrium is thus,

$$\lim_{p \to \infty} K(p, m, g) < y_0$$

We shall assume that this holds throughout the remainder of this chapter.

4. The Three Regimes

Like the models of the preceding chapters, this one will have three different regimes, also denoted A, B, and C (note, however, that regime C has a slightly different characterization because of upward wage flexibility):[2]

Excess supply on the output and labor markets (regime A)
Excess supply for labor, output market cleared (regime B)
Output and labor markets cleared (regime C)

As in the preceding chapters, the fourth potential regime is a degenerate one, as we shall see later. We shall now describe these three regimes in detail. In each case we shall compute the values p^*, w^*, y^*, and l^* of price, wage, output, and employment in the non-Walrasian equilibrium associated with the basic parameters $\bar{p}$, $\bar{w}$, m, and g. We shall particularly study the effects on employment and prices of the variables m and g, which are central to macroeconomic models.

Regime A: Excess Supply in Both Markets

With excess supply in the two markets, the price and wage are blocked at their minimum levels;

$$p = \bar{p} \qquad w = \bar{w}$$

There is excess supply in the output market, and the level of sales is thus given by the aggregate demand for goods:

$$y = Z(y, r, p) + g$$

The level of employment is equal to labor demand. Since the firm is constrained in the goods market, this demand for labor has the Keynesian form $F^{-1}(y)$, i.e., the quantity of labor just necessary to produce y, and thus,

$$l = F^{-1}(y)$$

[2]We consider in this classification only the output and labor markets since the bonds market always clears.

Finally, the interest rate clears the bonds market, which yields a fifth equation:

$$B(y, r, p) = b = r(pg - m + \bar{m})$$

The equilibrium values of the various variables are given by the solution of the system of five equations listed above. If we combine the IS equation and the bonds market equation into the aggregate demand curve $K(p, m, g)$, we find that p^*, w^*, y^*, and l^* are the solution of the following system;

$$y^* = K(p^*, m, g)$$
$$l^* = F^{-1}(y^*)$$
$$p^* = \bar{p}$$
$$w^* = \bar{w}$$

The two economic policy multipliers are immediately computed as:

$$\frac{\partial y^*}{\partial g} = K_g > 0 \qquad \frac{\partial y^*}{\partial m} = K_m > 0$$

Note that the government spending multiplier can be written as

$$K_g = \frac{1}{(1 - Z_y) + Z_r L_y / L_r}$$

It is thus already lower in this regime than the simplest Keynesian multiplier $1/(1 - Z_y)$ because of an indirect crowding-out effect working through the bonds market: Indeed, the increase in interest rate necessary to finance additional public spending reduces private spending and thus also the multiplier.

For regime A to obtain, the parameters $\bar{p}$, $\bar{w}$, m, and g must be such that there is actually excess supply in the output and labor markets, which yields, as in previous chapters, the following conditions:

$$y^* \leq F[F'^{-1}(w^*/p^*)]$$
$$l^* \leq l_0$$

Inserting the equilibrium values found earlier we obtain

$$K(\bar{p}, m, g) \leq F[F'^{-1}(\bar{w}/\bar{p})]$$
$$K(\bar{p}, m, g) \leq F(l_0) = y_0$$

These conditions can be represented graphically in $(\bar{p}, \bar{w})$ space, assuming g and m constant (Fig. 6.1). The corresponding subregion has been denoted as A.

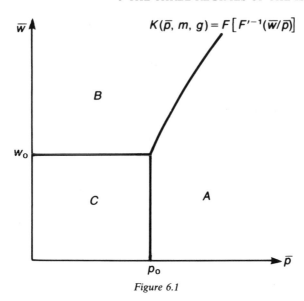

Figure 6.1

Regime B: Excess Supply in the Labor Market, Goods Market Cleared

In this regime, the price is not blocked at its minimum value but is determined instead by the condition of equality of supply and demand in the goods market. Sales are still equal to demand,

$$y = Z(y, r, p) + g$$

but the equation $p = \bar{p}$ must be replaced by an equation indicating that transactions are equal to the firm's supply in the output market. Since the firm is not constrained in the labor market, this supply is the neoclassical one, i.e.,

$$y = F[F'^{-1}(w/p)]$$

In the labor market, the wage is blocked at its minimum,

$$w = \bar{w}$$

and employment is determined by the demand for labor. Since the firm is not constrained in the goods market, this demand has the neoclassical form $F'^{-1}(w/p)$ and thus,

$$l = F'^{-1}(w/p)$$

Finally, we still have the market-clearing equation for bonds:

$$B(y, r, p) = b = r(pg - m + \bar{m})$$

The equilibrium values are solutions of the previous five equations. Combining again the IS and bonds market equations, we obtain the following simpler system in p^*, w^*, y^*, and l^*:

$$y^* = K(p^*, m, g)$$

$$y^* = F[F'^{-1}(w^*/p^*)]$$

$$l^* = F'^{-1}(w^*/p^*)$$

$$w^* = \bar{w}$$

We define, as in Chapter 4,

$$S(p, w) = F[F'^{-1}(w/p)] \qquad S_p > 0 \qquad S_w < 0$$

The economic policy multipliers are easily computed as

$$\frac{\partial y^*}{\partial g} = \frac{S_p K_g}{S_p - K_p} < K_g$$

$$\frac{\partial y^*}{\partial m} = \frac{S_p K_m}{S_p - K_p} < K_m$$

Comparing these with regime A above, we see that the effects of both fiscal and monetary policies are weaker here because of the induced price movements, which can be computed as

$$\frac{\partial p^*}{\partial g} = \frac{K_g}{S_p - K_p} > 0$$

$$\frac{\partial p^*}{\partial m} = \frac{K_m}{S_p - K_p} > 0$$

These price increases reduce private demand and thus the multipliers. We may also note that in this regime a reduction of the minimum wage $\bar{w}$ results in an increase in production and employment as well as a decrease in the price of output:

$$\frac{\partial y^*}{\partial \bar{w}} = \frac{-K_p S_w}{S_p - K_p} < 0$$

$$\frac{\partial p^*}{\partial \bar{w}} = \frac{-S_w}{S_p - K_p} > 0$$

We shall now characterize the set of parameters for which the equilibrium is of type B. The values w^*, p^*, y^*, l^* must be such that there is excess supply in the labor market and that the equilibrium price is above the minimum value:

$$l^* \le l_0 \qquad p^* \ge \bar{p}$$

Using the graphical representation of Fig. 6.2 (which will be explained in Section 5), it is easy to see that these two conditions are equivalent to the following:

$$K[\bar{w}/F'(l_0), m, g] \le y_0$$

$$K(\bar{p}, m, g) \ge F[F'^{-1}(\bar{w}/\bar{p})]$$

The corresponding subregion in $(\bar{p}, \bar{w})$ space has been denoted by B in Fig. 6.1.

Regime C: Both Markets Cleared

In this case, the price and wage are determined by the equality of supply and demand in the output and labor markets. The equations for the output market are the same as for regime B:

$$y = Z(y, r, p) + g$$

$$y = F[F'^{-1}(w/p)]$$

For the labor market to clear, the transaction l must be equal to both the effective supply l_0 and the effective demand, which, since the goods market

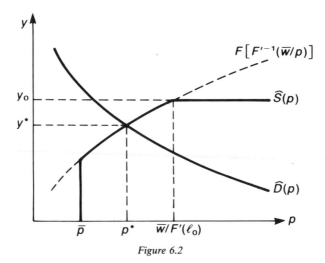

Figure 6.2

clears, has the neoclassical form $F'^{-1}(w/p)$:

$$l = l_0$$

$$l = F'^{-1}(w/p)$$

Finally, the bonds market equilibrium equation is

$$B(y, r, p) = b = r(pg - m + \bar{m})$$

Combining again this and the IS equation, we obtain the following system:

$$y^* = K(p^*, m, g)$$

$$y^* = F[F'^{-1}(w^*/p^*)]$$

$$l^* = F'^{-1}(w^*/p^*)$$

$$l^* = l_0$$

We see that in this case, both multipliers are equal to zero, since y^* is at the full-employment value y_0. All effects of fiscal and monetary policies on employment and production are canceled by the movements in price and interest rate caused by them. The equilibrium price and wage are given by:

$$y_0 = K(p^*, m, g)$$

$$w^* = p^* F'(l_0)$$

where we recognize the Walrasian values. We can compute

$$\frac{\partial p^*}{\partial g} = -\frac{K_g}{K_p} > 0$$

$$\frac{\partial p^*}{\partial m} = -\frac{K_m}{K_p} > 0$$

Parameters for which this regime obtains must be such that the equilibrium price and wage are above their minimum levels, i.e.,

$$p^* \geqslant \bar{p} \qquad w^* \geqslant \bar{w}$$

Using the values computed above, this yields

$$K(\bar{p}, m, g) \geqslant y_0$$

$$K[w/F'(l_0), m, g] \geqslant y_0$$

The corresponding subregion is denoted as C in Fig. 6.1.

The "Fourth" Regime

From a merely combinatorial point of view, there should exist in this model a fourth regime with excess supply of goods and the labor market cleared. One never sees in the literature, however, any IS-LM model with this structure and for a good reason. As we shall now show, the corresponding subregime degenerates into a limiting case, somehow "between" regimes A and C. Indeed, since there is excess supply of goods, the price and transaction in the output market are determined by

$$p = \bar{p}$$

$$y = Z(y, r, p) + g$$

Since the labor market clears, the level of employment is equal to both the supply and demand for labor. Because there is excess supply in the goods market, the demand for labor has the Keynesian form, and thus,

$$l = F^{-1}(y)$$

$$l = l_0$$

Finally, the bonds market clears:

$$B(y, r, p) = b = r(pg - m + \bar{m})$$

Combining this and the IS equation, one obtains

$$p^* = \bar{p}$$

$$y^* = K(p^*, m, g)$$

$$l^* = F^{-1}(y^*)$$

$$l^* = l_0$$

Note that the last three conditions yield an equilibrium price equal to the Walrasian one: $p^* = p_0$. Combining this with the first condition, we obtain $\bar{p} = p_0$, which is a first restriction on the set of possible parameters. Furthermore, for this regime to obtain, there must be excess supply in the output market, and the wage must be above its minimum level, i.e.,

$$y^* \leq F[F'^{-1}(w^*/p^*)]$$

$$w^* \geq \bar{w}$$

We can find a value of w^* satisfying both these conditions, provided that

$$\bar{w}/p_0 \leq F'(l_0)$$

Summing up, the set of parameters corresponding to this fourth regime is given by

$$\bar{p} = p_0$$

$$\bar{w}/p_0 \leqslant F'(l_0)$$

One sees graphically (Fig. 6.1) that this set corresponds to the line separating region A from region C. This regime is thus degenerate, and a local study of economic policy effects would be useless.

5. A Graphical Solution

As in the preceding chapters we shall give here a graphical representation of the three regimes of this model, very close to the traditional Keynesian aggregate demand and supply diagrams. If we look at the various systems of equations given earlier, we see that the equilibrium values p^* and y^* can be found at the intersection in (p, y) space of a demand and a supply curve denoted respectively as

$$y = \hat{D}(p) \qquad \text{and} \qquad y = \hat{S}(p)$$

The demand curve is simply the aggregate demand function constructed earlier:

$$\hat{D}(p) = K(p, m, g)$$

The supply curve $\hat{S}(p)$ consists of three parts (see Fig. 6.2 in Section 4): a vertical part with equation $p = \bar{p}$, a horizontal part with equation $y = y_0$, and an upward-sloping part with the equation

$$y = F[F'^{-1}(\bar{w}/p)]$$

Note that this upward-sloping part may not exist if $\bar{w}/\bar{p} < F'(l_0)$. One immediately sees that the equilibrium will be of type A if the two curves intersect in the vertical part of the supply curve, of type B if they intersect in the upward-sloping part, and of type C if they intersect in the horizontal part. Case B has been shown in Fig. 6.2. We have already indicated in Section 4 for which sets of parameters each of the three regimes obtains.

We may remark here that an equilibrium need not always exist. In Fig. 6.2 we see that this would correspond to a situation where $K(p, m, g)$ is greater than y_0 whatever the level of p. In such a case, a short-run Walrasian equilibrium would not exist either, since excess demand would prevail at all prices. However, we eliminated by assumption such a situation at the end of Section 3.

6. The IS-LM Model with a Rigid Real Wage

In order to find the three traditional versions of the IS-LM model, we considered in the preceding sections a specification of our model with downward rigidity of price and nominal wage. Clearly, we could work out the same model by introducing other assumptions on the formation of wages and prices, for example, wage indexation as in Chapter 5. As an example, we shall briefly describe what becomes of the IS-LM model if, as in Chapter 5 Section 4, we assume a rigid real wage ω. We shall assume that nominal wage and price are subject to the constraints

$$w = \omega p \qquad p \geq \bar{p}$$

Of course, we keep the IS-LM equations

$$y = Z(y, r, p) + g$$
$$L(y, r, p) = m$$

which combine into the aggregate demand equation

$$y = K(p, m, g)$$

As in Chapter 5, we shall have three regimes: A, B, and C, the first two being characterized by the presence of involuntary unemployment. We shall indicate how the equilibrium values y^* and p^* are determined in these three regimes. In each case, w^* and l^* can be deduced from these by the formulas

$$w^* = \omega p^* \qquad l^* = F^{-1}(y^*)$$

In regime A, we obtain the system

$$p^* = \bar{p}$$
$$y^* = K(\bar{p}, m, g)$$

Traditional Keynesian results already seen in this chapter are again valid. Notably, fiscal and monetary policies are effective against unemployment. In regime C, the system becomes

$$y^* = y_0$$
$$y^* = K(p^*, m, g)$$

In this case, since y is fixed at its full-employment value, the only effect of fiscal and monetary policies is to drive prices up, a result also seen before.

The most important change concerns of course regime B, where the equations determining activity and prices are

$$y^* = F[F'^{-1}(\omega)]$$

$$y^* = K(p^*, m, g)$$

We see here that even though there is some involuntary unemployment and demand is always satisfied, multipliers for fiscal and monetary policies are both equal to zero. The corresponding policies only increase the price level and, in the case of an increase in g, simply crowd out private consumption. We thus see that in this regime it is possible to obtain a result of ineffectiveness for fiscal and monetary policies in an IS-LM framework. This result is achieved without making any of the assumptions usually made by the "new classicals" on market clearing or expectations in order to achieve such results. It is enough to assume full indexation of wages on prices.

Globally, the level of activity is given by

$$y^* = \min\{K(\bar{p}, m, g), F[F'^{-1}(\omega)], y_0\}$$

which allows us to determine for each set of parameters $\bar{p}$, ω, m, g in which regime the economy is, as was done in Chapter 5.

7. Conclusions

In order to attain a synthesis with traditional IS-LM models, we formalized the hypothesis, implicit in most Keynesian models, according to which price and wage are flexible upward but rigid downward, the bonds market always clearing. We have seen that the resulting equilibria could be of three types, depending on the values of the minimum price and wage as well as the government's fiscal and monetary policy parameters m and g. It is interesting to note that these three types correspond to the three versions of the IS-LM model usually found in the literature. In each case we showed how production and employment were determined, and we computed the multipliers for fiscal and monetary policy. These multipliers are very different in the three cases, and it appears to be particularly important to specify rigorously in which regime the economy is assumed to be when the IS-LM model is used for prescribing economic policy.

We have furthermore studied a version of the IS-LM model with rigid real wage, which showed that ineffectiveness results for fiscal and monetary policies can be obtained, even in the presence of involuntary unemployment, an important result, although hardly ever mentioned in traditional expositions.

References

The model of this chapter is adapted from Benassy (1983). Models introducing bonds, while assuming price and wage completely rigid, can be found in Barro and Grossman (1976), Gelpi and Younès (1977), Hool (1980), Danthine and Peytrignet (1981), and Sneessens (1981). The three versions of the IS-LM model can be found, for example, in Branson (1979).

PART III

OPEN-ECONOMY MODELS

7

Economic Policies in an
Open Economy

1. Introduction

The framework of the preceding chapters was that of a closed economy. We shall now study the effectiveness of economic policies in an open economy by constructing a two-country model. This will allow us to study both the effects of various policies on the country pursuing them and their repercussions on a foreign country. We shall perform this analysis in regimes of both fixed and flexible exchange rates. Finally, we shall also study the influence of the country size on the effects of various economic policies.

In order to discuss these different points, we shall use a simple two-country extension of the model of Chapter 4. We shall consider two economies, denoted as 1 and 2, producing a unique homogeneous output the price of which clears the world market.[1] In each of the two countries, however, labor is a specific factor, and wages are assumed to be rigid.

2. The Model

We thus have two countries labeled 1 and 2. In each country there is a national market for labor. Wages are assumed rigid in the short run at the

---

[1]We thus do not assume a minimum price, contrary to the model of Chapter 4. Indeed, such an assumption could not be made here since the good is homogeneous, and exchange rates can vary. We shall reintroduce downward rigidity in Chapter 8, where goods produced in each country are differentiated.

levels w_1 and w_2. The internationally traded good is sold at the price p_1 in country 1 and p_2 in country 2. Let e be the level of the exchange rate, i.e., the value of country 2's money in terms of country 1's money. The values of p_1 and p_2 are related by the identity

$$p_1 = ep_2$$

since this is actually a single good and a single market. Implicit in this model is an exchange market where currencies of the two countries are exchanged at the rate e. This market always clears, either through the flexibility of e, in the case of flexible exchange rates, or through central banks' interventions in the case of fixed exchange rates. We shall no longer consider this market in what follows.

Agents

In each of the two countries the agents are similar to those of Chapter 4: a firm, a household, and the government. Firms have respectively production functions

$$F_1(l_1) \quad \text{and} \quad F_2(l_2)$$

Households have labor supplies l_{01} and l_{02} and consumption functions

$$C_1(y_1, p_1, \tau_1) \quad \text{and} \quad C_2(y_2, p_2, \tau_2)$$

Finally, governments levy taxes τ_1 and τ_2 in real terms and express demands for output of levels g_1 and g_2, respectively.

3. International Equilibrium

The model just described generally has four regimes, depending on whether labor markets in each of the two countries are in excess supply (unemployment) or in excess demand (full employment). We shall now consider the system of equations that gives the levels of employment, sales, and the balance of payments. Let us start with the definitional equations: first, the relation of equivalence for prices (the "law of one price") seen before:

$$p_1 = ep_2$$

then, the definition of the balance of payments surplus for country 1, which we shall express in this chapter in terms of the homogeneous good, and denote by B:

$$B = y_1 - C_1(y_1, p_1, \tau_1) - g_1$$

Of course, the surplus of country 1 is equal to the deficit of country 2. Let us now look at the equations that will determine the non-Walrasian equilibrium in this international framework.

One equation always holds, that which expresses that total sales of output on the world market $y_1 + y_2$ are equal to the total demand coming from households or governments, i.e.,

$$y_1 + y_2 = C_1(y_1, p_1, \tau_1) + g_1 + C_2(y_2, p_2, \tau_2) + g_2$$

The other equations, which intuitively represent the "supply side" for each country, are different, depending on whether one is in a situation of unemployment or full employment. We shall discuss them here briefly for country 1, since we have already seen them in Chapter 4.

If we are in a situation of unemployment, the firm carries out its "neoclassical" employment and sales plan, i.e.,

$$y_1 = F_1[F_1'^{-1}(w_1/p_1)]$$
$$l_1 = F_1'^{-1}(w_1/p_1)$$

If, on the contrary, full employment prevails, employment, production, and sales are fixed at the maximum level, i.e.,

$$l_1 = l_{01}$$
$$y_1 = y_{01} = F_1(l_{01})$$

If we set

$$S_1(p_1, w_1) = F_1[F_1'^{-1}(w_1/p_1)]$$

the determination of y_1 and l_1 can be summarized by

$$y_1 = \min\{S_1(p_1, w_1), y_{01}\}$$
$$l_1 = F_1^{-1}(y_1)$$

Similar formulas apply to country 2.

The Complete System

We can now write down the complete system of equations we shall work with, determining price, production, employment, exchange rate and the balance of payments:

$$y_1 + y_2 = C_1(y_1, p_1, \tau_1) + g_1 + C_2(y_2, p_2, \tau_2) + g_2$$

$$y_1 = \min\{S_1(p_1, w_1), y_{01}\}$$

$$y_2 = \min\{S_2(p_2, w_2), y_{02}\}$$

$$l_1 = F_1^{-1}(y_1)$$

$$l_2 = F_2^{-1}(y_2)$$

$$p_1 = ep_2$$

$$B = y_1 - C_1(y_1, p_1, \tau_1) - g_1$$

4. Flexible Exchange Rates

The case of flexible exchange rates is particularly easy to treat in this model. Indeed, in the absence of capital movements the balance of payments is identical to the trade balance, and the equation $B = 0$ transforms the demand-side equation for the output market into two independent equations one for each country:

$$y_1 = C_1(y_1, p_1, \tau_1) + g_1$$

$$y_2 = C_2(y_2, p_2, \tau_2) + g_2$$

We then see that the countries are "insulated" from each other by the system of flexible rates. For example, the equations concerning country 1 are written

$$y_1 = C_1(y_1, p_1, \tau_1) + g_1$$

$$y_1 = \min\{S_1(p_1, w_1), y_{01}\}$$

$$l_1 = F_1^{-1}(y_1)$$

$$e = p_1/p_2$$

We recognize here the equations derived for a closed economy (cf. Chapter 4), with one difference: Price increases lead here to a depreciation of the currency, as the fourth equation shows. We shall now recall the relevant multipliers, which will allow a comparison with the fixed-exchange-rate regime studied next in Section 5. Only the case of unemployment is considered here, however, since the level of employment is fixed in the case of an excess demand for labor, and thus the multipliers are equal to zero insofar as activity and employment are concerned.

Keynesian policies aimed at increasing demand ($dg_1 > 0$ or $d\tau_1 < 0$) lead to an increase in production and employment, to an increase in prices, and thus to a depreciation of the currency:[2]

$$\frac{\partial y_1^*}{\partial g_1} = \frac{1}{1 - C_{1y} - (C_{1p}/S_{1p})} > 0$$

$$\frac{\partial y_1^*}{\partial \tau_1} = \frac{C_{1\tau}}{1 - C_{1y} - (C_{1p}/S_{1p})} < 0$$

$$\frac{\partial p_1^*}{\partial g_1} = \frac{1}{S_{1p}(1 - C_{1y}) - C_{1p}} > 0$$

$$\frac{\partial p_1^*}{\partial \tau_1} = \frac{C_{1\tau}}{S_{1p}(1 - C_{1y}) - C_{1p}} < 0$$

Incomes policies ($dw_1 < 0$) lead not only to an increase in production and employment, but also to a decrease in prices and thus to an appreciation of the currency:

$$\frac{\partial y_1^*}{\partial w_1} = \frac{-S_{1w}C_{1p}}{S_{1p}(1 - C_{1y}) - C_{1p}} < 0$$

$$\frac{\partial p_1^*}{\partial w_1} = \frac{-S_{1w}(1 - C_{1y})}{S_{1p}(1 - C_{1y}) - C_{1p}} > 0$$

As we mentioned before, none of these policies has any effect on the internal variables of the foreign economy. This result would not hold in a more general model, especially if capital flows are included in the balance of payments.

5. Fixed Exchange Rates

We shall compute here the effects of Keynesian and classical policies against unemployment and compare them with their impact in a closed economy. We shall also see the effect of the size of the country on the efficacy of economic policies. In what follows we shall assume that by suitable normalization, the exchange rate e is equal to 1. We shall thus have

$$p_1 = p_2 = p$$

[2]As before, a subindex corresponds to a partial derivative. Subindex 1 or 2 is added depending on whether country 1 or 2 is concerned. For example, $C_{1y} = \partial C_1/\partial y_1$.

Moreover, we shall be interested in situations of unemployment in both countries, i.e., we shall take

$$y_1 = S_1(p, w_1)$$
$$y_2 = S_2(p, w_2)$$

We can obtain the corresponding results when one country is at full employment by setting the partial derivatives of the above functions equal to zero, i.e., replacing S_{1p} and S_{1w} by zero (if country 1 is at full employment) or S_{2p} and S_{2w} by zero (if country 2 is at full employment). The system with which we shall work is thus the following:

$$y_1 + y_2 = C_1(y_1, p, \tau_1) + g_1 + C_2(y_2, p, \tau_2) + g_2$$
$$y_1 = S_1(p, w_1)$$
$$y_2 = S_2(p, w_2)$$
$$B = y_1 - C_1(y_1, p, \tau_1) - g_1$$

Keynesian Policies

We shall consider here policies of government-spending increases ($dg_1 > 0$ and $dg_2 > 0$). Programs of tax reductions would have similar effects. In order to solve the previous system with respect to variations in g_1 and g_2, let us define

$$\lambda_1 = S_{1p}(1 - C_{1y}) - C_{1p} > 0$$
$$\lambda_2 = S_{2p}(1 - C_{2y}) - C_{2p} > 0$$

We immediately find by differentiation,

$$\frac{\partial p}{\partial g_1} = \frac{1}{\lambda_1 + \lambda_2} > 0$$

$$\frac{\partial y_1}{\partial g_1} = \frac{S_{1p}}{\lambda_1 + \lambda_2} > 0$$

$$\frac{\partial y_2}{\partial g_1} = \frac{S_{2p}}{\lambda_1 + \lambda_2} > 0$$

$$\frac{\partial B}{\partial g_1} = \frac{-\lambda_2}{\lambda_1 + \lambda_2} < 0$$

A few results are obvious from these formulas. First, the public spending multiplier is smaller in an open economy with fixed exchanged rates than in a closed economy (or in an open economy with flexible exchange rates but without capital movements, as we saw in Section 4), where we would have

$$\frac{\partial y_1}{\partial g_1} = \frac{S_{1p}}{\lambda_1} > \frac{S_{1p}}{\lambda_1 + \lambda_2}$$

The reason is that part of the extra effective demand is spent abroad. This reduces the multiplier and has the two supplementary effects of increasing activity in the foreign economy $(\partial y_2/\partial g_1 > 0)$ and worsening the balance of payments $(\partial B/\partial g_1 < 0)$. Furthermore, in this very simple model the effects of an increase in government spending on activity and prices are the same, independent of which country actually pursues that policy, since

$$\frac{\partial y_1}{\partial g_1} = \frac{\partial y_1}{\partial g_2} = \frac{S_{1p}}{\lambda_1 + \lambda_2}$$

It is thus clearly in the interest of each country that the other pursue Keynesian policies, since this increases its own activity without worsening its balance of payments. We may then think of concerted Keynesian policies that would preserve the balance of payments. We can compute that

$$dB = \frac{\lambda_1 \, dg_2 - \lambda_2 \, dg_1}{\lambda_1 + \lambda_2}$$

and thus such coordinated Keynesian policies should be such that

$$\frac{dg_1}{\lambda_1} = \frac{dg_2}{\lambda_2}$$

Note that λ_1 and λ_2 are positive, even if the corresponding country is at full employment. This formula thus implies that even in a country at full employment the government could be led to increase demand in such a framework, which of course may be difficult to obtain in practice.

Incomes Policies

We shall now consider incomes policies in country 1 $(dw_1 < 0)$. Solving the previous system, we obtain

$$\frac{\partial p}{\partial w_1} = \frac{(1 - C_{1y})S_{1w}}{\lambda_1 + \lambda_2} > 0$$

$$\frac{\partial y_1}{\partial w_1} = \frac{[S_{2p}(1 - C_{2y}) - C_{2p} - C_{1p}]S_{1w}}{\lambda_1 + \lambda_2} < 0$$

$$\frac{\partial y_2}{\partial w_1} = -\frac{S_{2p}(1 - C_{1y})S_{1w}}{\lambda_1 + \lambda_2} > 0$$

$$\frac{\partial B}{\partial w_1} = \frac{\lambda_2}{\lambda_1 + \lambda_2}(1 - C_{1y})S_{1w} < 0$$

From these formulas, we can draw a number of inferences. First, the effect of incomes policies is stronger in an open economy than in a closed economy, where the multiplier would be equal to $-C_{1p}S_{1w}/\lambda_1$, since

$$\frac{S_{2p}(1 - C_{2y}) - C_{2p} - C_{1p}}{\lambda_1 + \lambda_2} > -\frac{C_{1p}}{\lambda_1}$$

Indeed, a wage reduction in country 1 makes it more competitive, allowing it to appropriate part of country 2's demand. This increases the impact of a wage decrease and also improves country 1's balance of payments. If we now consider the effects on country 2, we see that contrary to Keynesian policies, incomes policies in country 1 have a negative effect on both activity and the balance of payments of the foreign economy, since

$$\frac{\partial y_2}{\partial w_1} > 0 \qquad \frac{\partial B}{\partial w_1} < 0$$

The positive results of incomes policies are thus partially obtained at the expense of the foreign economy.

The Effects of Size

We shall now examine briefly what happens if we vary the relative size of the two countries. At one extreme, if the size of the foreign country approaches zero, we find the results of a closed economy. At the other extreme, if the foreign economy becomes very large, we obtain at the limit the case of the "small country," which we can describe with our formulas by letting S_{2p}, S_{2w}, and C_{2p} approach infinity. We then obtain

$$\frac{\partial y_1}{\partial g_1} = 0 \qquad \frac{\partial B}{\partial g_1} = -1$$

Keynesian demand policies become completely ineffective. Moreover, every increase in demand leads to an equal balance-of-payments deficit. Incomes policies, on the contrary, are effective in increasing activity and employment and in improving the balance of payments:

$$\frac{\partial y_1}{\partial w_1} = S_{1w} < 0 \qquad \frac{\partial B}{\partial w_1} = (1 - C_{1y})S_{1w} < 0$$

These results have a very intuitive explanation when we observe that the small-country assumption is equivalent to assuming an exogenous price and a world demand infinitely elastic at that price. Such an hypothesis obviously rules out any traditional Keynesian effect.

6. Conclusions

In this chapter we have extended the models of the preceding chapters to a two-country framework by considering a simple model in which one homogeneous good is exchanged in all countries. This has allowed us to see that opening an economy could radically modify the relative efficiency of antiunemployment policies. We first studied briefly the case of flexible exchange rates: In the absence of capital flows, the assumption of balance of payments equilibrium leads in this model to the same results as in a closed economy, with the sole exception of exchange-rate variations. More interesting are the results in a fixed-exchange-rates regime, where one sees that the opening of the economy reduces the effectiveness against unemployment of Keynesian policies. Moreover, Keynesian demand policies create a deficit in the balance of payments, which may possibly force the government to practice restrictive demand policies in the future. Income policies, by contrast, create a surplus in the balance of payments and are more effective than in a closed economy.

We should note that in this model with a homogeneous good the real terms of trade cannot be modified, whereas changes in these terms of trade are an important element in studying issues such as currency devaluation. We shall thus introduce in Chapter 8 a differentiation of the goods produced by each country in order to study balance-of-payments problems.

References

The model of this chapter combines and extends models of international trade presented by Branson and Rotemberg (1980) and Dixit and Norman (1980). Devaluation has been studied in a similar framework by Schmid (1982). The small-country model had been introduced by Dixit (1978).

CHAPTER

8

The Balance of Payments

1. Introduction

Our purpose in this chapter is to construct a synthetic model of international trade that is consistent with the main theories of the balance of payments (elasticities, absorption, and monetary theories) and that can function under various regimes, going from full employment with price flexibility to unemployment with rigid prices. This exercise will allow us to show explicitly some particular assumptions that underlie these theories. The model deployed here is an extension of the one-country model of Chapter 4 to the case of two countries and two goods.

2. The Model

There are two countries, denoted as 1 and 2, each specialized in the production of one good. The goods are also indexed by 1 and 2. We shall assume that labor is fixed in each country, whereas goods circulate freely. As before, e is the exchange rate, i.e., the price of country 2's money in terms of country 1's money. The "law of one price" applies to each good, and thus good 1 has a price p_1 in country 1 and p_1/e in country 2; good 2 has a price p_2 in country 2 and ep_2 in country 1.

Description of Country 1

Country 1 has three agents: a firm, a household, and the government. The wage and the price of the national good are equal to w_1 and p_1 in terms of the national money. As in the model of Chapter 4 we shall assume that w_1 is given, whereas p_1 is flexible with a minimum level $\bar{p}_1$.

The firm has a production function $F_1(l_1)$ and sells a quantity of output y_1. The household has a supply of labor l_{01} and initial money holdings $\bar{m}_1$. The firm distributes all profits, and the household's income in terms of good 1 is thus y_1. It is faced with a price p_1 for the national good and a price $q_1 = ep_2$ for the imported good. It chooses its consumption of national good C_1 and imported good I_1 as a function of y_1, p_1, q_1,[1] according to the following two functions:

$$C_1(y_1, p_1, q_1) \qquad \text{and} \qquad I_1(y_1, p_1, q_1)$$

We shall assume that the partial derivatives have the following signs:

$$0 < C_{1y} < 1 \qquad C_{1p} < 0 \qquad C_{1q} > 0$$
$$I_{1y} > 0 \qquad I_{1p} > 0 \qquad I_{1q} < 0$$

The government has a demand g_1 for the national good, which is implicitly financed by money creation. To simplify the exposition of the model, we shall omit taxes in this chapter.

Description of Country 2

The description of country 2 is symmetrical to that of country 1; therefore it is sufficient to replace index 1 by index 2. For example, the consumption and import functions are

$$C_2(y_2, p_2, q_2) \qquad \text{and} \qquad I_2(y_2, p_2, q_2)$$

where $q_2 = p_1/e$.

3. Determination of Incomes and Prices in the Different Regimes

As indicated above, we make the following assumptions: Wages are fixed in the two countries, respectively equal to w_1 and w_2. Prices p_1 and p_2 are

---

[1] And of course of $\bar{m}_1$, which we shall omit as an argument since it is given in the period.

flexible but with lower bounds (in terms of national monies) equal to $\bar{p}_1$ and $\bar{p}_2$, respectively. The model evidently has a multiplicity of regimes. We may, however, classify them quite simply: If we consider each country separately, there are, as in a closed economy, three possible regimes, insofar as the national labor market and the market for the nationally produced good are concerned (cf. Chapter 4):

Excess supply of labor and national good (regime A).
Excess supply of labor with the national good market cleared (regime B).
Excess demand for labor with the national good market cleared (regime C).

Each country can be in any of these three regimes. There are thus nine possible combinations. We shall show here how y_1, y_2, p_1, p_2 are determined in these various cases and describe the equations that allow us to compute them. First, two equations are the same in all regimes. Indeed, the prices of goods being flexible upward, the demands for the national and foreign goods are always satisfied. Thus, the sales of each of the two goods are always equal to the sum of national and foreign demands for that good:

$$y_1 = C_1(y_1, p_1, ep_2) + I_2(y_2, p_2, p_1/e) + g_1 \tag{1}$$

$$y_2 = C_2(y_2, p_2, p_1/e) + I_1(y_1, p_1, ep_2) + g_2 \tag{2}$$

In order to fully determine the values of y_1, y_2, p_1, p_2, we must have two other equations, which depend on the regime prevailing in each country (A, B, or C). As we saw in Chapter 4, these equations are the following:

If the country is in regime A, the price is fixed at its minimum,

$$p_1 = \bar{p}_1$$

or

$$p_2 = \bar{p}_2$$

If the country is in regime B, sales of goods are equal to the neoclassical supply, i.e.,

$$y_1 = F_1[F_1'^{-1}(w_1/p_1)]$$

or

$$y_2 = F_2[F_2'^{-1}(w_2/p_2)]$$

If the country is in regime C, sales of goods are at the level of full-employment production,

$$y_1 = y_{01} = F_1(l_{01})$$

or

$$y_2 = y_{02} = F_2(l_{02})$$

Figure 8.1 represents the relation between y_1 and p_1 corresponding to this supply relation.

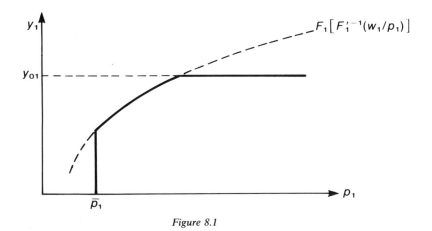

Figure 8.1

An Example: the Keynesian Two-Country Multiplier

As an example, consider the case where the two countries are in regime A, the exchange rate being given. We thus have the two basic equations,

$$y_1 = C_1(y_1, p_1, ep_2) + I_2(y_2, p_2, p_1/e) + g_1$$

$$y_2 = C_2(y_2, p_2, p_1/e) + I_1(y_1, p_1, ep_2) + g_2$$

and $p_1 = \bar{p}_1$, $p_2 = \bar{p}_2$, since both countries are in regime A. By differentiating we can immediately compute the effects in the two countries of a variation in public spending:

$$\frac{\partial y_1}{\partial g_1} = \frac{1 - C_{2y}}{(1 - C_{1y})(1 - C_{2y}) - I_{1y}I_{2y}}$$

$$\frac{\partial y_2}{\partial g_1} = \frac{I_{1y}}{(1 - C_{1y})(1 - C_{2y}) - I_{1y}I_{2y}}$$

where we recognize the traditional Keynesian international trade multipliers. One should thus note that these multipliers are valid only if the two countries are in regime A.

4. The Balance of Payments and the Three Traditional Approaches

We shall now show that the previous model is consistent with the three traditional approaches to the balance of payments. Let us first set down the definition of balance of payments. If B_1 is the surplus of country 1 (in terms of its own money) and B_2 that of country 2, we have

$$B_1 = p_1 I_2 - e p_2 I_1 = p_1 I_2 - q_1 I_1$$

$$B_2 = p_2 I_1 - (p_1/e) I_2 = p_2 I_1 - q_2 I_2$$

Of course, $B_1 + e B_2 = 0$.

The Absorption Approach

The absorption approach tells us that the balance of payments surplus is equal to the value of national production minus the value of absorption (i.e., the total spending by the agents of the country considered). To verify that it holds here, we define the absorption A_1 of country 1 as

$$A_1(y_1, p_1, q_1, g_1) = p_1 C_1(y_1, p_1, q_1) + q_1 I_1(y_1, p_1, q_1) + p_1 g_1$$

By using the equality $q_1 = e p_2$ and Eq. (1) above, we find that

$$B_1 = p_1 y_1 - A_1$$

which is the equality stated earlier.

The Monetary Approach

The monetary approach to balance of payments tells us that the surplus of a country is equal to the difference between the quantity of money that the agents desire to hold and the quantity of money created in the country. Note that we carried all our analysis without a demand function for money, but we can construct one from the budget constraints. Indeed, the budget constraint of country 1's household is

$$p_1 y_1 + \bar{m}_1 = p_1 C_1 + q_1 I_1 + m_1$$

where m_1 is the quantity of money held by country 1's household at the end of the period considered. If we consider this as its "demand for money," we can define via the above budget constraint a money demand function:

$$m_1^d(y_1, p_1, q_1) = p_1 y_1 + \bar{m}_1 - p_1 C_1(y_1, p_1, q_1) - q_1 I_1(y_1, p_1, q_1)$$

Combining this with the definition of B_1 and Eq. (1), we obtain

$$B_1 = m_1^d - \bar{m}_1 - p_1 g_1$$

That is, the balance-of-payments surplus is equal to the demand for money m_1^d minus the total quantity of money created internally in country 1 at the end of the period, i.e., $\bar{m}_1 + p_1 g_1$.

The Elasticities Approach

The elasticities approach has its starting point in the equations of equality between the exports of one country and the imports of the other. By differentiating logarithmically the corresponding equalities, the well-known traditional elasticities formulas are obtained (these will be seen later.) In the framework of our model, it is possible to obtain formulas of the same type by defining potential export functions X_1 and X_2 by

$$X_1(y_1, p_1, q_1, g_1) = y_1 - C_1(y_1, p_1, q_1) - g_1$$

$$X_2(y_2, p_2, q_2, g_2) = y_2 - C_2(y_2, p_2, q_2) - g_2$$

Using these new functions, Eqs. (1) and (2) can be rewritten:

$$X_1(y_1, p_1, ep_2, g_1) = I_2(y_2, p_2, p_1/e) \tag{3}$$

$$X_2(y_2, p_2, p_1/e, g_2) = I_1(y_1, p_1, ep_2) \tag{4}$$

Note that the import and export functions contain income arguments as well as price arguments. Equations (3) and (4) are thus not sufficient to derive the elasticity formulas, contrary to the usual approach where only price effects are taken into account. Here we must specify the regime in which each economy lies in order to add to Eqs. (3) and (4) the relation between price and production in each country, as we saw in Section 3.

5. The Effects of a Devaluation

In order to determine the effects of a devaluation (or, as well, of variations in g_1 or g_2), we must write the complete system of equations relevant to the regime considered. We first have Eqs. (1) and (2), which we rewrite as

$$X_1(y_1, p_1, ep_2, g_1) = I_2(y_2, p_2, p_1/e) \tag{3}$$

$$X_2(y_2, p_2, p_1/e, g_2) = I_1(y_1, p_1, ep_2) \tag{4}$$

We then have the balance-of-payments equation, where B is the surplus of country 1, expressed in terms of country 2's money[2] (this is the most generally used objective function):

$$B = \frac{p_1}{e} I_2(y_2, p_2, p_1/e) - p_2 I_1(y_1, p_1, ep_2) \tag{5}$$

Finally, the two remaining equations, linking, respectively, y_1 to p_1 and y_2 to p_2, depend on the regime each country is in, as we saw in Section 3. By differentiating logarithmically all these equations, we can obtain the effect of a devaluation. It is worth noting that in the general case (Appendix D) we have to take into account no less than four income elasticities, eight price elasticities, and two elasticities σ_1 and σ_2, which depend on the regime each country is in. We shall not develop this general case here; instead, we shall draw a bridge with the traditional formulas with two elasticities (Marshall–Lerner) or four elasticities by considering simple particular cases.

The Marshall–Lerner Conditions

The traditional Marshall–Lerner formula gives the effects of a devaluation as a function of the elasticities of the import function with respect to foreign-product prices, which are denoted here i_{1q} and i_{2q}.[3] If we call V the value of imports and exports in terms of country 2's money in the initial situation (we assume an initial balance of payments in equilibrium to simplify the formulas), this Marshall–Lerner formula is written

$$\frac{dB}{V} = -(1 + i_{1q} + i_{2q}) \frac{de}{e}$$

According to this formula, for a devaluation to be successful, it is necessary that $|i_{1q} + i_{2q}| > 1$, the Marshall–Lerner condition. This formula is assumed to be valid in the case where prices of goods expressed in terms of national money do not move after the devaluation (which corresponds in the framework of our model to both countries in regime A). One sees, however, that even in this case the Marshall–Lerner formula is not correct, since the devaluation will change income in both countries. It is no more valid in

---

[2] B is related to the values B_1 and B_2 seen before by $B = -B_2 = B_1/e$.

[3] The elasticities of the import and export functions are denoted by letters i (for import elasticities) and x (for export elasticities), with subindexes 1 or 2 (depending on the country) and p, q, or y (depending on the variable with respect to which the elasticity is computed). For example, $i_{1q} = (q_1/I_1) \, \partial I_1/\partial q_1$.

the other regimes where price changes as well will follow the devaluation. The complete formula, obtained by logarithmically differentiating Eq. (5), is

$$\frac{dB}{V} = -(1 + i_{1q} + i_{2q}) \frac{de}{e} + (1 + i_{2q} - i_{1p}) \frac{dp_1}{p_1}$$

$$+ (i_{2p} - i_{1q} - 1) \frac{dp_2}{p_2} + i_{2y} \frac{dy_2}{y_2} - i_{1y} \frac{dy_1}{y_1}$$

One sees that to the first term, à la Marshall–Lerner, are added four other terms that depend on the variations of p_1, p_2, y_1, y_2 brought about by the devaluation. One can, however, obtain the Marshall–Lerner formula in *all* regimes if one assumes that at the same time as the devaluation the two countries adopt policies of deflation or expansion that cancel the devaluation's effects on prices and production. Assume that governments use for that purpose modifications in g_1 and g_2. These are easily found by computing the variations dg_1 and dg_2 associated with the exchange-rate variation de and consistent with the stability of prices and incomes. Assume thus:

$$dp_1 = 0 \qquad dp_2 = 0 \qquad dy_1 = 0 \qquad dy_2 = 0$$

and differentiate logarithmically Eqs. (3) and (4). We obtain

$$x_{1q} \frac{de}{e} + x_{1g} \frac{dg_1}{g_1} = -i_{2q} \frac{de}{e}$$

$$-x_{2q} \frac{de}{e} + x_{2g} \frac{dg_2}{g_2} = i_{1q} \frac{de}{e}$$

Since $x_{1g} = -g_1/X_1$ and $x_{2g} = -g_2/X_2$, these relations can be rewritten

$$\frac{dg_1}{X_1} = (x_{1q} + i_{2q}) \frac{de}{e} < 0$$

$$\frac{dg_2}{X_2} = -(x_{2q} + i_{1q}) \frac{de}{e} > 0$$

The Marshall–Lerner conditions thus hold if and only if the devaluing country pursues an adequate deflation policy while the other country expands its economy to compensate for the potential decrease in income. Unless such accompanying policies are pursued, the conventional Marshall–Lerner condition alone will not be enough to ensure a successful devaluation.

The Four-Elasticities Formula

In order to obtain the four-elasticities formula, one generally suppresses cross-elasticities: Exports are only a function of the price of exported goods, whereas imports are only a function of the price of imported goods. The following elasticities are thus assumed to be zero:

$$x_{1q} = x_{2q} = i_{1p} = i_{2p} = 0$$

Introducing this hypothesis in Eqs. (3)–(5), we get

$$X_1(y_1, p_1, g_1) = I_2(y_2, p_1/e)$$

$$X_2(y_2, p_2, g_2) = I_1(y_1, ep_2)$$

$$B = \frac{p_1}{e} I_2(y_2, p_1/e) - p_2 I_1(y_1, ep_2)$$

If we assume that both countries are in regime C, then y_1 and y_2 are fixed at their maximum level y_{01} and y_{02}. By differentiating logarithmically the previous three relations, we find

$$\frac{dB}{V} = \left[-1 - i_{1q}\left(\frac{1 + x_{2p}}{x_{2p} - i_{1q}}\right) - i_{2q}\left(\frac{1 + x_{1p}}{x_{1p} - i_{2q}}\right) \right] \frac{de}{e}$$

which is the four-elasticities formula with export elasticities x_{1p} and x_{2p} and import elasticities i_{1q} and i_{2q}. It should be noted that if only one of the two countries is not in regime C, the formula will be different, since variations in incomes will be present.

We shall not pursue further the exposition of the various other particular cases. The interested reader can find in Appendix D the complete method of calculation of the effects of a devaluation in the various regimes.

6. Conclusions

We have seen in this chapter that the three traditional approaches to the study of balance of payments (elasticities, absorption, monetary theory) are different ways of representing the same phenomenon, since all equations describing the three approaches derive from the same basic system. With our model we could show the particular assumptions implicit in some traditional models, like the Marshall–Lerner or four-elasticities models. More complete calculations, where income elasticities as well as price elasticities are present, are given in Appendix D. The main result is that the prevailing regime affects the equations needed to compute the balance of payments surplus or deficit and thus also influences the effect of a devaluation. In traditional expositions, each approach implicitly assumes a unique regime, which necessarily leads to particular results.

References

The model of this chapter is taken from Benassy (1984b), and an extension to the problem of tariffs is found in Benassy (1984c). A model with rigid prices and wages studying the effects of a devaluation has been presented by Younès (1978); see also Laussel and Montet (1983).

The elasticities approach is the oldest, since it apparently goes back to Marshall (1924) and Lerner (1944) for the two-elasticities formula, and to Bickerdike (1920), Robinson (1947), and Metzler (1949) for the four-elasticities formula. Mundell (1971) gives a formula with eight price elasticities, which corresponds to our model if both countries are at full employment. The absorption approach had been proposed by Alexander (1952), and elements of synthesis with the elasticities approach are found in Harberger (1950), Alexander (1959), and Tsiang (1961). For the monetary approach, classic references are Meade (1951), Hahn (1959), Mundell (1968, 1971), and Frenkel and Johnson (1976).

PART IV

DYNAMIC MODELS

CHAPTER

9

Theories of Inflation

1. Demand and Cost Inflation

For a long time two schools have been debating on what causes inflation:
On one side, believers in demand inflation think that inflation is the response
of prices to "exogenous" increases in demand (notably due to expansionist
government monetary or fiscal policies); on the other side believers in cost
inflation blame exogenous increases in costs, such as wages, social contributions, or primary materials.

The debates between these two schools have not been conclusive. One
reason of course is the absence of a common theoretical framework between
the two schools. In this chapter we shall construct a simple synthetic model
where cost and demand inflations appear as the dynamic response of the
same system to different shocks. The two types of inflation will thus correspond to two dynamic subregimes of a single model.

2. The Model

We shall study here the evolution over time of an aggregated model very
similar to the models of Chapters 3–5 insofar as markets and agents are
concerned. We shall, however, make different assumptions on the formation
of wages and prices.

Time is represented by a sequence of periods indexed by t. In each period, prices and quantities are determined by a short-run non-Walrasian equilibrium where the wage is given; the price of goods is determined by firms in a framework of imperfect competition similar to that studied in Chapter 7, Section 7. The wage itself evolves from period to period according to a simple indexation formula.

Markets and Agents

Let us recall briefly the characteristics of the economy considered. There are two markets: output against money where a quantity y is exchanged at a price p; labor against money where a quantity of labor l is exchanged at the wage w. Agents in this economy are a firm, a household, and the government.

The firm has a production function $F(l)$, carries no inventories, and maximizes its short-period profit $py - wl$. The household has a labor supply l_0 and a consumption function that we shall take of the form

$$\tilde{c} = C(y, \bar{m}/p, \tau)$$

We thus assume that consumption demand is a function of real money balances and not, as before, of $\bar{m}$ and p separately.[1] This homogeneity property, very traditional in macroeconomics, allows us to simplify greatly the exposition of the dynamic properties of the system. As an example, we shall give in various places some explicit calculations for a consumption function that is linear in disposable real income $y - \tau$ and real money balances $\bar{m}/p$:

$$\tilde{c} = \alpha(y - \tau) + \beta(\bar{m}/p)$$

The government collects taxes τ in real terms. It has an effective demand for goods $\tilde{g}$, which, as we shall see, is always satisfied. The transaction g^* is thus equal to $\tilde{g}$, and we shall denote both by g. The government's deficit in money terms is equal to $p(g - \tau)$.

The Formation of Wages and Prices

We assume that the level of wages is the subject of collective bargaining at the beginning of each period t and remains fixed for the whole period. Wage earners want to obtain a "desired real wage," which we shall denote

---

[1] Only the variable p appears explicitly in the short-run models seen in the preceding chapters, $\bar{m}$ being a datum in the period considered.

by $\omega(t)$ for period t. However, the object of the negotiation is the nominal wage $w(t)$, and we shall assume that it is given by the following formula:

$$w(t) = \omega(t)p(t-1)$$

This formula reflects in the simplest possible manner the idea that there is some "lag" in wage adjustments with respect to prices, due to the fact that in period t wages are announced before the price level is known. Chapter 10 includes expectational elements in a similar model, but we shall retain here this simpler formula in order to simplify exposition.

Once the wage is known, the firm determines its price in a framework of imperfect competition. As we saw in Chapter 1, Section 7, the firm must estimate its demand curve in order to assess the effects of its price decisions on quantity demanded. This estimated curve is the perceived demand curve. We shall assume here that the potential demand curves considered by the firm are isoelastic curves, with elasticity $\nu > 1$, assumed fixed in all that follows. Perceived demand curves will be of the general form $\eta p^{-\nu}$, where η is a position parameter that can vary from period to period.

3. Temporary Equilibria and Dynamics

In each period the wage level w is given, and the variables l, y, and p are jointly determined within an equilibrium with monopolistic competition analogous to those studied in Chapter 2, Section 7. We shall first study these short-run equilibria, separating a "demand side" and a "supply side" for expositional convenience, and we shall then describe the dynamic equations governing the evolution of these short-run equilibria.

The Supply Side

When determining its price the firm faces (1) in the labor market a given wage w and a fixed supply of labor l_0, and (2) in the goods market a quantitative constraint given by the perceived demand curve $\eta p^{-\nu}$. The profit maximizing price p, sales y, and employment l, which maximize profit, are thus solutions to the following program:

$$\text{Maximize } py - wl \quad \text{s.t.}$$

$$y \leq F(l)$$

$$y \leq \eta p^{-\nu}$$

$$l \leq l_0$$

These solutions are thus all functions of η. It is more convenient for what follows, however, to represent the solutions of this program in the form of a "supply curve" relating p and y directly, the equation of which is

$$y = \min\left\{ F\left[F'^{-1}\left(\frac{\nu}{\nu - 1} \cdot \frac{w}{p} \right) \right], F(l_0) \right\} = \hat{S}(p)$$

Indeed, two cases can occur in the resolution of the previous program: (1) If the constraint $l \leqslant l_0$ is binding, then y is blocked at the value $y_0 = F(l_0)$. (2) If the constraint $l \leqslant l_0$ is not binding, the solution is characterized by the usual equality between marginal revenue and marginal cost, which is

$$p\left(1 - \frac{1}{\nu}\right) = \frac{w}{F'(l)} = \frac{w}{F'[F^{-1}(y)]}$$

Combining these two cases, one obtains the supply curve seen before and represented in Fig. 9.1. The level of employment l is related to y by the inverse production relation $l = F^{-1}(y)$.

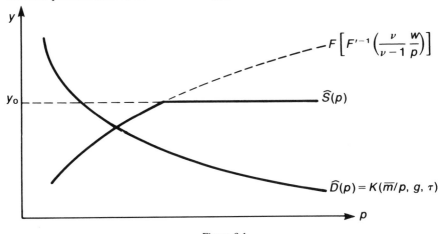

Figure 9.1

The Demand Side

We know (Chapter 1, Section 7) that a price-making firm chooses a price level such that it will be willing to satisfy all demand addressed to it. In each period the level of transactions on the output market is thus equal to the sum of consumption demand and government spending, i.e., with the form of the consumption function seen above,

$$y = C(y, \bar{m}/p, \tau) + g$$

This equation can be solved, as we have already done several times (notably in Chapters 4 and 5) in the form of an aggregate demand equation, represented in Fig. 9.1:

$$y = K(\bar{m}/p, g, \tau) = \hat{D}(p)$$

where the function K is increasing in $\bar{m}/p$ (and thus decreasing in p), increasing in g and decreasing in τ. For example, with the linear consumption function seen before we find

$$K(\bar{m}/p, g, \tau) = \frac{1}{1 - \alpha}\left[\frac{\beta\bar{m}}{p} + g - \alpha\tau\right]$$

where we recognize a traditional multiplier formula. For what follows, it is also useful to solve for $\bar{m}/p$ the demand-side equation, and we then obtain the solution in the form

$$\frac{\bar{m}}{p} = \mu(y, g, \tau)$$

with

$$\mu_y > 0 \qquad \mu_g < 0 \qquad \mu_\tau > 0$$

Continuing with the example of the linear consumption function, we find

$$\mu(y, g, \tau) = (1/\beta)[(1 - \alpha)y - g + \alpha\tau]$$

The Two Types of Equilibrium

The short-run equilibrium values of y and p are given by the solution to the system of the two demand- and supply-side equations seen before, i.e.,

$$y = \min\left\{F\left[F'^{-1}\left(\frac{\nu}{\nu - 1} \cdot \frac{w}{p}\right)\right], y_0\right\} = \hat{S}(p)$$

$$y = K(\bar{m}/p, g, \tau) = \hat{D}(p)$$

the level of employment being derived by $l = F^{-1}(y)$. One immediately sees in Fig. 9.1, which represents these two equations, that two types of equilibria (unemployment or full employment) can exist, depending on whether the curves intersect at a level y less than or equal to y_0. Figure 9.1 depicts the case of a short-run equilibrium with unemployment. We may remark that a short-run equilibrium exists if and only if (Fig. 9.1),

$$\lim_{p \to \infty} K(\bar{m}/p, g, \tau) < y_0$$

a condition that is more easily expressed, using the function μ defined before, by

$$\mu(y_0, g, \tau) > 0$$

We shall assume in what follows that g and τ always satisfy this condition, which yields, for example, with the linear consumption function seen above,

$$g < (1 - \alpha)y_0 + \alpha\tau$$

Dynamics

As we indicated at the beginning of this chapter, the evolution of the economy in time is represented by a succession of short-run equilibria, which we have just described. The link between successive periods is made through the wage equation seen before:

$$w(t) = \omega(t)p(t-1)$$

Furthermore, the household's money balances at the beginning of each period evolve according to the formula

$$\bar{m}(t+1) = \bar{m}(t) + p(t)g(t) - p(t)\tau(t)$$

that is, in each period the increase in money balances is equal to the government deficit. The evolution of "exogenous" parameters $\omega(t)$, $g(t)$, $\tau(t)$ determines the path of the system in time. In what follows, we shall examine the response of the system to changes in these exogenous variables and show how the results relate to traditional demand and cost inflations.

4. Demand Inflation

The cause of inflation here is an increase in governmental demand g beyond the level g_0 that can be financed by taxes, i.e., $g_0 = \tau$. Let us thus assume that the government attempts to permanently increase its spending in real terms from g_0 to $g > g_0$ without increasing taxes τ (which will be assumed fixed in what follows). We shall see that this will create some demand inflation, which will itself generate the forced savings necessary to finance the extra government spending. We shall now formalize this process in the framework of our model.

Typically, we are in a situation where the demand curve cuts the supply curve in its horizontal part.[2] Employment and production are at their maximum level:

$$y(t) = y_0 \qquad l(t) = l_0$$

We find the price level in period t by equating the level of demand to y_0, i.e., using the aggregate demand function (Fig. 9.1):

$$K[\bar{m}(t)/p(t), g(t), \tau] = y_0$$

an equation that can also be written by using the function μ defined above:

$$\frac{\bar{m}(t)}{p(t)} = \mu[y_0, g(t), \tau]$$

which immediately yields the price level in period t:

$$p(t) = \frac{\bar{m}(t)}{\mu[y_0, g(t), \tau]}$$

This price level is finite since, as we assumed above, $\mu(y_0, g, \tau)$ is always strictly positive. If the target real wage is constant in time and equal to ω, the dynamic equations are for the nominal values,

$$w(t) = \omega p(t - 1)$$

$$p(t) = \frac{\bar{m}(t)}{\mu[y_0, g(t), \tau]}$$

$$\bar{m}(t + 1) = \bar{m}(t) + p(t)g(t) - p(t)\tau$$

Combining these last two equations with appropriate lags, we find the rate of increase in prices from one period to the next:

$$\frac{p(t)}{p(t - 1)} = \frac{\mu[y_0, g(t - 1), \tau] + g(t - 1) - \tau}{\mu[y_0, g(t), \tau]} = 1 + \pi(t)$$

where $\pi(t)$ is the inflation rate in t. The stationary rate of inflation π is simply obtained by making $g(t - 1) = g(t) = g$:

$$\pi = \frac{g - \tau}{\mu(y_0, g, \tau)}$$

[2]Of course, ω must not be too high, otherwise we would be in a situation of cost inflation, studied next in Section 5.

which yields, as an example, with the linear consumption function,

$$\pi = \frac{\beta(g - \tau)}{(1 - \alpha)y_0 - g + \alpha\tau}$$

We indicated earlier that government spending beyond $g_0 = \tau$ was somehow "financed" by forced savings. The previous formula allows us to display this mechanism very intuitively. Indeed, if we rewrite it as

$$g - \tau = \pi\mu$$

we see that the extra government spending in real terms, $g - \tau$, is financed by the "inflationary tax" on money balances expressed in real terms, i.e., $\pi\mu$.

5. Cost Inflation

Inflation here is caused by an increase in the target real wage ω. The initial result is to displace the supply curve toward the right. This increases the price level, which leads to wage increases in the next period because of indexation and thus to further price increases, and so on. However, this "wage-price spiral" will not develop indefinitely unless the demand curve itself shifts upwards. Such upward shifts of the demand curve can happen in our model by an increase in government spending, which may itself result from Keynesian antiunemployment policies. In what follows, we shall study the dynamics of the model with or without such an endogenous spending policy.

The Unemployment–Inflation Dilemma

Typically, after an increase in ω, we are in a situation where the demand curve cuts the supply curve in its nonhorizontal part (Fig. 9.1). In this case, $y(t)$ and $p(t)$ are related by

$$y(t) = F\left[F'^{-1}\left(\frac{\nu}{\nu - 1} \cdot \frac{w(t)}{p(t)}\right)\right]$$

Since $y(t) = F[l(t)]$ and $w(t) = \omega(t)p(t - 1)$, we obtain by inverting the above relation,

$$\frac{p(t)}{p(t - 1)} = \frac{\nu}{\nu - 1} \cdot \frac{\omega(t)}{F'[l(t)]}$$

an equation which can also be written in terms of $u(t)$, the level of unemployment in period t, and $\pi(t)$, the inflation rate:

$$1 + \pi(t) = \frac{\nu}{\nu - 1} \cdot \frac{\omega(t)}{F'[l_0 - u(t)]}$$

This yields a negative relation between inflation and unemployment in each period. Let us define

$$\chi(t) = \frac{\nu}{\nu - 1} \frac{\omega(t)}{F'(l_0)}$$

The parameter $\chi(t)$ is somehow an index of conflict between the workers' target real wage $\omega(t)$ and the firm's price-making behavior summarized by the parameter ν. If $\chi(t) > 1$, there is inconsistency between the two, and one cannot have both full employment and price stability. We obtain a family of unemployment–inflation tradeoff curves indexed by χ, with equations

$$1 + \pi = \chi \cdot \frac{F'(l_0)}{F'(l_0 - u)}$$

Note that $\chi(t) > 1$ if $\omega(t) > F'(l_0)(\nu - 1)/\nu$ and we may thus have a conflict even if the target real wage is below the Walrasian real wage $F'(l_0)$. A typical tradeoff curve is shown in Fig. 9.2. The greater is χ compared to 1, the further is the curve from the origin. For a given value of χ, the

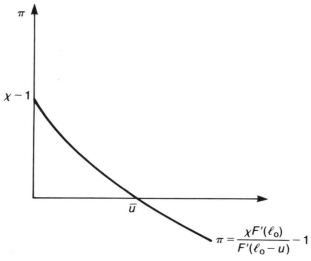

Figure 9.2

unemployment level $\bar{u}$ corresponding to zero inflation (Fig. 9.2) is determined by the solution in $\bar{u}$ to the equation

$$F'(l_0 - \bar{u}) = \chi F'(l_0)$$

This "noninflationary rate of unemployment" is thus an increasing function of the conflict parameter χ.

For given χ, the point (u, π) giving the unemployment and inflation rates remains on the curve defined by χ. Movements and final position along each tradeoff curve are determined by governmental policy, summarized by the parameters g and τ. In Section 6, we shall study the steady states that the system can reach. Before that, we shall examine the role of government policy in the process of cost inflation.

Government Policy and Cost Inflation

We shall ask the following question: Is inconsistency between the firm's price strategy and the workers' wage strategy (i.e., $\chi > 1$) a sufficient condition for an inflationary wage-price spiral to go on indefinitely, or is a policy of "monetary accommodation," e.g., through public spending, necessary for inflation to persist? We shall not give a general answer here, rather, we shall show the dynamic effects of an increase in χ with or without such a policy of monetary accommodation.

Let us first assume that because of an exogenous increase in ω, $\chi(t)$ goes from 1 to $\chi > 1$, whereas the government remains financially neutral by maintaining $g(t) = \tau$. We can follow the dynamic path of activity and prices in a supply–demand diagram (Fig. 9.3). Since $g(t) = \tau$, the quantity $\bar{m}(t)$

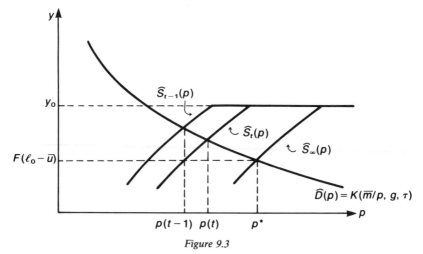

Figure 9.3

remains constant in time, and thus the aggregate demand curve $K(\bar{m}/p, g, \tau)$ will be invariant in the process. The supply curve, however, will move toward the right. The displacement from one period to the next can be represented quite simply (Fig. 9.3): The equation for the nonhorizontal part of the supply curve, as we saw before, is

$$y(t) = F\left[F'^{-1}\left(\frac{\nu}{\nu-1} \cdot \frac{w(t)}{p(t)}\right)\right]$$

Since $w(t) = \omega p(t-1)$ and by definition $\omega\nu/(\nu-1) = \chi F'(l_0)$, this part of the supply curve in period t, $\hat{S}_t(p)$, can be written as

$$y(t) = F\left[F'^{-1}\left(\chi F'(l_0)\frac{p(t-1)}{p(t)}\right)\right]$$

If we make $p(t) = p(t-1)$, we find

$$y(t) = F[F'^{-1}(\chi F'(l_0))] = F(l_0 - \bar{u})$$

where $\bar{u}$ is the noninflationary rate of unemployment defined before. The supply curve in t thus goes through the point of coordinates $\{p(t-1), F(l_0-\bar{u})\}$, which has been represented in Fig. 9.3. Using this fact we see graphically that supply curves will gradually move to the right until the level of unemployment reaches $\bar{u}$, and the price reaches its long-term value p^*.

This process can also be followed in the unemployment–inflation diagram (Fig. 9.4). As soon as $\chi(t)$ has taken the value $\chi > 1$, all corresponding

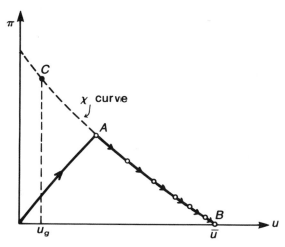

Figure 9.4

points are on the unemployment-inflation tradeoff curve associated with the parameter χ. After an initial increase in both unemployment and inflation (point A), the unemployment level continues to increase, converging as we saw before toward the unemployment level $\bar{u}$ (point B), and the inflation rate steadily declines toward zero. We see that in this model, without a policy of monetary accommodation, cost inflation does not persist. On the contrary, a wage-profits conflict (i.e., $\chi > 1$) leads to unemployment in the long run.

Assume now that in order to fight unemployment, the government adopts a "Keynesian" policy of the following form:

$$g(t) - g(t-1) = \xi[u(t-1) - u_g]$$

where u_g is an unemployment level that is "acceptable" to the government and ξ a reaction coefficient. The government thus increases its demand as long as the unemployment level is above the acceptable level. It is difficult to give a simple graphical or analytical representation of the process, because the aggregate supply and demand curves move simultaneously. One may observe, though, that all points in (u, π) space will be on the curve corresponding to χ. Moreover, a steady state of such a process must be such that g is constant, and thus such that $u = u_g$. Therefore the system, if it is stable,[3] will converge toward point C in Fig. 9.4, characterized by an unemployment level equal to u_g, an inflation rate $\pi > 0$, and government spending $g > \tau$. We thus see that in this case, a governmental policy of monetary accommodation is a necessary condition for cost inflation to proceed indefinitely.

6. Steady States

If the values of the exogenous parameters ω, g, τ remain constant through time, we generally obtain a steady state where unemployment and inflation rates are also constant. We shall now see how these steady-state values u^* and π^* are computed and determine the influence of exogenous parameters on them. For this we shall construct two relations relating π and u in steady states.

The first relation comes from the equation of price formation, which can be written as we saw before,

$$p(t) \geqslant \frac{\nu}{\nu - 1} \frac{w(t)}{F'[l(t)]} = \frac{\nu}{\nu - 1} \frac{\omega(t)p(t-1)}{F'[l_0 - u(t)]}$$

---

[3]Computer simulations actually indicate that the system is stable provided that the coefficient ξ is not too high.

with strict equality if the unemployment level is strictly positive. Using the definition of χ seen before, this yields

$$\frac{p(t)}{p(t-1)} \geqslant \frac{\chi(t)F'(l_0)}{F'[l_0 - u(t)]}$$

Taking stationary values for χ, u, and π, we obtain

$$1 + \pi \geqslant \frac{\chi F'(l_0)}{F'(l_0 - u)}$$

with strict equality if u is positive. This relation, which is represented graphically in Fig. 9.5, consists of two parts: a vertical part for $u = 0$ and $\pi \geqslant \chi - 1$, and a negatively sloped part for $u \geqslant 0$ with the equation

$$\pi = \frac{\chi F'(l_0)}{F'(l_0 - u)} - 1$$

which cuts the horizontal axis at the noninflationary unemployment level $\bar{u}$ given by the equation seen before

$$F'(l_0 - \bar{u}) = \chi F'(l_0)$$

We see that this first steady-state relation displays a tradeoff between inflation and unemployment. This relation depends only on the degree of

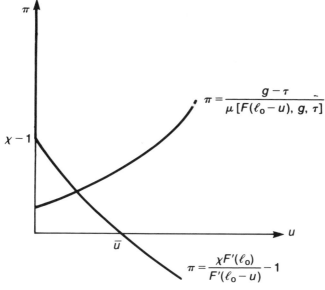

Figure 9.5

inconsistency between workers' wage strategies and firms' price strategies, which is summarized by the "conflict" parameter χ. The tradeoff is less favorable the higher is χ.

In order to find out where the long-run equilibrium will be on this curve, we need a second relation between u and π. This is found by combining the equation giving the time path of money balances,

$$\bar{m}(t+1) = \bar{m}(t) + p(t)g(t) - p(t)\tau(t)$$

and the demand-side equation for the output market, which we shall write here in the form

$$\frac{\bar{m}(t)}{p(t)} = \mu[y(t), g(t), \tau(t)]$$

Combining these two relations with appropriate lags, we obtain

$$\frac{p(t+1)}{p(t)} = \frac{\mu[y(t), g(t), \tau(t)] + g(t) - \tau(t)}{\mu[y(t+1), g(t+1), \tau(t+1)]}$$

In a steady state the variables y, g, and τ are constant, and thus,

$$\pi = \frac{g - \tau}{\mu(y, g, \tau)}$$

Using $y = F(l_0 - u)$, we obtain the second steady-state relation between π and u:

$$\pi = \frac{g - \tau}{\mu[F(l_0 - u), g, \tau]}$$

We may remark that this relation depends only on government policy parameters g and τ. The corresponding curve, represented in Fig. 9.5, has a positive slope if $g \geq \tau$, which we shall assume.

The long-run unemployment and inflation rates are determined by the intersection of these two steady-state curves (Fig. 9.5). We see that there will be two types of equilibria: one with zero unemployment and the other with positive unemployment. In the case where unemployment is greater than zero (which corresponds to $\chi > 1$ if $g \geq \tau$), it is easy to find graphically and mathematically that

$$\frac{\partial u^*}{\partial g} < 0 \qquad \frac{\partial \pi^*}{\partial g} > 0$$

$$\frac{\partial u^*}{\partial \tau} > 0 \qquad \frac{\partial \pi^*}{\partial \tau} < 0$$

$$\frac{\partial u^*}{\partial \chi} > 0 \qquad \frac{\partial \pi^*}{\partial \chi} > 0$$

We thus see that only a reduction in χ, which may come from incomes restraint, decrease in monopoly power, or productivity increases, can reduce inflation and unemployment at the same time. On the contrary, government "demand" policies (i.e., variations in g or τ) at best allow one to choose a "preferred" combination of unemployment and inflation, since any improvement in one of these two targets is made at the expense of the other.

In the case where unemployment is zero, a decrease in g or an increase in τ reduces inflation, whereas a variation in χ has no effect.

The Case of an Excess Demand for Labor

So far we have defined the unemployment variable u as the difference between the aggregate supply of labor (here fixed and equal to l_0) and the level of employment actually realized. This variable is thus equal to the excess supply of labor when positive, but it is zero when there is excess demand for labor. In this case we have no information on the size of this excess demand. We shall now extend the previous steady-state relations to the case where there is excess demand for labor by redefining u as the difference between the supply and the demand for labor, i.e.,

$$u = l^s - l^d = l_0 - l^d$$

This new variable u is equal to the preceding one when its value is positive, but it can become negative in case of an excess demand for labor. We now have to define the firm's labor demand l^d, including the case where it may be greater than the supply of labor. In accordance with earlier definitions of effective demand, we shall take l^d to be equal to the quantity of labor that the firm would like to employ in the absence of the labor market constraint $l \leq l_0$. In such a case, the firm would equate marginal revenue and marginal cost; i.e.,

$$\frac{w}{F'(l)} = p\left(1 - \frac{1}{\nu}\right)$$

which immediately yields labor demand as the solution in l of the previous equation:

$$l^d = F'^{-1}\left(\frac{\nu}{\nu - 1} \cdot \frac{w}{p}\right)$$

We shall now derive the steady-state relations between π and the new variable u. In order to obtain the first, let us combine the equality $u = l_0 - l^d$ with the definition of l^d before. We get

$$p = \frac{\nu}{\nu - 1} \frac{w}{F'(l_0 - u)}$$

If we now put time indices in this equation and use the equality $p(t) = \omega(t)p(t-1)$, we obtain

$$\frac{p(t)}{p(t-1)} = \frac{\nu}{\nu - 1} \frac{\omega(t)}{F'[l_0 - u(t)]} = \frac{\chi(t)F'(l_0)}{F'[l_0 - u(t)]}$$

Considering a steady state, we obtain a first long-run relation between π and u:

$$1 + \pi = \frac{\chi F'(l_0)}{F'(l_0 - u)}$$

This relation, which was previously valid only for positive u, now holds for both positive and negative values of u. It is represented in Fig. 9.6.

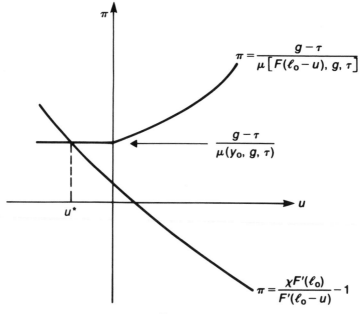

Figure 9.6

In order to obtain the second steady-state relation between π and u, let us use the equality seen before:

$$\pi = \frac{g - \tau}{\mu(y, g, \tau)}$$

If there is excess demand for labor $(u < 0)$, y is at the full-employment level y_0, and this formula becomes

$$\pi = \frac{g - \tau}{\mu(y_0, g, \tau)} \qquad \mu \leqslant 0$$

In the case where u is positive, we of course still have the relation already seen

$$\pi = \frac{g - \tau}{\mu[F(l_0 - u), g, \tau]} \qquad u \geqslant 0$$

The full relation has been represented in Fig. 9.6. We now have two steady-state relations between u and π, valid for positive or negative u. Their intersection (Fig. 9.6) yields the long-run unemployment and inflation rates u^* and π^*. The case where an excess demand for labor, corresponding to a negative u, is obtained is displayed in Fig. 9.6.

7. Conclusions

We have seen in this chapter that the two traditionally antagonistic theories of cost and demand inflation can be formalized in a synthetic manner, both types of inflation appearing as the response of the same dynamic system to different shocks. In the simple model of this chapter, demand inflation results from an increase in public spending not financed by taxes, whereas cost inflation is the consequence of an incompatibility between the target real wage of workers and the markup practiced by firms. Cost inflation, however, can be maintained indefinitely only if the government has an accommodating monetary policy.

In order to follow effectively the dynamics of the two types of inflation, we made some particularly simple assumptions by supposing that the "strategic" parameters were exogenous (except for government spending, which adapted endogenously in the cost-inflation process). In the real world, however, a mechanism such as the wage-formation process does not of course depend on purely exogenous parameters; rather, through complex socioeconomic processes, it is influenced by endogenous variables such as unemployment and inflation. We shall see in Chapter 10 how such effects can be included in the model.

References

This chapter is adapted from Benassy (1976d, 1978, 1982). A classic review article on cost versus demand inflation may be found in Bronfenbrenner and Holzman (1963).

CHAPTER

10

Phillips Curves, Conflicts, and Expectations

1. Introduction

The model of Chapter 9 was based on very simple assumptions in order to highlight the various regimes under which it could function in response to exogenous shocks. The wage equation was particularly simplified, being essentially based on the idea of a target real wage; however, we generally find in the literature wage equations that depend on demand variables as well as inflationary expectations. The corresponding functions, often known as the "Phillips curves," usually have the following form:

$$\frac{\dot{w}}{w} = \phi(u) + \lambda \pi^e \qquad 0 \leq \lambda \leq 1 \qquad \phi'(u) < 0$$

where π^e is the expected rate of inflation for output prices. The curve $\phi(u)$ has generally the shape shown in Fig. 10.1. The unemployment level $\hat{u}$ such that $\phi(\hat{u}) = 0$ is often called the natural rate of unemployment, i.e., the rate of unemployment supposed to result from the free functioning of the labor market taking into account all frictions inherent in this functioning.

In this chapter we shall attempt a synthesis between the literature on the Phillips curve and the inflation model seen in Chapter 9. We shall thus construct a short-run equilibrium model similar to that of Chapter 9 and study its dynamics when the wage equation simultaneously takes into

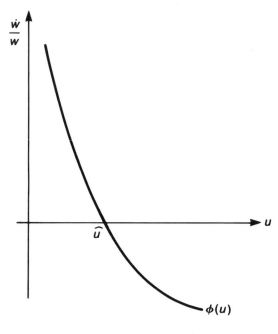

Figure 10.1

account demand elements and expectations, as in the literature on the Phillips curve, and autonomous "wage-push" elements in order to achieve a target real wage as in Chapter 9.

Within this model we shall be particularly interested in the tradeoffs between inflation and unemployment both in the short and the long run, a subject often debated in the traditional literature on the Phillips curve, to which we shall add some elements of "cost inflation." Moreover, we shall explicitly treat the determination of activity and prices in the short run, since these are determined within a short-run non-Walrasian equilibrium. For our model to be comparable with traditional models, we shall adopt here a continuous time version, which we shall now describe.

2. The Model

We shall thus have here a continuous time version of the model of Chapter 9. Let us start the description with the wage equation, which changes the most.

The Wage Equation

We shall take in this chapter the following general form for the wage equation:

$$\frac{\dot{w}}{w} = \phi(u) + \delta \max\left\{\frac{p\omega}{w} - 1, 0\right\} + \lambda\pi^e$$

where π^e is again the expected inflation rate and ω a target real wage as in Chapter 9. We thus adopt the traditional form of the Phillips curve with expectations, adding one term, the second in the equation, which represents an autonomous wage-push effect, say, due to the influence of trade unions in collective wage bargaining. Because of that effect, if the real wage w/p is below its target value ω, there will be an additional wage push proportional to the discrepancy between ω and w/p. Note that in our formula this effect is assumed to be asymmetrical because if the real wage is above ω, the corresponding term becomes equal to zero, an assumption that seems fairly realistic. Indeed, if the real wage attains a level equal to or greater than ω (for example, because of some boost in the demand for labor), there is clearly no reason for wage earners to push toward a wage decrease.

The Rest of the Model

For given wage w and money balances m^1 the short-run model is exactly the same as that of Chapter 9: The level of price p and sales y are determined by the intersection of a demand curve $\hat{D}(p)$ and a supply curve $\hat{S}(p)$ (Fig. 10.2). The equations for these two curves, respectively, are

$$y = K(m/p, g, \tau) = \hat{D}(p)$$

$$y = \min\left\{F\left[F'^{-1}\left(\frac{\nu}{\nu - 1}\frac{w}{p}\right)\right], y_0\right\} = \hat{S}(p)$$

The values of p and y in the short run are determined as the solutions of these two equations. Employment l and unemployment u are deduced from these by

$$l = F^{-1}(y) \qquad u = l_0 - l$$

---

[1]Since the model is in continuous time, we need not distinguish between initial and final money balances, $\bar{m}$ and m, which was necessary in the discrete time model of Chapter 9. The two are the same here and are both represented by m.

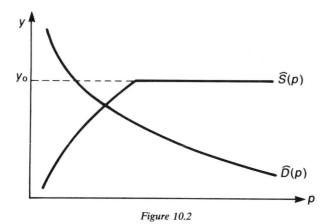

Figure 10.2

The dynamics of the model is determined by the equations of evolution of the wage level and money balances. Increase in money balances is the counterpart to government deficits,

$$\dot{m} = p(g - \tau)$$

and wages move according to the equation given before:

$$\frac{\dot{w}}{w} = \phi(u) + \delta \max\left\{\frac{p\omega}{w} - 1, 0\right\} + \lambda \pi^e$$

Note that in order to have a complete dynamic system, we would have to specify how inflationary expectations π^e are formed. Since we shall be mostly interested in steady states where realized inflation π and expected inflation π^e are assumed to be the same, we actually need not specify any particular form for π^e.

3. The Short Run: Equilibrium and the Phillips Curve

In the short run, the level of prices, sales, and employment are determined by a short-run equilibrium characterized by the following equations:

$$y = K(m/p, g, \tau)$$

$$y = \min\left\{F\left[F'^{-1}\left(\frac{\nu}{\nu - 1}\frac{w}{p}\right)\right], y_0\right\}$$

$$y = F(l)$$

We may note that since the curve $\phi(u)$ defined before tends to infinity when u goes to zero, the intersection will always belong to the nonhorizontal part of the supply curve (Fig. 10.2). Also note that this section of the supply curve can be rewritten as a price equation:

$$p = \frac{\nu}{\nu - 1} \cdot \frac{w}{F'(l)}$$

We shall now characterize the short-run Phillips curve, that is, the relation between the rate of increase in wages and the level of unemployment. Let us recall the wage equation seen earlier:

$$\frac{\dot{w}}{w} = \phi(u) + \delta \max\left\{\frac{p\omega}{w} - 1, 0\right\} + \lambda \pi^e$$

Combining this, the price equation just given, and the identity $l = l_0 - u$, we obtain

$$\frac{\dot{w}}{w} = \phi(u) + \delta \max\left\{\frac{\nu}{\nu - 1} \frac{\omega}{F'(l_0 - u)} - 1, 0\right\} + \lambda \pi^e$$

an equation which may be rewritten, using the coefficient χ defined in Chapter 9 as $\omega \nu / (\nu - 1) F'(l_0)$,

$$\frac{\dot{w}}{w} = \phi(u) + \delta \max\left\{\frac{\chi F'(l_0)}{F'(l_0 - u)} - 1, 0\right\} + \lambda \pi^e$$

The second term of this equation introduces the possibility of a rise in the short-run Phillips curve due to conflicts in income distribution, provided that the "conflict coefficient" χ is greater than 1. Indeed, it is easy to see that if $\chi \leq 1$, the second term is zero, and the expression reduces to the "traditional" curve $\phi(u) + \lambda \pi^e$. If $\chi > 1$, the curve will shift upward from it, and the higher χ is, the greater will be the shift. More precisely, the curve will be above the curve $\phi(u) + \lambda \pi^e$ for all unemployment levels such that

$$F'(l_0 - u) < \chi F'(l_0)$$

We thus see that taking into account such effects allows us to formalize a rise in the Phillips curve. The element inducing this rise in the Phillips curve may be an autonomous increase in the target real wage ω or the desire to maintain a historically attained real wage level, even when production conditions become less favorable (an increase in the cost of some primary materials is an evident example).

4. Steady States and the
Unemployment–Inflation Dilemma

We shall now characterize the steady states that the system can reach, assuming that the various exogenous variables ω, g, τ are constant. Let us recall briefly the equations giving the short-run equilibrium and the dynamics:

$$y = K(m/p, g, \tau)$$

$$y = F\left[F'^{-1}\left(\frac{\nu}{\nu - 1} \cdot \frac{w}{p} \right) \right]$$

$$\dot{m} = p(g - \tau)$$

$$\frac{\dot{w}}{w} = \phi(u) + \delta \max\left\{ \frac{p\omega}{w} - 1, 0 \right\} + \lambda \pi^e$$

The Unemployment–Inflation Tradeoff

We shall construct here a first relation, often called the long-run Phillips curve, relating unemployment and inflation in the steady states. This curve has a negative slope; it thus displays a tradeoff between inflation and unemployment. To obtain it we combine the second and fourth equations given above, together with the condition that in a steady state of this model, the rate of increase in wages, the actual inflation rate, and the expected inflation rate are equal:

$$\frac{\dot{w}}{w} = \pi = \pi^e$$

We then obtain immediately

$$\pi = \frac{1}{1 - \lambda}\left[\phi(u) + \delta \max\left\{ \frac{\chi F'(l_0)}{F'(l_0 - u)} - 1, 0 \right\} \right]$$

We shall first consider the case where $\lambda = 0$, i.e., where inflationary expectations are not taken into account in the wage-formation equation. In this case the formula for π becomes

$$\pi = \phi(u) + \delta \max\left\{ \frac{\chi F'(l_0)}{F'(l_0 - u)} - 1, 0 \right\}$$

A typical case is shown in Fig. 10.3. We see that the long-run Phillips curve is partially above $\phi(u)$ if $\chi \geq 1$. One may be particularly interested in what is usually called in the literature the "noninflationary rate of unemployment," i.e., the unemployment $\bar{u}$ such that long-run inflation is zero. It is defined by the equation

$$\phi(\bar{u}) + \delta \max\left\{\frac{\chi F'(l_0)}{F'(l_0 - \bar{u})} - 1, 0\right\} = 0$$

It is obvious that $\bar{u}$ is always equal to or greater than $\hat{u}$, the natural rate of unemployment. Equality of $\bar{u}$ to $\hat{u}$ will obtain if and only if

$$\chi \leq \frac{F'(l_0 - \hat{u})}{F'(l_0)} \qquad \text{or} \qquad \omega \leq \frac{\nu - 1}{\nu} F'(l_0 - \hat{u})$$

that is, if the target real wage is consistent with the firms' markup and the marginal productivity of labor at the natural employment level $l_0 - \hat{u}$. Otherwise, the noninflationary unemployment level $\bar{u}$ is greater than the "natural" one $\hat{u}$.

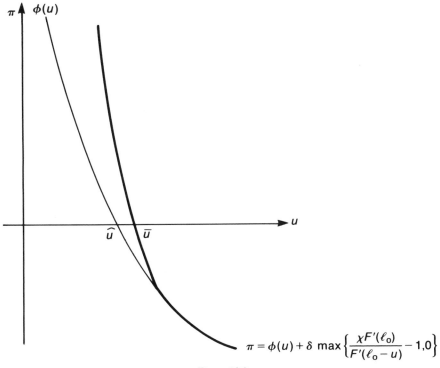

$$\pi = \phi(u) + \delta \max\left\{\frac{\chi F'(\ell_0)}{F'(\ell_0 - u)} - 1, 0\right\}$$

Figure 10.3

It is now easy to revert to the general case where λ is nonzero, i.e., where expectations matter, by multiplying by $1/(1 - \lambda)$ the value given by the formula without expectations. The resulting curve still goes through the point $(\bar{u}, 0)$ corresponding to the noninflationary unemployment rate, but its slope is higher in absolute terms than in the case without expectations, a traditional result. In the literature, one often comes across the extreme case where $\lambda = 1$; i.e., where wage increases adjust fully to the expected inflation rate. In such a case the curve becomes vertical at the noninflationary value of unemployment $\bar{u}$, which is given as before by the formula

$$\phi(\bar{u}) + \delta \max\left\{\frac{\chi F'(l_0)}{F'(l_0 - \bar{u})} - 1, 0\right\} = 0$$

The important point to note is that the curve can become vertical for a level of unemployment $\bar{u}$, which is higher than the natural one $\hat{u}$.

Steady States

The long-run Phillips curve just studied only gives us one steady-state relation between inflation and unemployment. In order to obtain a second, let us consider the first and third equations given at the beginning of this section:

$$y = K(m/p, g, \tau)$$
$$\dot{m} = p(g - \tau)$$

We saw in Chapter 9 that the first equation can also be written as

$$\frac{m}{p} = \mu(y, g, \tau)$$

Combining with the second equation, we obtain immediately,

$$\frac{\dot{m}}{m} = \frac{g - \tau}{\mu(y, g, \tau)}$$

In a steady state of this model, the rate of increase of money balances and the rate of inflation are the same. We thus have, taking into account $y = F(l_0 - u)$, a second steady-state relation between inflation and unemployment:

$$\pi = \frac{g - \tau}{\mu[F(l_0 - u), g, \tau]}$$

We may remark that this relation, which depends on the government policy parameters g and τ, relates u and π positively (provided that $g \geq \tau$).

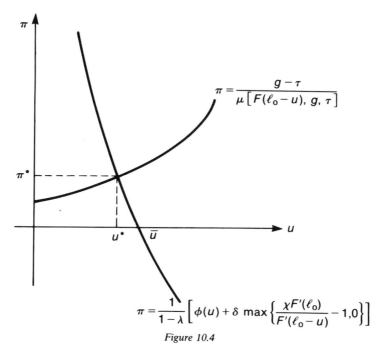

$$\pi = \frac{g - \tau}{\mu\left[F(\ell_0 - u),\, g,\, \tau\right]}$$

$$\pi = \frac{1}{1 - \lambda}\left[\phi(u) + \delta \max\left\{\frac{\chi F'(\ell_0)}{F'(\ell_0 - u)} - 1,\, 0\right\}\right]$$

Figure 10.4

Steady-state unemployment and inflation rates can be found at the intersection of this curve and the long-run Phillips curve found earlier

$$\pi = \frac{1}{1 - \lambda}\left[\phi(u) + \delta \max\left\{\frac{\chi F'(l_0)}{F'(l_0 - u)} - 1,\, 0\right\}\right]$$

$$\pi = \frac{g - \tau}{\mu[F(l_0 - u),\, g,\, \tau]}$$

This has been represented in Fig. 10.4. We see mathematically and graphically that an increase in χ increases both unemployment and inflation, whereas an increase in g (or a reduction in τ) diminishes unemployment but increases inflation. In the extreme case where λ is equal to 1, these last measures have no effect on unemployment; they merely increase the rate of inflation.

5. Conclusions

In this chapter we combined the inflation model of Chapter 9 with the traditional literature on Phillips curves. The explicit use of a non-Walrasian short-run equilibrium concept allows us to determine the level of employment, aggregate output, and prices at every instant. Following the model of Chapter 9, we could also incorporate the effects of conflicts on income distribution that enable us to explain not only displacements of the short-run Phillips curve, but also some modifications in the long-run tradeoff between inflation and unemployment.

References

This chapter synthesizes the model of Chapter 9 and the traditional contributions on the Phillips curve. This curve was originally presented in Phillips (1958). Expectations were introduced by Phelps (1967) and Friedman (1968).

11

A Model of the Business Cycle

1. Introduction

In this chapter we shall draw a bridge between the theory of non-Walrasian equilibria and a traditional topic in macroeconomic theory: the problem of business cycles. We shall show how the dynamic evolution of a short-run equilibrium of the IS-LM type can generate cycles. The driving element in the cycle is unstable quantity dynamics, which comes, as in most traditional cycle models, from an investment accelerator and from the dynamic adjustment of demand expectations. If these effects are sufficiently strong, the system will be unstable around its long-run equilibrium. However, there are also stabilizing effects, namely, the effect of the price level on global demand and wage movements along a Phillips curve, which tend to drive the system back toward its long-run equilibrium. The combination of these stabilizing and destabilizing elements can create a cyclical evolution, as we shall see.

The model to be presented here brings a number of improvements with respect to traditional nonlinear cycle models: (1) The short run is described rigorously as a non-Walrasian equilibrium, whereas most existing models do not have such a structure; (2) we only need fairly usual assumptions on all functions used, whereas earlier models required rather ad hoc assumptions on these functions, such as sigmoid shapes for the investment function or the Phillips curve.

2. The Model

The Short Run

In the short run, the structure of the model is that of a traditional IS-LM model with a fixed wage and a flexible price level. We shall assume as in Chapter 6 that there is an inelastic labor supply l_0 and a production function with decreasing returns $F(l)$. The "demand block" consists of the following two IS-LM equations:

$$y = C(y, p) + I(x, r, p)$$

$$L(y, r, p) = \bar{m}$$

where x represents expected demand, and $\bar{m}$ is the quantity of money in the economy. This system differs from that considered in Chapter 6 mainly on two points. First, we simplify the equations by leaving out any government intervention, which allows us to have a constant quantity of money $\bar{m}$ through time. Second, we explicitly introduce expected demand x in the investment function, which corresponds to the "natural" formulation of this function. In the traditional IS-LM system this expected demand is often replaced by the level of current sales y, which presupposes an implicit expectations function relating expected demand to current sales. We shall assume that all these functions are continuously differentiable and that their partial derivatives have the following signs:

$$0 < C_y < 1 \qquad C_p < 0$$

$$I_x > 0 \qquad I_r < 0 \qquad I_p < 0$$

$$L_y > 0 \qquad L_r < 0 \qquad L_p > 0$$

We shall also assume, in accordance with the usual formulations, that consumption is positive even if income is zero, which implicitly assumes some type of real balance effect. Mathematically, $C(0, p)$ is strictly positive for all finite values of the price p.

Dynamics

We shall now describe the dynamic equations governing the system. Since the quantity of money is fixed, we have to describe only the behavior of the wage w and of the expected demand x. We shall assume that wage variations depend negatively on the level of unemployment u, according to a Phillips curve;[1]

$$\dot{w} = \phi(u) \qquad \phi'(u) < 0$$

We omit inflationary expectations in this Phillips curve for two reasons. First, their inclusion would make the model too complex to handle with available mathematical cycle theories. Second, quantity expectations rather than inflationary expectations are our subject of interest in this chapter. We shall assume that the function ϕ has the traditional form represented in Fig. 11.1. In particular, it is assumed that $\phi(u)$ tends to infinity when u

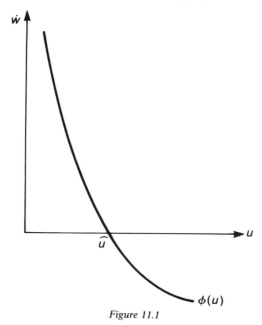

Figure 11.1

goes to zero. We shall denote by $\hat{u}$ the noninflationary level of unemployment such that $\phi(\hat{u}) = 0$. We can note that since y and l are related through the production function, we can also rewrite the previous Phillips curve as

$$\dot{w} = \varphi(y)$$

with

$$\varphi(y) = \phi[l_0 - F^{-1}(y)] \qquad \varphi'(y) > 0$$

[1]Note that we take $\phi(u)$ to represent the absolute increases in w and not the relative increases as is usually done and was done in Chapter 10. This is done only to make the exposition more elegant. The reader can check that all results would hold as well with the traditional formulation. It is enough to use, starting with Section 5, log w instead of w as the working variable and adapt accordingly the graphs and stability condition.

The function $\varphi(y)$ tends to infinity when y tends to $y_0 = F(l_0)$ and is equal to zero for the value $\hat{y} = F(l_0 - \hat{u})$.

As for demand expectations, we shall assume that they adaptatively adjust to the value of demand observed in the current period, i.e.,

$$\dot{x} = \theta(y - x) \qquad \theta > 0$$

3. Short-Run Equilibrium

We shall now study in more detail the equations determining the short-run equilibrium for given values of w and x. As in the preceding chapters we shall separate a demand side and a supply side.

The Demand Side

We have already seen the two IS-LM equations that form the demand side:

$$y = C(y, p) + I(x, r, p)$$

$$L(y, r, p) = \bar{m}$$

Let us call $K(x, p)$ the solution in y of this system. This function is obviously very close to the Keynesian aggregate demand function that we have seen before in some chapters. We can compute its partial derivatives:

$$K_x = \frac{I_x L_r}{(1 - C_y)L_r + L_y I_r} > 0$$

$$K_p = \frac{(C_p + I_p)L_r - I_r L_p}{(1 - C_y)L_r + L_y I_r} < 0$$

Some functions $K(x, p)$ for particular values of x have been represented in (y, p) space (Fig. 11.2). Note that $K(x, p)$ is always strictly positive, since $C(0, p) > 0$ for all p.

Furthermore, as shown in Fig. 11.2, we shall make two quite plausible assumptions about the behavior of the function $K(x, p)$ for extreme values of the price p. More specifically, we shall assume that

$$\lim_{p \to 0} K(0, p) > y_0 \qquad \lim_{p \to +\infty} K(y_0, p) < \hat{y}$$

The first assumption can be naturally justified by invoking a real balance-type effect in the consumption function; for the second, it is sufficient to observe that the price acts negatively on global demand through three

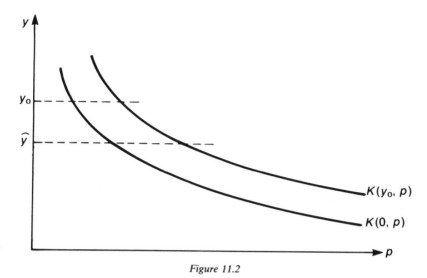

Figure 11.2

different channels that become clear if the term K_p is written as:

$$K_p = \frac{C_p + I_p - I_r L_p / L_r}{(1 - C_y) + L_y I_r / L_r}$$

Here we see that price has a direct negative influence on consumption and investment (terms C_p and I_p in the numerator) and an indirect negative influence on investment via the interest rate and the demand for money (the term $I_r L_p / L_r$). We thus assume that even with relatively optimistic expectations $(x = y_0)$, if the price level tends to infinity, consumption and investment will diminish so much via these three effects that the equilibrium level of income $K(x, p)$ will fall below $\hat{y}$ (which will turn out to be the long-run equilibrium value of y). Such an hypothesis is quite weak and plausible.

The Supply Side

We assume here that the goods market clears competitively,[2] which implies that y and p are related by the following equation:

$$y = \min\{F[F'^{-1}(w/p)], y_0\}$$

Indeed, if the firm is not constrained on the labor market, it will be on the

---

[2] We could also assume that the price of output is determined in an imperfect competition framework, as in Chapters 9 and 10. The "competitive" assumption simplifies the notation somewhat.

neoclassical supply curve $F[F'^{-1}(w/p)]$. If, however, this neoclassical supply is above the full-employment production $y_0 = F(l_0)$, the firm's production will be limited to y_0.

Short-Run Equilibrium

The short-run equilibrium is determined by the two IS-LM equations and the previous supply-side equation. In particular, y and p are determined by the system

$$y = K(x, p)$$

$$y = \min\{F[F'^{-1}(w/p)], y_0\}$$

The solution of this system has been represented in Fig. 11.3. We see graphically that a solution exists for all values of x such that

$$\lim_{p \to \infty} K(x, p) < y_0$$

The assumptions made before about the function K ensure that a short-run equilibrium exists for at least all values of x between 0 and y_0. In general, a short-run equilibrium will also exist for higher values of x, but we shall not need it for what follows.

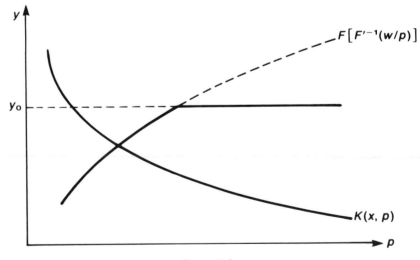

Figure 11.3

4. Dynamics and Long-Run Equilibrium

A priori, the short-run equilibrium determined before could be an equilibrium with full employment or an equilibrium with unemployment; however, the form we have adopted for the Phillips curve implies that full employment will never be attained in the dynamic evolution of the system since wage increases become infinite as y goes to y_0. The supply side of the model is thus defined by

$$y = F[F'^{-1}(w/p)]$$

and the values of y, r, p at the short-run equilibrium are determined by the following system:

$$y = C(y, p) + I(x, r, p)$$

$$L(y, r, p) = \bar{m}$$

$$y = F[F'^{-1}(w/p)]$$

We shall call $H(x, w)$ the solution in y of this system; $H(x, w)$ is also a solution of the simpler system

$$y = K(x, p)$$

$$y = F[F'^{-1}(w/p)]$$

Let us write down, as we have done in previous chapters,

$$S(p, w) = F[F'^{-1}(w/p)] \qquad S_p > 0 \qquad S_w < 0$$

Then, the partial derivatives of the function H are

$$H_x = \frac{S_p K_x}{S_p - K_p} > 0$$

$$H_w = \frac{-K_p S_w}{S_p - K_p} < 0$$

We have in Fig. 11.4 a few curves giving $H(x, w)$ as a function of w for given values of x. Note that as a consequence of the assumptions made about function K, we have

$$\lim_{w \to 0} H(0, w) > y_0 \qquad \lim_{w \to \infty} H(y_0, w) < \hat{y}$$

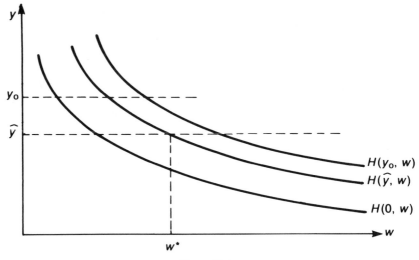

Figure 11.4

We shall see later that these conditions are sufficient to ensure the existence of a long-run equilibrium. Note also that H_x is higher the higher is I_x. Indeed, combining the previous formulas we obtain

$$H_x = \frac{S_p L_r I_x}{S_p L_y I_r + S_p(1 - C_y)L_r - (C_p + I_p)L_r + I_r L_p}$$

The Dynamic System

The full dynamic system can now be summarized by the equations

$$y = H(x, w)$$
$$\dot{w} = \varphi(y)$$
$$\dot{x} = \theta(y - x)$$

The long-run equilibrium of this system is given by the following relations:

$$y^* = x^* = \hat{y}$$
$$H(\hat{y}, w^*) = \hat{y}$$

Such an equilibrium exists if the second equation has a solution in w^*. We see immediately in Fig. 11.4 that the long-run equilibrium exists and is unique. We shall now study the stability properties of the model and show that it is either stable around the long-run equilibrium or unstable, in which case there will be at least one limit cycle.

5. Stability of the Long-Run Equilibrium

If we linearize the previous dynamic system around the long-run equilibrium, we obtain the following system in matrix form:

$$\begin{bmatrix} \dot{w} \\ \dot{x} \end{bmatrix} = \begin{bmatrix} \varphi'(\hat{y})H_w & \varphi'(\hat{y})H_x \\ \theta H_w & \theta(H_x - 1) \end{bmatrix} \begin{bmatrix} w - w^* \\ x - x^* \end{bmatrix}$$

where the partial derivatives H_x and H_w are evaluated at the long-run equilibrium point (x^*, w^*). The stability of the system depends on the sign of the roots ρ_1 and ρ_2 of the characteristic polynomial of the matrix, which is

$$\rho^2 - T\rho + \Delta = 0$$

where T is the trace of the matrix and Δ its determinant. This determinant is equal to $-\theta\varphi'(\hat{y})H_w$, which is always positive. The local stability of the system thus depends entirely on the value of the trace T of the matrix. This is equal to

$$T = \varphi'(\hat{y})H_w + \theta(H_x - 1)$$

If the trace is negative, the two roots have a negative real part, and the system is locally stable. If, however, $T > 0$, i.e., if

$$\theta(H_x - 1) > -\varphi'(\hat{y})H_w$$

the system is locally unstable, since both roots have a positive real part. This happens in particular if the acceleration coefficient I_x, and thus H_x, is high. We shall see later that in this case there exists a limit cycle. We have drawn in Fig. 11.5 two typical phase diagrams. The curves $\dot{w} = 0$ and $\dot{x} = 0$, respectively, have the equations

$$\dot{w} = 0 \Leftrightarrow H(x, w) = \hat{y}$$

$$\dot{x} = 0 \Leftrightarrow H(x, w) = x$$

The curve $\dot{w} = 0$ always has a positive slope. The curve $\dot{x} = 0$ has a positive slope if $H_x > 1$ and a negative slope if $H_x < 1$. We thus see that in the case presented in Fig. 11.5a, there is always local stability, whereas an unstable long-run equilibrium implies that the curve $\dot{x} = 0$ has a positive slope at the point (w^*, x^*), as in Fig. 11.5b. Let us also note that since

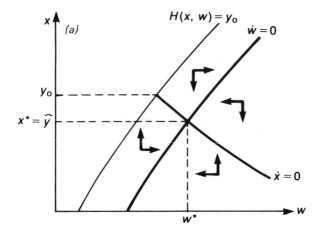

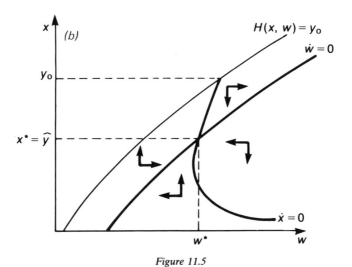

Figure 11.5

$H(x, w)$ is always positive, the curve $\dot{x} = 0$ is strictly above the horizontal axis.

6. Existence of Cycles

We shall now show that our model can generate cycles and for that we shall use the Poincaré–Bendixson theorem. This theorem says in particular that there is at least a limit cycle in a two-dimensional dynamic system if the following conditions are satisfied: (1) The long-run equilibrium is unique and locally unstable; (2) there exists a bounded compact set in the (x, w) space such that the dynamic system points into this compact on every point in its frontier. With the help of this theorem we can now prove the following proposition.

Proposition. *Assume that at the long-run equilibrium (x^*, w^*) one has*

$$\theta(H_x - 1) > -\varphi'(\hat{y})H_w$$

Then there exists at least a limit cycle.

Proof. The condition in the proposition is sufficient for the long-run equilibrium to be unstable, as we saw before in Section 5. It is thus enough, in order to use the Poincaré–Bendixson theorem, to construct a compact set in (w, x) space such that the dynamic system points inward. This compact set has been drawn in Fig. 11.6 as the set bounded by the line $ABCDE$. The line AC corresponds to the equation

$$H(x, w) = y_m$$

where y_m must be "sufficiently" close to y_0 (later we shall give sufficient conditions for y_m). The equation for the line CD is $x = y_0$ and that for the

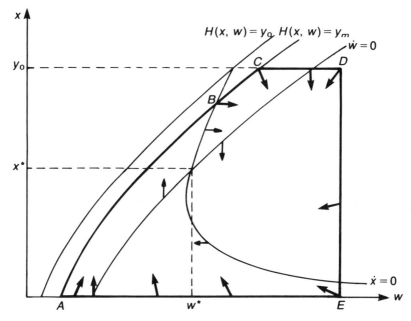

Figure 11.6

line DE is $w = w_m$, where w_m is sufficiently high that $H(y_0, w_m) < \hat{y}$. Finally, the segment EA is along the horizontal axis.

Note that as shown in Fig. 11.6, along the frontier $ABCDE$ the dynamic system points unambiguously toward the interior of the compact, except along the segment AB where this is ambiguous. We must thus choose a value of y_m sufficiently high for the dynamic system to point inward along AB as well. Since this segment is characterized by a constant value of y, it is enough to show that $\dot{y} < 0$ along AB. Since $y = H(x, w)$, we obtain

$$\dot{y} = H_x \dot{x} + H_w \dot{w}$$

$$= \theta(y - x)H_x + \varphi(y)H_w$$

Because we consider a compact where $x \geq 0$ and $y < y_0$, the first term on the right-hand side is less than $\theta y_0 H_x$ and thus,

$$\dot{y} < \theta y_0 H_x + \varphi(y)H_w$$

A sufficient condition for $\dot{y} < 0$ is to choose y_m such that along the segment AB,

$$\theta y_0 H_x + \varphi(y_m)H_w < 0$$

or

$$\varphi(y_m) > -\frac{\theta y_0 H_x}{H_w}$$

which is possible since $\varphi(y)$ tends to infinity when y tends to y_0.

Q.E.D

7. Conclusions

The model presented in this chapter allows us to draw a bridge between traditional short-run equilibrium analyses and the theories of the business cycle by describing a cycle as a succession of non-Walrasian short-run equilibria. The results obtained are very intuitive: If the investment accelerator is sufficiently strong compared to the stabilizing "price effects," there will be a cyclical evolution. Otherwise, the model will be locally stable around its long-run equilibrium. Furthermore, the model sheds light on the importance of quantity expectations, whose adjustment speed also plays a role in the stability results.

The model of this chapter was purposely simplified to the extreme in order to obtain simple analytical results using the Poincaré–Bendixson theorem, which only applies to two-dimensional systems. If not for this technical constraint, supplementary variables could have been incorporated, such as expected inflation as in Chapter 10. In particular, since there is an investment function in the model, it would have been natural to add an equation describing the evolution of productive capacities based on this function, which would have introduced some elements of growth in the model. All these themes should be the subject of future research.

References

The model of this chapter is adapted from Benassy (1984a). The traditional models of the cycle with an investment accelerator are Kalecki (1935), Samuelson (1939), Kaldor (1940), Hicks (1950), and Goodwin (1951).

The Poincaré–Bendixson technique has been applied in various cycle models by Rose (1967, 1969), Chang and Smyth (1971), Schinasi (1982), and Dana and Malgrange (1983, 1984).

PART V

EXPECTATIONS

CHAPTER

12

The Role of Expectations

1. Introduction

In many of the macroeconomic models presented in the preceding chapters, agents' expectations were not explicitly taken into account. However, as we have emphasized, notably in Chapters 1 and 2, all the non-Walrasian equilibrium concepts that we use depend, implicitly or explicitly, on the price-quantity expectations schemes of the agents, an element that also plays a key role in Keynesian method. The theory we have developed allows us to incorporate any expectation scheme depending on information available in the period considered, which thus includes not only past and present price-quantity signals but also any other available information, notably concerning government policies.[1]

In order to simplify exposition, we have thus far not made the expectations schemes explicit in those chapters devoted to macroeconomic models except where absolutely necessary for construction of a specific model, as in Chapter 11. In this chapter, as well as in Chapters 13 and 14, we shall construct a few simple models that incorporate expectations explicitly, which will enable us to focus on their specific role.

We shall start be developing a model with parametric expectations, which has the advantage of showing us both the effects of "exōgenous" expectations and expectational errors, as we shall see in what follows.

[1]Note that these government policies did not appear explicitly in the models of Chapter 2, where an exchange economy without government was considered. The method developed there generalizes, however, trivially to this case.

2. The Model

The model we shall study in this chapter is an extension incorporating expectations of the closed-economy model seen at the end of Chapter 5. Let us briefly recall its characteristics: There are two markets, labor and output. It is assumed that the real wage is rigid, whereas the price is flexible upward but rigid downward, which is expressed by

$$p \geq \bar{p} \qquad w = \omega p$$

where ω is the level of the real wage, assumed given in the short run. As we saw, this model has many advantages: It allows us to obtain regimes with very clearcut and different properties, similar to those of models with fixed price and wage (cf. Chapter 3) while avoiding demand rationing on the goods market, which makes it more realistic and closer to traditional macroeconomic models.

The Agents

There are three agents: The household, the firm, and the government. We continue to assume that the firm has a production function $F(l)$ with decreasing returns to scale, and it maximizes its short-run profits without investing or building up inventories. The firm, thus, need not form any expectations. Government spends g in real terms, and to simplify the exposition, we shall assume that there are no taxes. The household has a supply of labor l_0. Its consumption function, however, will depend on its expectations.

The Consumption Function

It is actually traditional in theories of consumption to assume that it depends on expected incomes and prices. We shall thus introduce in the consumption function an index of expected income, which we shall denote by y^e, and an index of expected prices, which we shall denote by p^e. These arguments appear in the consumption function together with the arguments y and p already seen in previous models. This function then becomes

$$C(y, p, y^e, p^e)$$

We have seen in Chapter 1, Section 6, an example of construction of such a consumption function. We shall assume the following partial derivatives:

$$C_y > 0 \qquad C_p < 0 \qquad C_{ye} > 0 \qquad C_{pe} > 0$$

with

$$C_{ye} = \frac{\partial C}{\partial y^e} \qquad C_{pe} = \frac{\partial C}{\partial p^e}$$

As we saw in the general formalization of Chapter 2, the expectations y^e and p^e may be formed from all information available at the time considered, notably, past and present values of income and prices. These expectations can also be influenced by information or expectations about current and forthcoming government policies. However, in order to highlight in the simplest possible manner the specific influence of expectations, in this chapter we shall take y^e and p^e as given parameters in the period. The results we shall obtain have a number of interesting interpretations.

The first and most direct is to consider y^e and p^e as expectations mostly inherited from the past, similar in spirit to the "state of long-run expectations" of Keynesian theory. Changes in y^e and p^e would then correspond to exogenous changes in these expectations, which might be produced by announcements of future government policies.

Another fruitful interpretation of the results on changes in y^e and p^e is to consider these parameters with reference to what they would be in the "benchmark" situation of perfect foresight (such a perfect-foresight situation is studied next in Chapter 13). Exogenous changes in y^e and p^e can then be treated as expectational errors, and our results directly show the effects of such errors in expectations.

3. The Structure of Equilibria

We shall first state the characteristics of Walrasian equilibria and then indicate the structure of non-Walrasian equilibria for any value of ω and $\bar{p}$.

Walrasian Equilibria

Again, let p_0 and w_0 be the values of current price and wage at the Walrasian equilibrium. They are given by the equations

$$C(y_0, p_0, y^e, p^e) + g = y_0$$
$$w_0 / p_0 = F'(l_0)$$

As before, the Walrasian equilibrium real wage is equal to full-employment productivity, but the general price level p_0 and the nominal wage w_0 depend on expectations. More specifically,

$$\frac{\partial p_0}{\partial y^e} = -\frac{C_{ye}}{C_p} > 0$$

$$\frac{\partial p_0}{\partial p^e} = -\frac{C_{pe}}{C_p} > 0$$

We see that it is impossible to say that a wage–price system corresponds to a Walrasian equilibrium by looking only at the current parameters, because expectations must also be taken into account. We shall encounter this problem again later since for given values of current parameters ω, $\bar{p}$, and g, the nature of imbalances observed will also depend on expectations.

Non-Walrasian Equilibria

Let us now assume that ω and $\bar{p}$ are given. Although the equations are a little different, the structure of non-Walrasian equilibria is the same as in Chapter 5. Depending on the values of the various parameters, we shall thus have three regimes; A, B, and C. In Section 4 we shall compute the impact of economic policies and the effect of changes on the expectational parameters y^e and p^e in each of these regimes. For that we shall have to compute the equilibrium values of the variables y, p, and w, and we shall thus need three equations. The structure is the same as in Chapter 5, and two equations will be invariant in the three regimes:

$$y = C(y, p, y^e, p^e) + g$$
$$w = \omega p$$

The first equation says that output sales are equal to total demand; the second expresses the rigidity of the real wage. The third equation, depending on the regime, is

$$p = \bar{p} \qquad \text{regime A}$$
$$y = F[F'^{-1}(\omega)] \qquad \text{regime B}$$
$$y = y_0 \qquad \text{regime C}$$

4. The Effects of Economic Policies and Expectations

We shall now study in each regime the effect of variations in the various parameters on activity and prices. We shall essentially study two categories of parameters: (1) the economic policy parameters ω and g, respectively representing classical and Keynesian policies, and (2) the expectational parameters y^e and p^e, which, as we have already indicated, may represent either the exogenous state of expectations or expectational errors.

As we would expect, variations in these parameters have quite different effects, depending on the regime considered. We may note in anticipation the similarity of the results on economic policies with those obtained in the model without explicit expectations.

Regime A

In this case, the system of equations determining y, p, and w is

$$y = C(y, p, y^e, p^e) + g$$

$$p = \bar{p}$$

$$w = \omega p$$

If we first examine the impact of economic policies, we see that income policies have no effect on activity, whereas government-spending policies have beneficial effects on both activity and private consumption, since

$$\frac{\partial y}{\partial g} = \frac{1}{1 - C_y} > 0 \qquad \frac{\partial c}{\partial g} = \frac{C_y}{1 - C_y} > 0$$

Turning now to the study of the impact of exogenous changes in expectations, one sees that an increase in y^e (i.e., more "optimistic" expectations) results in an increase in current production and employment:

$$\frac{\partial y}{\partial y^e} = \frac{C_{ye}}{1 - C_y} > 0$$

Such a result conforms to the Keynesian tradition, where favorable expectations (appearing in the marginal efficiency of capital schedule) are associated with a higher employment level. If we now take the expectational errors interpretation, we see that incorrect foresight may have beneficial effects in this regime, since overoptimistic expectations lead to an increase in output and employment.

In a similar manner, an exogenous increase in expected price also has a favorable effect on activity because of its positive impact on consumption:

$$\frac{\partial y}{\partial p^e} = \frac{C_{pe}}{1 - C_y} > 0$$

Regime B

In this regime, the equations determining y, p, and w become

$$y = C(y, p, y^e, p^e) + g$$

$$y = F[F'^{-1}(\omega)]$$

$$w = \omega p$$

One immediately sees that the effectiveness of employment policies changes completely compared with the preceding regime: A decrease in ω brings an increase in y (and a decrease in price and wage), whereas an increase in g has no effect on y and, moreover, increases prices, thereby crowding out consumption completely:

$$\frac{\partial y}{\partial g} = 0 \qquad \frac{\partial c}{\partial g} = -1 \qquad \frac{\partial p}{\partial g} = -\frac{1}{C_p} > 0$$

With regard to expectations, their impact is just as different in this regime, since exogenous changes in these expectations have no impact on activity, but lead only to price changes:

$$\frac{\partial p}{\partial y^e} = -\frac{C_{ye}}{C_p} > 0 \qquad \frac{\partial y}{\partial y^e} = 0$$

$$\frac{\partial p}{\partial p^e} = -\frac{C_{pe}}{C_p} > 0 \qquad \frac{\partial y}{\partial p^e} = 0$$

In particular, overoptimistic expectations do not bring about expansion as in regime A, but, instead, only inflation.

Regime C

In this regime the equations become

$$y = C(y, p, y^e, p^e) + g$$

$$y = y_0$$

$$w = \omega p$$

Production being at its full employment level, government economic policies have no effect on the level of activity. Government spending, though, still creates a full crowding-out effect on private consumption via price increases. As for expectations, they affect only prices, as in Regime B:

$$\frac{\partial p}{\partial y^e} = -\frac{C_{ye}}{C_p} > 0$$

$$\frac{\partial p}{\partial p^e} = -\frac{C_{pe}}{C_p} > 0$$

5. Global Analysis

Having analyzed the impact of the various parameters in each regime, we shall now see how the regime itself is a function of these parameters. We start with a graphical representation of the problem.

A Graphical Representation

As we have done before, we shall represent the equilibrium solution in (y, p) space as the intersection of a supply curve and a demand curve (Fig. 12.1). The demand curve corresponds to the solution in y of the equation

$$y = C(y, p, y^e, p^e) + g$$

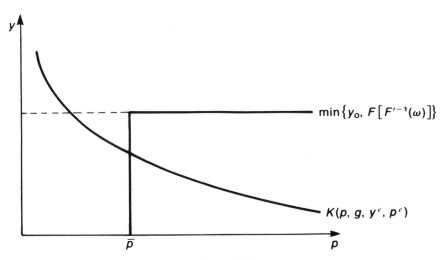

Figure 12.1

which we shall represent, with the usual notation, by

$$y = K(p, g, y^e, p^e)$$

The supply curve has two parts (Cf. Chapter 5, Section 4): a vertical part with equation $p = \bar{p}$ and a horizontal part with the equation

$$y = \min\{F[F'(\omega)], y_0\}$$

One immediately sees in Fig. 12.1 that the solution in y can be written as

$$y = \min\{K(\bar{p}, g, y^e, p^e), F[F'(\omega)], y_0\}$$

This formula allows us both to compute the level of activity for each set of parameters and to delimit the regimes, as we shall now see.

The Delimitation of Regimes

From the previous formula we can very simply find the subspace of parameters corresponding to each regime by determining which of the three possible expressions for y has the smallest value. So, regime A is characterized by values $\bar{p}, \omega, g, y^e, p^e$ such that

$$K(\bar{p}, g, y^e, p^e) \leqslant y_0$$
$$K(\bar{p}, g, y^e, p^e) \leqslant F[F'^{-1}(\omega)]$$

regime B by

$$F[F'^{-1}(\omega)] \leqslant K(\bar{p}, g, y^e, p^e)$$
$$F[F'^{-1}(\omega)] \leqslant y_0$$

regime C by

$$y_0 \leqslant K(\bar{p}, g, y^e, p^e)$$
$$y_0 \leqslant F[F'^{-1}(\omega)]$$

The corresponding regions in $(\omega, \bar{p})$ space are represented in Fig. 12.2, where they are separated by the bold lines.

It is important to note that the nature of the prevailing regime is defined not only by the values of current variables, but also, in a fundamental way, by price–quantity expectations. In particular, point W, which corresponds to the temporary Walrasian equilibrium, has an abscissa p_0 that is higher the higher are y^e and p^e since, as we saw earlier, p_0 depends positively on these two variables. Similarly, the previous formulas show that an increase

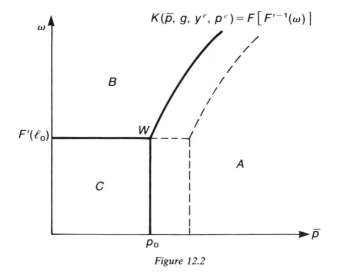

Figure 12.2

in y^e and or p^e reduces the "size" in $(\omega, \bar{p})$ space of region A, since it is defined by:

$$K(\bar{p}, g, y^e, p^e) \leqslant y_0$$
$$K(\bar{p}, g, y^e, p^e) \leqslant F[F'^{-1}(\omega)]$$

and the function K is increasing in y^e and p^e. In Fig. 12.2, the dashed lines represent the new separating lines corresponding to higher values of y^e and p^e. One sees that optimistic expectations reduce the size of region A, which corresponds to the traditional Keynesian regime.

6. Conclusions

We have seen in this chapter that expectations play a very central role in non-Walrasian macroeconomic models, since notably the nature of the regime the economy is in is determined not only by the values of current parameters, but by expectational parameters as well. Furthermore, we have noted that exogenous changes in these expectations had very different effects, depending on the regime, leading to either price or quantity movements. The interpretation of parametric expectations in terms of expectational errors also showed us that such errors have quite different effects, depending on the regime. For example, overoptimistic expectations could lead to either expansion or inflation. All this shows quite clearly that if we want to study the problem of expectations, a correct specification of the nature of possible market imbalances is quite fundamental.

We also found in this chapter a differentiation of the effects of economic policies quite similar to that found in the chapters where expectations were not made explicit. However, we only considered here parametric expectations, thus allowing some expectational errors. One might naturally ask which results would obtain if, as is often done nowadays, a perfect-foresight assumption was made. This is what we shall examine next in Chapter 13.

References

Expectations were introduced in general models of non-Walrasian equilibria by Benassy (1973, 1975a). Expectations have been introduced in the standard macroeconomic model with fixed price and wage by K. Hildenbrand and W. Hildenbrand (1978), Muellbauer and Portes (1978), Benassy (1982a, b), Neary and Stiglitz (1983), and Persson and Svensson (1983).

Non-Walrasian Prices and
Perfect Foresight

1. Introduction

Thus far we have assumed, explicitly or implicitly, that agents' expectations about future events are based on information available when the agent is forming these expectations, which is obviously the most realistic way to consider the problem. Such expectations, formed historically on the basis of past and present information clearly allow for errors in expectations even if economic agents learn over time. But we have seen more and more in the literature some authors of the "new classical economics" claim that the results of traditional Keynesian-type macroeconomics, notably those results about effectiveness of economic policy, are due only to expectational errors by economic agents. For the adepts of this school, who generally use models described as "rational expectations models," perfect foresight would be sufficient to make economic policies almost completely ineffective.

A number of authors in the Keynesian tradition have replied that the primary reason why government policy might be ineffective in the so-called rational expectations models is not so much the assumption about expectations, but rather the assumption of general market clearing, which is quite commonly made by the "new classicals," but the implications of which they unfortunately do not emphasize.

To shed some light on this controversy, we shall describe in this chapter a very simple non-Walrasian equilibrium model where all errors in expectations are excluded, since we shall assume perfect foresight in both prices and quantities.[1] In this model it turns out that economic policies have no effect on activity if the economy is at the Walrasian equilibrium (one thus finds in this particular case the new classical position), but such is not the case if non-Walrasian equilibria are considered. The effectiveness of each policy will then depend on the regime that the economy is in, and we shall see as well that the traditional Keynesian results are valid only in some regimes.

2. The Model

We shall consider here a model dealing explicitly with two periods denoted 1 and 2. In each of these periods there is a market for output (at prices p_1 and p_2, respectively) and a market for labor (at wages w_1 and w_2). There are three agents in the economy: a household, a firm, and the government.

The Agents

We shall assume that the firm does not invest and does not build up inventories. It has a specific production function in each period, respectively,

$$F_1(l_1) \quad \text{and} \quad F_2(l_2)$$

The government spends g_1 and g_2 in the two periods. As in Chapter 12, we ignore taxes to keep the notation simple. Finally, the household is endowed with quantities of labor l_{01} and l_{02} in the two periods and has a utility function that we assume has the form

$$U(c_1, c_2, m_2, \psi)$$

where c_1 and c_2 are the first- and second-period consumptions, respectively, and m_2 the quantity of money saved at the end of the second period. The first two arguments of this function obviously represent the direct utility of consumptions c_1 and c_2. The third and fourth arguments correspond, in the form of an indirect utility for money, to the expected utility of all consumptions after period 2. In accordance with the method developed in Chapters 1 and 2, the arguments of this indirect utility function are the quantity of

---

[1]The mathematical structure of such an intertemporal non-Walrasian equilibrium model with perfect foresight is actually the same as that of a single-period model, where the number of markets would have been multiplied by the number of periods considered. It is thus a particular case of the concepts studied in Chapter 2.

money m_2 saved at the end of the second period and a variable ψ, which represents all price–quantity expectations about periods after the second. Since we are interested explicitly in second-period expectations only, this variable ψ is treated as a fixed parameter in what follows.

Prices and Wages

In order to obtain simple and clearcut results, as in Chapter 13, we shall assume rigid real wages in each period ω_1 and ω_2 and prices flexible upward but rigid downward. This is expressed mathematically by

$$p_1 \geqslant \bar{p}_1 \qquad w_1 = \omega_1 p_1$$

$$p_1 \geqslant \bar{p}_2 \qquad w_2 = \omega_2 p_2$$

3. The Consumption Function

In this model the firm does not need to form expectations, since it neither invests nor accumulates inventories. Only the consumer's behavior is influenced by the prices and quantities he expects and this through his consumption function, which we shall now construct. The household's budget constraints in periods 1 and 2 are written, respectively,

$$p_1 c_1 + m_1 = p_1 y_1 + \bar{m}_1 \qquad m_1 \geqslant 0$$

$$p_2 c_2 + m_2 = p_2 y_2 + m_1 \qquad m_2 \geqslant 0$$

where $\bar{m}_1$ is the quantity of money held by the household at the beginning of the first period, and m_1 and m_2 are the quantities held at the end of each of the two periods. The household's consumption is very simply determined by the solution in c_1 and c_2 of the following program:

$$\text{Maximize } U(c_1, c_2, m_2, \psi) \qquad \text{s.t.}$$

$$p_1 c_1 + m_1 = p_1 y_1 + \bar{m}_1 \qquad m_1 \geqslant 0$$

$$p_2 c_2 + m_2 = p_2 y_2 + m_1 \qquad m_2 \geqslant 0$$

where p_1, p_2, y_1, y_2 are taken as exogenous parameters by the household. Note that we do not need to take into account any other price or quantity signal, since the constraints on the household's labor supply in the two periods have already been taken into account in y_1 and y_2, and there is no constraint on consumption purchases themselves because prices are flexible upward in each period. The solutions in c_1 and c_2 of the program just given yield two consumption functions (we omit the parameter ψ, which is assumed to be given in all that follows):

$$C_1(y_1, y_2, p_1, p_2) \quad \text{and} \quad C_2(y_1, y_2, p_1, p_2)$$

where the second function is an expected consumption function. Expected consumption is actually equal to the true second-period consumption because of the perfect-foresight assumption. We shall assume in what follows that both goods and money are normal and gross substitutes, which notably implies that:[2]

$$C_{1y1} > 0 \quad C_{1y2} > 0 \quad C_{1p1} < 0 \quad C_{1p2} > 0$$

$$C_{2y1} > 0 \quad C_{2y2} > 0 \quad C_{2p1} > 0 \quad C_{2p2} < 0$$

4. The Intertemporal Walrasian Equilibrium

Let p_{01}, p_{02}, w_{01}, and w_{02} be the prices and wages corresponding to a Walrasian intertemporal equilibrium. They are determined by the conditions of market clearing in the output and labor markets. Market clearing for labor in periods 1 and 2 implies

$$w_{01}/p_{01} = F_1'(l_{01})$$

$$w_{02}/p_{02} = F_2'(l_{02})$$

We set $y_{01} = F_1(l_{01})$ and $y_{02} = F_2(l_{02})$, the full employment output levels. The conditions of equality between supply and demand in the two output markets imply

$$y_{01} = C_1(y_{01}, y_{02}, p_{01}, p_{02}) + g_1$$

$$y_{02} = C_2(y_{01}, y_{02}, p_{01}, p_{02}) + g_2$$

These four equations determine p_{01}, p_{02}, w_{01}, and w_{02}. Note that in this Walrasian framework, public-spending policies g_1 and g_2 have no positive effect on employment. Moreover, through crowding-out effects they have a negative effect on private consumption. One thus finds in this very simple framework the positions of the new classical school. However, as we shall see later, the conclusions are modified outside the intertemporal Walrasian equilibrium.

---

[2]We adopt here the convention, not very elegant but explicit, according to which $C_{1y1} = \partial C_1/\partial y_1$, etc.

5. The Structure of Non-Walrasian Equilibria

Assume now that the levels of real wages ω_1 and ω_2 and of minimum prices $\bar{p}_1$ and $\bar{p}_2$ are given. We shall indicate in which regimes the system can be and which are the equations determining the levels of activity, prices, and wages in the two periods for each case considered. The structure of this type of model is by now familiar. In each period there are three possible regimes: A, B, or C, which yields nine possible overall combinations since there are two periods. We shall be interested in the equilibrium values of p_1, p_2, y_1, and y_2, which are determined by four equations. Two of these, which represent the equality between transactions on the goods market in each period and the demand of that period, are the same for all regimes:

$$y_1 = C_1(y_1, y_2, p_1, p_2) + g_1$$
$$y_2 = C_2(y_1, y_2, p_1, p_2) + g_2$$

The two other equations, which are specific to each period, depend on the regime the economy is in during that period. For example, for period 1 this equation is, depending on the regime

$$p_1 = \bar{p}_1 \qquad \text{regime A}$$
$$y_1 = F_1[F_1'^{-1}(\omega_1)] \qquad \text{regime B}$$
$$y_1 = y_{01} \qquad \text{regime C}$$

and symmetrically for period 2. We shall now examine the effectiveness of economic policies according to the regime the economy is in for each of the two periods.

6. The Effects of Economic Policies

We shall now compute the effects of economic policies in the various regimes. In order not to burden the exposition, we shall limit ourselves to studying the impact on current activity y_1 of variations in the parameters g_1 and ω_1, representing respectively a Keynesian or a classical policy in the current period. From this point of view, although there are nine possible regimes, only four different cases emerge insofar as the effects on current activity are concerned. These are summarized in the following combinations: (1) regime A in the two periods; (2) regime A in the first period, regime B or C in the second period; (3) regime B in the first period, any regime in the second; (4) regime C in the first period, any regime in the second. We shall examine in turn these various cases.

Regime A in the Two Periods

In this case, the four equations determining y_1, y_2, p_1, p_2 are the following:

$$y_1 = C_1(y_1, y_2, p_1, p_2) + g_1$$
$$y_2 = C_2(y_1, y_2, p_1, p_2) + g_2$$
$$p_1 = \bar{p}_1$$
$$p_2 = \bar{p}_2$$

One first sees that a classical policy of reduction in ω_1 has no impact on the level of activity. However, an increase in government spending g_1 improves the employment situation, since,

$$\frac{\partial y_1}{\partial g_1} = \frac{1 - C_{2y2}}{(1 - C_{1y1})(1 - C_{2y2}) - C_{1y2}C_{2y1}} > 0$$

The denominator of this fraction is indeed positive, since the assumption that money is a normal good implies that positive variations in y_1 or y_2 lead to an increase in the quantity of money saved, i.e.,

$$1 - C_{1y1} - \frac{p_2}{p_1}C_{2y1} > 0$$

$$1 - C_{2y2} - \frac{p_1}{p_2}C_{1y2} > 0$$

Combining these two inequalities, we obtain

$$(1 - C_{1y1})(1 - C_{2y2}) > C_{2y1}C_{1y2}$$

and the denominator is thus positive. We may note that this multiplier is higher than the "naive" multiplier $1/(1 - C_{1y1})$ as can be clearly seen by rewriting it in the form

$$\frac{\partial y_1}{\partial g_1} = \frac{1}{(1 - C_{1y1}) - C_{1y2}C_{2y1}/(1 - C_{2y2})}$$

The explanation is straightforward: A variation dy_1 leads to a change $C_{1y1}\,dy_1$ in first-period consumption, hence the first term in the denominator, but it also leads (cf. the second of the four equilibrium equations) to a variation $C_{2y1}\,dy_1$ in second-period consumption and, since regime A prevails, to a change in second-period activity equal to

$$dy_2 = \frac{C_{2y1}}{1 - C_{2y2}}\,dy_1$$

Since this variation is perfectly foreseen, it leads to an indirect change in C_1 equal to

$$C_{1y2}\, dy_2 = \frac{C_{1y2}C_{2y1}}{1 - C_{2y2}}\, dy_1$$

hence the second term in the denominator, which thus represents an "indirect propensity to consume" via second-period expectations. Furthermore, the first-period consumption level is a positive function of g_1, since

$$\frac{\partial c_1}{\partial g_1} = \frac{C_{1y1}(1 - C_{2y2}) + C_{1y2}C_{2y1}}{(1 - C_{1y1})(1 - C_{2y2}) - C_{1y2}C_{2y1}} > 0$$

There is no crowding-out effect, quite to the contrary. The results are thus similar to those obtained in regime A in the one-period model, even though the multipliers are more complex.

Regime A in the First Period, Regime B or C in the Second

We shall first consider the case where regime C prevails in the second period. In this case, the equations are the following:

$$y_1 = C_1(y_1, y_2, p_1, p_2) + g_1$$
$$y_2 = C_2(y_1, y_2, p_1, p_2) + g_2$$
$$p_1 = \bar{p}_1$$
$$y_2 = y_{02}$$

In case regime B prevails in the second period, we only have to replace y_{02} by $F_2[F_2'^{-1}(\omega_2)]$ in the previous equation, which changes nothing when we consider how ω_1 or g_1 affect y_1. We see that in this case, as in the preceding one, a classical policy of reduction in ω_1 has no effect on activity and employment. One can, however, compute the public-spending multiplier:

$$\frac{\partial y_1}{\partial g_1} = \frac{1}{(1 - C_{1y1}) + (C_{1p2}C_{2y1}/C_{2p2})} > 0$$

Here, also, the multiplier differs from the naive multiplier $1/(1 - C_{1y1})$. Indeed, an increase dy_1 leads to a rise in second-period prices equal to (cf. the second equation):

$$dp_2 = -\frac{C_{2y1}}{C_{2p2}}\, dy_1$$

hence an indirect variation of first-period consumption:

$$C_{1p2}\, dp_2 = -\frac{C_{1p2}C_{2y1}}{C_{2p2}}\, dy_1$$

which corresponds to the second term in the denominator. The multiplier is higher than the naive multiplier if, as we assumed, C_{1p2} is positive.

Regime B in the First Period

In this case, regardless of the second-period regime, there are three invariant equations:

$$y_1 = C_1(y_1, y_2, p_1, p_2) + g_1$$
$$y_2 = C_2(y_1, y_2, p_1, p_2) + g_2$$
$$y_1 = F_1[F_1'^{-1}(\omega_1)]$$

The fourth equation will depend on the second-period regime. One sees that the level of activity is entirely determined by the third equation, i.e.,

$$y_1 = F_1[F_1'^{-1}(\omega_1)]$$

Only a classical policy of reduction of ω_1 can increase the activity level, whereas government spending has no effect. Moreover, the first equation shows that an increase in g_1 diminishes private consumption by the same quantity. There is thus full crowding out. On these various points, the results are similar to those in the one-period model.

Regime C in the First Period

In this case, whatever the second-period regime, there are three invariant equations:

$$y_1 = C_1(y_1, y_2, p_1, p_2) + g_1$$
$$y_2 = C_2(y_1, y_2, p_1, p_2) + g_2$$
$$y_1 = y_{01}$$

Activity y_1 being fixed at the full-employment level y_{01}, neither variations in ω_1 nor in g_1 will change its level. An increase in g_1 still creates a one-hundred per cent crowding-out effect. There, again, the results are those of the one-period model.

7. Expectations of Government Policy

When we computed the first-period government-spending multipliers, we implicitly assumed that government could bring about variations in g_1 without changing the other variables and particularly while maintaining g_2 constant. However, an argument often invoked in support of ineffectiveness of government policies is that an expansionist policy today will require a deflationary policy tomorrow. If we combine the two effects, assumed perfectly foreseen by private agents, the impact of Keynesian demand policies might be annihilated, even in the "Keynesian zone." We shall scrutinize here this argument, assuming that the economy is in regime A in both periods. In this case, as we saw before, the equations determining activities and prices are

$$y_1 = C_1(y_1, y_2, p_1, p_2) + g_1$$
$$y_2 = C_2(y_1, y_2, p_1, p_2) + g_2$$
$$p_1 = \bar{p}_1$$
$$p_2 = \bar{p}_2$$

We should first note that variations in g_2, i.e., in future government spending, have an effect of the same sign on first-period activity, since

$$\frac{\partial y_1}{\partial g_2} = \frac{C_{1y2}}{(1 - C_{1y1})(1 - C_{2y2}) - C_{2y1}C_{1y2}} > 0$$

We shall now compute the decrease in g_2 associated with an increase in g_1, which would just cancel the impact on first-period activity. For this we differentiate the previous equations, setting dy_1 equal to zero. This yields

$$C_{1y2}\, dy_2 + dg_1 = 0$$
$$C_{2y2}\, dy_2 + dg_2 = dy_2$$

The first equation says that one should expect a deterioration in future income ($dy_2 < 0$). This deterioration is caused by a negative variation in g_2 equal to

$$dg_2 = -\frac{1 - C_{2y2}}{C_{1y2}}\, dg_1$$

Money being a normal good, we have, as seen before,

$$1 - C_{2y2} - \frac{p_1}{p_2} C_{1y2} > 0$$

Combining these two equations, we obtain immediately

$$p_1 \, dg_1 + p_2 \, dg_2 < 0$$

For the effect on first-period activity to be canceled, the government should thus actually have an overall *deflationary* policy over the two periods, the total spending being negative.

8. Conclusions

We have seen in this chapter that the perfect foresight assumption, whether on prices, quantities, or government actions, does not imply at all that economic policies have no impact on activity. We found indeed that in some of the regimes, classical or Keynesian policies are quite effective against unemployment, some multipliers being even greater than those found in one-period models.

Expectations are certainly a very important factor, as we have seen notably in Chapter 12, but the nature of market imbalances, current and expected, is in all circumstances a fundamental element in assessing the effectiveness of the various economic policies.

References

A similar model with fully rigid prices and wages has been constructed by Neary and Stiglitz (1983). The argument that the ineffectiveness of economic policies essentially stems from the assumption that all markets clear is found, for example, in Tobin (1980).

CHAPTER

14

Expectations, Information, and Dynamics

1. Introduction

In Chapters 12 and 13 we have studied the introduction of various expectations schemes in the framework of a static macroeconomic model. In this chapter we shall construct a *dynamic* model of similar inspiration, which will allow us to follow the evolution in time of a given economy under alternative assumptions about expectations schemes. This exercise will enable us to highlight a number of ideas.

The first point pertains to the "realism" of various expectations mechanisms. We shall see that in a model where expectations are formed from historically accumulated data, the perfect-foresight assumption may be very hard to justify, given the information available to the agents, and "imperfect" expectations might be more realistic.

Second, our model will allow us to appreciate the very partial and limited character of the generally admitted notion according to which the inefficiency of non-Walrasian equilibria results from "false prices," i.e., from non-Walrasian prices. This notion of false prices becomes very ambiguous indeed as soon as we take expectations and, notably, quantity expectations into account, since, as we saw in Chapter 12, the short-run Walrasian price system depends on these expectations. As an illustration, we shall construct a non-Walrasian equilibrium with positive unemployment, even though the price system is, for all periods, the intertemporal

Walrasian equilibrium price system. Such a situation will arise, as we shall see, from the fact that in the absence of future markets, agents cannot transmit to each other information on exchanges that they would like to carry in future periods. The cause of unemployment in that case is not so much a problem of false prices as the absence of institutional mechanisms that might allow agents to transmit some relevant information to each other.

2. The Model

We shall study here a dynamic discrete time model with overlapping generations. This is a monetary economy, and in each period t two markets are open: labor at wage w, and output at price p. Agents in the economy are a firm, which lasts forever, and households–consumers living two periods each. In each period there are thus three agents: the firm, a young consumer, and an old consumer.

The firm has the same production function in all periods, and we shall denote it by

$$q = F(l) \quad \text{with} \quad F'(l) > 0 \quad F''(l) < 0$$

where q is the production level. We shall assume that the firm can carry inventories without cost and has a planning horizon of one period. Note that since inventories are present, production q can be different from output sales y.

The consumer of generation t (i.e., "born" in t) lives in periods t and $t + 1$. He is endowed with a quantity of labor l_0 in t and zero in period $t + 1$. He has no money in the first period but owns all production of period t. The consumer chooses his first- and second-period consumptions c_1 and c_2 according to the utility function

$$U(c_1, c_2) = \alpha_t \log c_1 + (1 - \alpha_t) \log c_2 \quad 0 < \alpha_t < 1$$

The parameter α_t is somehow the propensity to consume of the young consumer. Indeed, he determines his consumption demand in t, $c_1(t)$, by solving the following program:

$$\text{Maximize } \alpha_t \log c_1 + (1 - \alpha_t) \log c_2 \quad \text{s.t.}$$

$$p(t)c_1 + m = p(t)q(t)$$

$$p^e(t + 1)c_2 = m$$

where $p^e(t+1)$ is the price expected to prevail at period $t+1$, and m is the quantity of money saved. The solution of this program is

$$c_1(t) = \alpha_t q(t)$$

α_t is thus the fraction of period t's production that is spent by the young consumer in this same period.

3. A Stationary Intertemporal Equilibrium

As a reference path we shall first study the case where all generations of households have the same utility function with $\alpha_t = \alpha$ for all periods. We shall then have a stationary intertemporal equilibrium. Let $\bar{m}$ be the total quantity of money in the economy (assumed constant in time) and $q_0 = F(l_0)$ the full-employment production level. The Walrasian wage and price are denoted by w_0 and p_0, respectively. For the labor market to clear, the real wage must be equal to full-employment productivity, i.e.,

$$\frac{w_0}{p_0} = F'(l_0)$$

Furthermore, for the goods market to clear, the supply of goods coming from the firm must be equal to the sum of consumption demands of the two households alive in each period. The old consumer, who holds all the money $\bar{m}$, demands a quantity $\bar{m}/p$. The young consumer demands αq_0, and the Walrasian equilibrium price p_0 is thus solution in p of

$$q_0 = \frac{\bar{m}}{p} + \alpha q_0$$

which yields immediately

$$p_0 = \frac{\bar{m}}{(1 - \alpha)q_0}$$

In the corresponding stationary equilibrium, each household consumes αq_0 in his first period and $(1 - \alpha)q_0$ in his second period.

Two Expectations Schemes

The previous intertemporal equilibrium solution is defined implicitly under the assumption of perfect foresight for all agents for the prices and quantities relevant to them. We may remark that this equilibrium would be the same if we had made the assumption of static expectations on quantities, the firm expecting for the next period the same demand as in the current period. In this stationary reference path, both expectations schemes yield the same result.

We shall now consider a temporary "deflationary" shock in a specific period θ, more specifically a diminution of the propensity to consume of the generation θ household, the propensity to consume of the following generations returning to the value on the reference path. As in previous chapters we shall assume that the real wage is rigid (and equal to its Walrasian value), whereas the price is rigid downward. Since we shall consider a deflationary shock, prices and wages will remain at their values on the Walrasian stationary path p_0 and w_0, and we shall assume in all cases that agents correctly forecast these values (there is thus perfect foresight on prices). We shall, however, consider two expectations schemes for quantities, perfect foresight and static expectations, and we shall study the dynamics of the system under these two assumptions.

4. A Temporary Deflationary Shock

As indicated before, we now assume that generation θ has a propensity to consume less than that of the other generations. More specifically, we shall assume that household θ has a utility function

$$\beta \log c_1 + (1 - \beta) \log c_2 \qquad \text{with} \quad \beta < \alpha$$

This generation thus wants to save a higher fraction $(1 - \beta)$ of its income than the other generations.

Perfect Foresight

The temporary shock described earlier has been chosen so that it does not modify in any period the intertemporal Walrasian equilibrium price and wage. These are still p_0 and w_0 in each period. As for quantities in this new equilibrium, there is still full employment, and the firm produces q_0 in each period. All consumers, except those of generation θ, consume αq_0 in the first period and $(1 - \alpha)q_0$ in the second period. The consumer of generation θ consumes βq_0 in the first period and $(1 - \beta)q_0$ in the second period. One thus sees that in period θ, total consumption is $(1 + \beta - \alpha)q_0$, which is less than production q_0. The difference $(\alpha - \beta)q_0$ is held as inventories and is added to production q_0 in period $\theta + 1$, which allows the firm to satisfy the total consumption in $\theta + 1$, equal to $(1 + \alpha - \beta)q_0$. In subsequent periods, the economy reverts to the stationary reference path.

Static Expectations

We shall now consider as an example the case where the firm has "static" expectations,[1] i.e., where it expects future demand to be equal to the current one. With such expectations it is easy to see that the firm does not build any inventories. It produces only for the current-period demand, and production is thus equal to sales in each period:

$$q(t) = y(t) \qquad \forall t$$

In period θ, the demand of generation $\theta - 1$ is equal to $\bar{m}/p_0$, and the demand of generation θ is $\beta q(\theta) = \beta y(\theta)$. Sales and production in θ are thus determined by

$$y(\theta) = \frac{\bar{m}}{p_0} + \beta y(\theta)$$

$$q(\theta) = y(\theta) = \frac{1}{1 - \beta}\frac{\bar{m}}{p_0} = \frac{1 - \alpha}{1 - \beta}q_0 < q_0$$

We see that sales and production are less than their full-employment value. The difference between them can be written as

$$y(\theta) - q_0 = -\frac{(\alpha - \beta)q_0}{1 - \beta}$$

The reduction in activity is thus equal to the multiplier in period θ, $1/(1 - \beta)$, multiplied by the "autonomous" fall in consumption in period θ, $-(\alpha - \beta)q_0$. For all subsequent periods, sales and production revert to the value q_0.

5. An Interpretation

We saw in Section 4 that in case of static quantity expectations, the transitory shock considered led to unemployment, whereas full employment prevailed in case of perfect foresight. The interpretation of this inefficiency will show us that the problem is only apparently a problem of "false prices,"

---

[1] Other "adaptive" schemes would lead to similar, though more complex, results.

but that the true underlying cause is that agents cannot transmit to each other information on their future exchange intentions. In this respect, the perfect-foresight assumption does not appear to be credible in this dynamic context.

False Prices

If one limits the analysis to period θ, one sees that the apparent cause is that the price and wage are different from their temporary Walrasian equilibrium values. Indeed, under static expectations, production and income are equal:

$$q = y$$

If we want these two quantities to reach the full-employment levels q_0, the price level must satisfy

$$\frac{\bar{m}}{p} + \beta q_0 = q_0$$

which yields

$$p = \frac{\bar{m}}{(1 - \beta)q_0} < \frac{\bar{m}}{(1 - \alpha)q_0} = p_0$$

a level lower than the value p_0 at which the price is fixed in period θ because of its downward rigidity. A quick analysis of the problem would thus lead to the conclusion that there is unemployment because the price and wage are too high. However, we must not forget that the price p_0 prevailing in period θ is the intertemporal Walrasian equilibrium price, so it is difficult to call it a false price. We must therefore characterize the cause of inefficiency in a more subtle way.

The Cause of Inefficiency

In order to analyze the cause of inefficiency in the case of static expectations, it is useful to compare the prevailing situation with the reference situation where all generations would have the same first-period propensity to consume, α. In this reference situation, the intertemporal equilibrium is stationary, and the solutions corresponding to perfect foresight and static expectations are the same.

With respect to this reference situation, the consumer of generation θ decides to transfer a part of his consumption, equal to $(\alpha - \beta)q_0$, from the first to the second period. If there is perfect foresight, the producer knows this and thus compensates the lack of demand in period θ by building up inventories aimed at satisfying the increase in consumption forecast for period $\theta + 1$, and the economy remains at full employment. In traditional Keynesian terms, the extra savings in period $\theta, (\alpha - \beta)q_0$, have been matched by an equal increase in investment in the form of inventories.

One may, however, seriously question the realism of the perfect-foresight assumption in our dynamic framework. Indeed, when consumer θ goes on the goods market, he transmits only the signal of a decrease in his demand in θ, not the signal of an increase of his demand in $\theta + 1$. Since this information is not communicated to the firm, the hypothesis of perfect foresight on quantities seems very arbitrary.

In the absence of a signal of increased future consumption, it is more natural to think that the firm, in view of current declining demand, will forecast a future demand that is also decreasing (or in any case not increasing) with respect to the reference path. The consequence of this, however, as we have seen, is an inefficient unemployment situation.

We may note that this problem had been very lucidly seen by Keynes, since he wrote:

> An act of individual saving means—so to speak—a decision not to have dinner to-day. But it does *not* necessitate a decision to have a dinner or to buy a pair of boots a week hence or a year hence or to consume any specified thing at any specified date. Thus it depresses the business of preparing to-day's dinner without stimulating the business of making ready for some future act of consumption. It is not a substitution of future consumption-demand for present consumption-demand—it is a net diminution of such demand . . . .
>
> If saving consisted not merely in abstaining from present consumption but in placing simultaneously a specific order for future consumption, the effect might indeed be different . . . .
>
> The trouble arises, therefore, because the act of saving implies, not a substitution for present consumption of some specific additional consumption which requires for its preparation just as much immediate economic activity as would have been required by present consumption equal in value to the sum saved, but a desire for "wealth" as such, that is for a potentiality of consuming an unspecified article at an unspecified time.

6. Conclusions

This chapter has led us to do some further thinking on the widespread idea according to which any lack of market clearing can only be due to false prices, possibly manipulated by agents having some market power.

Such phenomena are obviously a fundamental cause of potential imbalances in the dynamic evolution of an economy, as we have seen, notably in Chapters 9 and 10. However, we have showed in this chapter that unemployment may appear because agents cannot, for lack of adequate institutional mechanisms, transmit to each other their future desires for exchange and therefore form correct expectations on the quantities they will be able to trade. There are thus potential causes for imbalance in the expectations-formation schemes as much as in price-formation schemes.

Furthermore, we have seen that the perfect-foresight assumption might not be very realistic, taking into account information actually available to agents and the absence of some future markets. Since no expectation scheme appears *a priori* to be better than others, it is important, in order to build a truly dynamic theory, to specify agents' learning behavior in their expectations-formation processes. This is particularly important since, as we saw in this chapter, the interaction between assumptions about expectations and price flexibility has a very significant effect on production and employment.

References

The model of this chapter is adapted from Benassy (1982b). Models with overlapping generations have been introduced by Samuelson (1958). The quotation is from Keynes (1936, Chapter 16) and is reproduced by permission of Harcourt, Brace, Jovanovich, Inc.

APPENDIXES

A

Existence Theorems

We shall present here a few brief proofs of the existence theorems for the non-Walrasian equilibrium concepts developed in Chapter 2, Sections 5–7. Before that we shall prove a property of optimality of the effective demand function mentioned in Section 4 of that chapter.

Effective Demand

We shall prove here that the effective demand function $\tilde{\zeta}_i$ "leads" to the optimal transaction vector ζ_i^*. Before proving the corresponding proposition, let us redefine these two vectors: the vector of optimal transactions $\zeta_i^*(p, \bar{d}_i, \bar{s}_i)$ is the solution in z_i of the following program (A):

$$\text{Maximize } U_i(x_i, m_i, \sigma_i) \quad \text{s.t.}$$

$$x_i = \omega_i + z_i \geq 0$$

$$m_i = \bar{m}_i - pz_i \geq 0 \tag{A}$$

$$-\bar{s}_{ik} \leq z_{ik} \leq \bar{d}_{ik} \qquad k = 1, \ldots, l$$

The vector of effective demands $\tilde{\zeta}_i(p, \bar{d}_i, \bar{s}_i)$ is constructed component by component as follows: $\tilde{\zeta}_{ih}(p, \bar{d}_i, \bar{s}_i)$ is a solution in x_{ih} of the following program (B_h):

$$\text{Maximize } U_i(x_i, m_i, \sigma_i) \qquad \text{s.t.}$$

$$x_i = \omega_i + z_i \geqslant 0$$

$$m_i = \bar{m}_i - pz_i \geqslant 0 \qquad\qquad\qquad (B_h)$$

$$-\bar{s}_{ik} \leqslant z_{ik} \leqslant \bar{d}_{ik} \qquad k \neq h$$

If the utility function U_i is strictly concave in x_i, ζ_i^* and $\tilde{\zeta}_i$ are functions. We shall now prove the following proposition, stated earlier in Chapter 2, Section 4.

Proposition.   *If U_i is concave in x_i and m_i, with strict concavity in x_i, then whatever the values of p, $\bar{d}_i$ and $\bar{s}_i$, we have*

$$\zeta_i^*(p, \bar{d}_i, \bar{s}_i) = \min\{\bar{d}_i, \max[-\bar{s}_i, \tilde{\zeta}_i(p, \bar{d}_i, \bar{s}_i)]\}$$

Proof.   Define

$$z_i^* = \min\{\bar{d}_i, \max[-\bar{s}_i, \tilde{\zeta}_i(p, \bar{d}_i, \bar{s}_i)]\}$$

We shall prove the proposition by proving the equality of z_i^* and ζ_i^* componentwise; i.e., that $z_{ih}^* = \zeta_{ih}^*$ for all h. There are three possibilities:

$(a) \quad -\bar{s}_{ih} \leqslant \tilde{\zeta}_{ih} \leqslant \bar{d}_{ih}$

This inequality implies, from the definition of z_i^*, that $z_{ih}^* = \tilde{\zeta}_{ih}$. Furthermore, in this case the constraints on market h are not binding, and the solution of programs (A) and (B_h) is the same, which implies $\zeta_{ih}^* = \tilde{\zeta}_{ih}$. The previous two equalities yield immediately

$$z_{ih}^* = \zeta_{ih}^*$$

$(b) \quad \tilde{\zeta}_{ih} > \bar{d}_{ih}$

This inequality implies, by the definition of z_i^*, that $z_{ih}^* = \bar{d}_{ih}$. Moreover, the constraint $\bar{d}_{ih}$ is binding, and because of the strict concavity of U_i, we have $\zeta_{ih}^* = \bar{d}_{ih}$. Combining these two equalities, we obtain again

$$z_{ih}^* = \zeta_{ih}^*$$

$(c) \quad \tilde{\zeta}_{ih} < -\bar{s}_{ih}$

Taking into account this inequality, the definition of z_i^* leads to $z_{ih}^* = -\bar{s}_{ih}$. Furthermore, the constraint $\bar{s}_{ih}$ is binding, and from the strict concavity of U_i we have $\zeta_{ih}^* = -\bar{s}_{ih}$. Again, we find

$$z_{ih}^* = \zeta_{ih}^*$$

The equality $z_{ih}^* = \zeta_{ih}^*$ has been shown to hold in the three possible cases: The proposition is thus proved.   Q.E.D.

Existence of a Fixprice K-Equilibrium

We shall now prove the existence of a K-equilibrium associated with a given price system p. Let us recall the definition: A K-equilibrium associated with a price system p and with rationing schemes F_i, $i = 1, \ldots, n$, is a set of vectors $\tilde{z}_i$, z_i^*, $\bar{d}_i$, and $\bar{s}_i$ such that

$$\tilde{z}_i = \tilde{\zeta}_i(p, \bar{d}_i, \bar{s}_i) \qquad i = 1, \ldots, n \tag{1}$$

$$z_i^* = F_i(\tilde{z}_i, \tilde{Z}_i) \qquad i = 1, \ldots, n \tag{2}$$

$$\bar{d}_i = G_i^d(\tilde{Z}_i) \qquad i = 1, \ldots, n \tag{3}$$

$$\bar{s}_i = G_i^s(\tilde{Z}_i) \qquad i = 1, \ldots, n$$

where the effective demand function $\tilde{\zeta}_i$ has been defined earlier and where the functions G_i^d and G_i^s are deduced component by component from the functions F_i through the following definition:

$$G_{ih}^d(\tilde{Z}_{ih}) = \max\{\tilde{z}_{ih} \,|\, F_{ih}(\tilde{z}_{ih}, \tilde{Z}_{ih}) = \tilde{z}_{ih}\}$$

$$G_{ih}^s(\tilde{Z}_{ih}) = -\min\{\tilde{z}_{ih} \,|\, F_{ih}(\tilde{z}_{ih}, \tilde{Z}_{ih}) = \tilde{z}_{ih}\}$$

We can now prove the following theorem.

Theorem A.1. *Let us make the following assumptions.*

(a) *All prices are strictly positive*:

$$p_h > 0 \qquad h = 1, \ldots, l$$

(b) *The functions $U_i(x_i, m_i, \sigma_i)$ are continuous in their arguments, concave in x_i and m_i, with strict concavity in x_i.*

(c) *The rationing schemes F_i are continuous and nonmanipulable.*

Then, a K-equilibrium corresponding to p and $\{F_i\}$, $i = 1, \ldots, n$ exists.

Proof. Consider the following mapping:

$$\{\tilde{z}_i \,|\, i = 1, \ldots, n\} \to \{\tilde{z}_i' \,|\, i = 1, \ldots, n\}$$

which associates to an initial set of effective demands $\tilde{z}_i$ a new set of $\tilde{z}_i'$ defined by

$$\tilde{z}_i' = \tilde{\zeta}_i(p, \bar{d}_i, \bar{s}_i)$$

$$\bar{d}_i = G_i^d(\tilde{Z}_i)$$

$$\bar{s}_i = G_i^s(\tilde{Z}_i)$$

This mapping is a continuous function. Indeed, $\tilde{\zeta}_i$ is continuous in its arguments and since the functions F_i are continuous, the functions G_i^d and G_i^s are also continuous by construction. Furthermore, the "new" effective demands are bounded:

$$-\omega_{ih} \leq \tilde{z}'_{ih} \leq (p\omega_i + \bar{m}_i)/p_h$$

If we limit the mapping to the bounded set defined by the above inequalities, we obtain a continuous function from a convex compact into itself. By Brouwers' theorem, this mapping has a fixed point that yields the effective demands at equilibrium. The transactions and perceived constraints are deduced through the equalities

$$z_i^* = F_i(\tilde{z}_i, \tilde{Z}_i)$$

$$\bar{d}_i = G_i^d(\tilde{Z}_i)$$

$$\bar{s}_i = G_i^s(\tilde{Z}_i)$$ Q.E.D.

Expectations and the Existence of a K-equilibrium with Rigid Prices

The existence Theorem A.1, is based on the properties of the indirect utility function $U_i(x_i, m_i, \sigma_i)$. In Section 6 of Chapter 2 we showed how such a function could be constructed from the original elements, i.e., the direct utility function $V_i(x_i, x_i^e)$ and the expectation schemes $\sigma_i^e = \psi_i(\sigma_i)$. We shall now give an existence theorem bearing directly on these basic data.

Theorem A.2.   *We assume the following.*

(a)   *Current prices are strictly positive:*

$$p_h > 0 \qquad h = 1, \ldots, l$$

(b)   *The direct utility function V_i is continuous and strictly concave in its arguments.*

(c)   *$\psi_i(\sigma_i)$ is continuous, and expected prices are strictly positive when current prices are.*

Then there exists a K-equilibrium corresponding to the price system p and to the rationing functions F_i, $i = 1, \ldots, n$.

Proof.   It is sufficient to prove that properties (b) and (c) lead to indirect utility functions $U_i(x_i, m_i, \sigma_i)$ possessing properties (b) of Theorem A.1, which can then be used directly. The concavity proof, trivial but heavy, is left to the reader. As for continuity, we recall that the function $U_i(x_i, m_i, \sigma_i)$ is defined in two steps. First, we construct a function $U_i^e(x_i, m_i, \sigma_i^e)$ by

$$U_i^e(x_i, m_i, \sigma_i^e) = \max\{V_i(x_i, x_i^e) \,|\, x_i^e \in \gamma_i^e(m_i, \sigma_i^e)\}$$

where $\gamma_i^e(m_i, \sigma_i^e)$ is the set of consumptions that are expected to be attainable in the second period and is defined by

$$x_i^e = \omega_i^e + z_i^e \geqslant 0$$

$$p^e z_i^e \leqslant m_i$$

$$-\bar{s}_i^e \leqslant z_i^e \leqslant \bar{d}_i^e$$

The vector p^e being strictly positive, the set $\gamma_i^e(m, \sigma_i^e)$ depends continuously on its arguments, and by the theorem of the maximum, the function $U_i^e(x_i, m_i, \sigma_i^e)$ is continuous in its arguments. Since the function U_i is itself defined from U_i^e by

$$U_i(x_i, m_i, \sigma_i) = U_i^e[x_i, m_i, \psi_i(\sigma_i)]$$

the continuity of U_i results from the continuity of U_i^e and ψ_i.   Q.E.D.

Existence of a K-Equilibrium with Bounded Prices

We shall now consider the problem of existence of a K-equilibrium with bounded prices. Let $\bar{p}$ and $\bar{\bar{p}}$ be the lower and upper bounds and $\tilde{z}_h$ the total excess demand on a market h:

$$\tilde{z}_h = \sum_{i=1}^{n} \tilde{z}_{ih}$$

A K-equilibrium associated with bounds $\bar{p}$ and $\bar{\bar{p}}$, and rationing schemes F_i, $i = 1, \ldots, n$, is a set of vectors $\tilde{z}_i, z_i^*, \bar{d}_i, \bar{s}_i, i = 1, \ldots, n$, and a price system p^* such that

(1) $\{\tilde{z}_i, z_i^*, \bar{d}_i, \bar{s}_i \,|\, i = 1, \ldots, n\}$ form a K-equilibrium for the price p^*;
(2) $\bar{p} \leqslant p^* \leqslant \bar{\bar{p}}$;
(3) $\tilde{z}_h < 0 \Rightarrow p_h^* = \bar{p}_h, \quad \forall\, h$;
      $\tilde{z}_h > 0 \Rightarrow p_h^* = \bar{\bar{p}}_h, \quad \forall\, h.$

As we shall now see, provided that the bounds $\bar{p}$ and $\bar{\bar{p}}$ are neither zero nor infinite, the existence conditions are fairly weak and quite similar to those for existence of a fixprice K-equilibrium.

Theorem A.3. *Let us assume the following.*

(a)   *The bounds are neither zero nor infinite:*

$$\bar{p}_h > 0 \qquad \bar{\bar{p}}_h < +\infty \qquad h = 1, \ldots, l$$

(b)   *The functions $U_i(x_i, m_i, \sigma_i)$ are continuous in their arguments, concave in x_i and m_i with strict concavity in x_i.*

(c)   *The rationing schemes F_i are continuous and nonmanipulable.*

Then there exists a K-equilibrium associated with the bounds $\bar{p}$ and $\bar{\bar{p}}$ and the rationing schemes F_i, $i = 1, \ldots, n$.

Proof.   We shall consider here a mapping from the set of prices and effective demands into itself, which associates to "initial values" of effective demands $\tilde{z}_i$ and prices p_h new values $\tilde{z}'_i$ and p'_h:

$$\{\tilde{z}_i \,|\, i = 1, \ldots, n\} \rightarrow \{\tilde{z}'_i \,|\, i = 1, \ldots, n\}$$

$$\{p_h \,|\, h = 1, \ldots, l\} \rightarrow \{p'_h \,|\, h = 1, \ldots, l\}$$

The mapping on effective demands is the same as that considered in Theorem A.1:

$$\tilde{z}'_i = \tilde{\zeta}_i[\, p, G_i^d(\tilde{Z}_i), G_i^s(\tilde{Z}_i)]$$

whereas the mapping on prices is a translation of the idea that each price p_h varies in accordance with the sign of $\tilde{z}_h$ while remaining between the bounds $\bar{p}_h$ and $\bar{\bar{p}}_h$:

$$p'_h = \min\{\bar{\bar{p}}_h, \max[\,\bar{p}_h, p_h + \lambda\tilde{z}_h]\}$$

where λ is any strictly positive real number. The mapping is a continuous function, for the same reasons as in Theorem A.1. Prices are evidently bounded by $\bar{p}$ and $\bar{\bar{p}}$. Effective demands $\tilde{z}'_{ih}$ are also bounded because

$$-\omega_{ih} \leq \tilde{z}'_{ih} \leq (\bar{\bar{p}}\omega_i + \bar{m}_i)/\bar{p}_h$$

The restriction of the mapping to prices $\bar{p} \leq p \leq \bar{\bar{p}}$ and to the set of effective demands bounded by the inequalities above is a continuous function from a convex compact into itself. It thus has a fixed point characterized by p^* and $\tilde{z}_i$. Using the second mapping on prices, it is easy to verify that

$$\bar{p} \leq p^* \leq \bar{\bar{p}}$$

$$\tilde{z}_h < 0 \Rightarrow p_h^* = \bar{p}_h$$

$$\tilde{z}_h > 0 \Rightarrow p_h^* = \bar{\bar{p}}_h \qquad\qquad \text{Q.E.D.}$$

B

Manipulation

In Chapters 1 and 2 we mainly treated the case of nonmanipulable rationing schemes, indicating that manipulable schemes would lead agents to express effective demands that are bigger than true desires of exchange and would prevent the establishment of any stable configuration of demands and transactions in the market. We shall now formalize this problem in this appendix.

The Framework of Analysis

Since the problems indicated above appear even if we do not consider multiple markets, in order to simplify the exposition, we shall study here a unique market where a particular good (the index of which will be omitted) is exchanged against money. The price p of this good is assumed to be given. On this market there are n agents indexed by $i = 1, \ldots, n$. Each of these agents has initial endowments of the good and money, which we shall denote by ω_i and $\bar{m}_i$, respectively. His preferences are represented by a strictly concave utility function $U_i(x_i, m_i)$, where x_i and m_i are the final holdings of the good and money. If z_i is the transaction realized by agent i on the market, then x_i and m_i are given by

$$x_i = \omega_i + z_i$$
$$m_i = \bar{m}_i - pz_i$$

In what follows it will be interesting to compare the effective demand to the Walrasian demand $\hat{z}_i(p)$, which is equal to the optimal transaction that agent i can realize at the price p and is thus the solution in z_i of the program

$$\text{Maximize } U_i(x_i, m_i) \qquad \text{s.t.}$$

$$x_i = \omega_i + z_i$$

$$m_i = \bar{m}_i - pz_i$$

More simply, $\hat{z}_i(p)$ corresponds to the maximum in z_i of the function $U_i(\omega_i + z_i, \bar{m}_i - pz_i)$. In what follows, since p is given, the Walrasian demand will be noted $\hat{z}_i$. In the absence of quantity signals, agent i would express this Walrasian demand. We shall now see how the existence of a manipulable rationing scheme has an effect on the level of effective demand, which we shall particularly compare with $\hat{z}_i$.[1]

Effective Demand: Principles of Determination

The Walrasian demand is determined under the assumption that the realized transaction will be equal to the demand. Since the market may not clear, we obviously cannot maintain this hypothesis of equality between transaction and demand. Each agent must, however, perceive a relation between them in order to link his actions (the demands) to their consequences (the transactions). We shall call this relation the *expected rationing scheme*, by an evident analogy with the "true" relation, i.e., the rationing scheme prevailing on the market considered. The expected rationing scheme gives us the transaction that the agent expects to realize as a function of the effective demand or supply he will express. If expectations are deterministic, which we shall assume here for simplicity, the expected rationing scheme is a function that we shall denote as

$$z_i = \rho_i(\tilde{z}_i)$$

We shall generally assume that the function ρ_i is nondecreasing and that agent i believes that voluntary exchange holds, which yields the conditions

$$\tilde{z}_i \cdot \rho_i(\tilde{z}_i) \geq 0$$

$$|\rho_i(\tilde{z}_i)| \leq |\tilde{z}_i|$$

In the case where the rationing scheme is manipulable, the expected scheme has a shape similar to that shown in Fig. B.1.

[1]Note that since we study a unique market, effective demand would be equal to $\hat{z}_i$ if the rationing scheme was nonmanipulable.

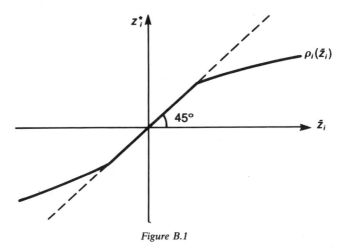

Figure B.1

For a given expected rationing scheme, the effective demand is that which maximizes the utility of the resulting transaction, and it is thus the solution in $\tilde{z}_i$ of the following program:

$$\text{Maximize } U_i(\omega_i + z_i, \bar{m}_i - pz_i) \qquad \text{s.t.}$$

$$z_i = \rho_i(\tilde{z}_i)$$

Manipulation, Overbidding, and Absence of an Equilibrium

If we apply the previous method to a manipulable rationing scheme, one observes a phenomenon of overbidding that may be explosive and thus prevent the system from reaching any kind of quantity equilibrium. Consider, indeed, an agent who expects to be rationed in the case where he would announce his optimal transaction, i.e., an agent such that

$$0 \leqslant \rho_i(\hat{z}_i) < \hat{z}_i \qquad \text{for a demander}$$

$$0 \geqslant \rho_i(\hat{z}_i) > \hat{z}_i \qquad \text{for a supplier}$$

In order to obtain his optimal transaction $\hat{z}_i$, he will be led to announce an effective demand $\tilde{z}_i$ equal to $\rho_i^{-1}(\hat{z}_i)$ and thus greater in absolute value than this desired transaction, as is shown in Fig. B.2, which represents the case of a demander. There will thus be artificially inflated demands, corresponding to an attempt at manipulating the rationing scheme. Note that this phenomenon would be limited if the expected rationing schemes were invariant in time. However, if many constrained agents modify their demands in the way we have just described, the expected rationing schemes

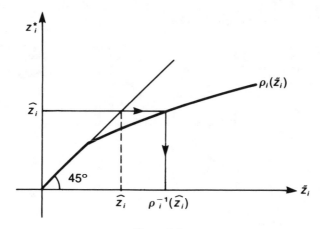

Figure B.2

will change over time in such a way that the same demand will yield lower and lower transactions. Agents will thus express higher and higher demands, hoping in this way to manipulate the rationing scheme to their advantage. Unless supplementary constraints restrict the demands, the process will be explosive and lead to no stable configuration, as the following example shows.

An Example

Consider a market functioning in a sequence of periods indexed by t under a proportional rationing scheme: This scheme is thus written (going back to the notation of Chapter 1),

$$d_i^*(t) = \tilde{d}_i(t) \times \min\left[1, \frac{\tilde{S}(t)}{\tilde{D}(t)}\right]$$

$$s_i^*(t) = \tilde{s}_i(t) \times \min\left[1, \frac{\tilde{D}(t)}{\tilde{S}(t)}\right]$$

$$\tilde{D}(t) = \sum_{i=1}^{n} \tilde{d}_i(t) \qquad \tilde{S}(t) = \sum_{i=1}^{n} \tilde{s}_i(t)$$

We assume excess Walrasian demand, i.e., that

$$\hat{D} = \sum_{i=1}^{n} \hat{d}_i > \sum_{i=1}^{n} \hat{s}_i = \hat{S}$$

In general, demanders will be rationed. Let $\mu(t)$ be the rationing coefficient,

$$\mu(t) = \frac{\tilde{S}(t)}{\tilde{D}(t)}$$

Since suppliers are not rationed, they will express in each period their Walrasian supply,

$$\tilde{s}_i(t) = \hat{s}_i \qquad \forall\, t$$

Demanders, however, being on the long side will be led to exaggerate their demands. Assume that each demander expects for period t a rationing coefficient equal to that of period $t - 1$. The expected rationing scheme in t is thus,

$$\rho_i^t(\tilde{d}_i) = \mu(t - 1) \cdot \tilde{d}_i$$

One finds the effective demand in t by equating this expected transaction to the optimal transaction $\hat{d}_i$, which yields

$$\tilde{d}_i(t) = \frac{\hat{d}_i}{\mu(t - 1)}$$

Adding these demands, one finds the new rationing coefficient in t:

$$\mu(t) = \frac{\hat{S}}{\sum \tilde{d}_i(t)} = \frac{\hat{S}}{\hat{D}}\mu(t - 1)$$

from which we immediately derive

$$\tilde{d}_i(t) = \frac{\hat{D}}{\hat{S}} \cdot \tilde{d}_i(t - 1)$$

which is a divergent process, since $\hat{D} > \hat{S}$.

C

Effective Demand under Uncertainty

We shall in this appendix study briefly the theory of effective demand under uncertainty. As we shall see, introducing elements of uncertainty also will shed light on our formulation of effective demand in the deterministic case. In order to introduce the discussion intuitively, let us start by considering the simple situation seen in Chapter 2 of the Edgeworth box described by Fig. C.1 and representing two agents A and B exchanging a single good

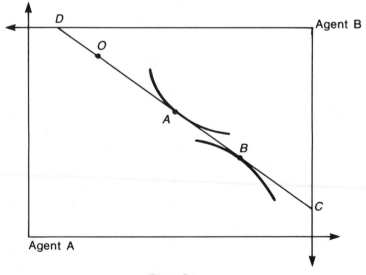

Figure C.1

(measured horizontally) against money. We described in Chapter 2 the equilibrium in this simple economy as follows: A announces an effective demand equal to OA,[1] B an effective supply OB, and the equilibrium transaction is the minimum of the two, i.e., OA. In the deterministic equilibrium considered there, each agent is assumed to know exactly the quantity constraint he faces; i.e., A knows that he is facing the supply OB, and B knows that he is facing the demand OA. We noted that in such a case, our definition of effective demand and supply was, at least for constrained agents, a particular selection among the set of possible signals. Consider indeed agent B who is subject to the binding constraint: For him, announcing any supply between OA and OC would yield the optimal transaction OA. Moreover, all of these except OA "reveal" that he is constrained. So the question may be, why, besides its simplicity of construction, choose OB as the expressed effective supply?

To understand this, let us no longer consider an equilibrium situation. Instead, assume that we are in a (more realistic) decentralized trading process functioning in real time, where each agent announces his demand or supply before knowing what those of the other agents will be. In particular, B does not know before trading what the demand of trader A will be. In such a case, the *only* supply that yields the best transaction against any possible demand of agent A is OB, i.e., the level of supply given by our definition. In this case, uncertainty about trading possibilities leads agent B to unambiguously choose OB as his optimal strategy. We shall now formalize this heuristic argument.

General Principles

Let us now turn to the general problem of determining effective demands and supplies in the case where the outcome of a particular decision is not deterministic but stochastic. The general method is the same as that seen in Chapter 2 or in Appendix B: Effective demands and supplies are signals that an agent sends to the market in order to obtain the best possible transactions. Since we are in a stochastic framework, the agent will attempt to maximize the *expected* utility of his transactions.[2] Of course, in order to be able to take a decision, each agent must link his actions (the effective demands and supplies) to their consequences (the resulting transactions). For this, each agent has in mind an expected rationing scheme, a concept

---

[1]Again, to simplify the exposition, we measure demands, supplies, etc., along the budget line OC.

[2]The signals sent must also be such that the resulting transactions are feasible with probability 1.

that we have already seen in Appendix B for the deterministic case. In the stochastic framework considered here, the expected rationing scheme is not a function: Rather, it associates to every demand and supply a probability distribution of the resulting transactions. If voluntary exchange is assumed to hold, then these probability distributions should be such that with a probability of 1, purchases are less than or equal to demands and sales less than or equal to supplies.

We saw in Appendix B that manipulability of rationing schemes leads to overbidding and totally unreliable effective demands and supplies, an unfortunate feature that applies to stochastic schemes as well. We shall thus essentially study stochastic nonmanipulable rationing schemes. Such a scheme has the following general form for an agent i in a market h,

$$d_{ih}^* = \min(\tilde{d}_{ih}, \bar{d}_{ih})$$

$$s_{ih}^* = \min(\tilde{s}_{ih}, \bar{s}_{ih})$$

or in algebraic notation,

$$z_{ih}^* = \begin{cases} \min(\tilde{z}_{ih}, \bar{d}_{ih}) & \tilde{z}_{ih} \geq 0 \\ \max(\tilde{z}_{ih}, -\bar{s}_{ih}) & \tilde{z}_{ih} \leq 0 \end{cases}$$

where $\bar{d}_{ih}$ and $\bar{s}_{ih}$ are random variables whose probability distributions are *independent* of $\tilde{z}_{ih}$. We shall now indicate a few examples of effective demand determination in such a case.

One Market

We shall study here the market for the exchange of a single good (whose index h is omitted) against money. Consider, as in Appendix B, an agent i with endowments of this good and money respectively equal to ω_i and $\bar{m}_i$ and with a utility function $U_i(x_i, m_i)$, where

$$x_i = \omega_i + z_i \qquad m_i = \bar{m}_i - pz_i$$

Let $\hat{z}_i$ be his Walrasian demand. Recall that $\hat{z}_i$ is the solution of the program

$$\text{Maximize } U_i(\omega_i + z_i, \bar{m}_i - pz_i) \qquad \text{s.t.}$$

$$\omega_i + z_i \geq 0$$

$$\bar{m}_i - pz_i \geq 0$$

To simplify the exposition, we assume that the Walrasian demand of agent i is positive, i.e., that $\hat{z}_i > 0$. The relevant part of the expected rationing scheme is that which concerns the expected constraint on demand $\bar{d}_i$, and we shall assume that it is distributed according to a cumulative probability distribution $\psi_i(\bar{d}_i)$. For an effective demand $\tilde{z}_i$, the resulting transaction is $\min(\tilde{z}_i, \bar{d}_i)$. Then, the optimal effective demand is that which maximizes the expected utility of the transaction, i.e., the solution in $\tilde{z}_i$ of

$$\text{Maximize} \int_0^\infty U_i[\omega_i + \min(\tilde{z}_i, \bar{d}_i), \bar{m}_i - p \min(\tilde{z}_i, \bar{d}_i)] \, d\psi_i(\bar{d}_i)$$

subject to the condition that the final endowments, respectively,

$$\omega_i + \min(\tilde{z}_i, \bar{d}_i) \quad \text{and} \quad \bar{m}_i - p \min(\tilde{z}_i, \bar{d}_i)$$

are positive with probability 1. Very simple calculations show that if $\psi_i(\hat{z}_i) < 1$, i.e., if there is some chance of being unconstrained, then $\hat{z}_i$ is the only solution to the previous maximization problem. We thus find rigorously the result that we arrived at heuristically in the Edgeworth box example given earlier.

Many Markets

We shall now consider several markets $h = 1, \ldots, l$. We continue to assume a nonmanipulable rationing scheme on each market,

$$z_{ih}^* = \begin{cases} \min(\tilde{z}_{ih}, \bar{d}_{ih}) & z_{ih} \geqslant 0 \\ \max(\tilde{z}_{ih}, -\bar{s}_{ih}) & z_{ih} \leqslant 0 \end{cases}$$

and we assume that the expected constraints are independently distributed across markets, i.e., that for each market we have a specific probability distribution denoted by $\psi_{ih}(\bar{d}_{ih}, \bar{s}_{ih})$.

When expected constraints are stochastic, the timing of trading becomes quite important, and we shall make the realistic assumption that markets are visited sequentially rather than many simultaneously (an argument for this is given later). Then, the determination of successive effective demands and supplies is found by applying the method of stochastic dynamic programming. Instead of giving the details of such maximization, we shall present a result that is a natural extension of what we saw for a single market.[3] Indeed, it is possible to show that the optimal demand in a particular market h depends on transactions realized in previous markets, as well as on the probability distributions of expected constraints in future markets, but *not* on the probability distribution of expected constraints for

[3]See Futia (1975) and Benassy (1977b, 1982b) for more complete developments.

the *current* market. This is a natural stochastic analog of our definition of effective demand in the deterministic case (Chapters 1 and 2) where the perceived constraints in the market itself were ignored when computing the effective demand. As a consequence, whenever an agent is constrained on a market, this is revealed by an effective demand (or supply) greater than his transaction.

We may now return briefly to our assumption of sequential trading. This is what is actually observed in reality, but we can also give a heuristic argument indicating that it is preferable for the agents to trade sequentially, in order to take advantage of the sequential acquisition of information.

Indeed, consider a worker offering his labor (assumed indivisible to simplify the exposition) to a large number of potential employers, each with a small but positive probability of giving him employment. If he had to make simultaneous labor-supply propositions, he would have to offer his labor to only one employer so as to make sure that his labor transactions are feasible with probability 1. If, on the contrary, he acts sequentially, he will successively offer his labor to all potential employers, in the order of his own preferences, until he finds one willing to employ him. He will therefore greatly increase his chances of being employed.

This last example also clearly shows that although effective demands and supplies have the nice property of revealing when an agent is constrained, they should not be used without caution if one wants to measure some kind of market imbalance. Indeed, in that example a single unemployed worker offers his labor supply to many different potential employers, so a statistician aggregating all these labor-supply signals might overstate the number of workers actually looking for work.

D

The Effects of a Devaluation

We gave in Chapter 8 several examples of determining the effects of a devaluation, mainly to show the assumptions that lead to the most traditional results in the literature. We shall present here a complete set of calculations for the general case. Let us again set down the equations of the model. First, we have the equation giving the balance of payments surplus in terms of country 2's currency:

$$B = \frac{p_1}{e} I_2(y_2, p_2, p_1/e) - p_2 I_1(y_1, p_1, ep_2)$$

The income–price variables y_1, y_2, p_1, and p_2 are themselves determined by a system of four equations. The first two are the same in all regimes:

$$X_1(y_1, p_1, ep_2, g_1) = I_2(y_2, p_2, p_1/e)$$

$$X_2(y_2, p_2, p_1/e, g_2) = I_1(y_1, p_1, ep_2)$$

The other two equations, however, depend on the regime each country is in. So, for country 1 this equation is

$$p_1 = \bar{p}_1 \qquad \text{regime A}$$

$$y_1 = F_1[F_1'^{-1}(w_1/p_1)] \qquad \text{regime B}$$

$$y_1 = y_{01} \qquad \text{regime C}$$

and symmetrically for country 2. In order to obtain the effects of a devaluation, we only have to differentiate logarithmically these five equations. First, the definitional equation

$$\frac{dB}{V} = -(1 + i_{1q} + i_{2q})\frac{de}{e} + (1 + i_{2q} - i_{1p})\frac{dp_1}{p_1}$$

$$+ (i_{2p} - i_{1q} - 1)\frac{dp_2}{p_2} + i_{2y}\frac{dy_2}{y_2} - i_{1y}\frac{dy_1}{y_1}$$

where V is, let us recall, the value in terms of country 2's currency of imports and exports, assumed to balance in the initial state. The relative variations of y_1, y_2, p_1, and p_2 brought about by the devaluation can be computed by differentiating logarithmically the four other equations. The first two immediately yield

$$x_{1y}\frac{dy_1}{y_1} - i_{2y}\frac{dy_2}{y_2} + (x_{1p} - i_{2q})\frac{dp_1}{p_1} + (x_{1q} - i_{2p})\frac{dp_2}{p_2} = -(i_{2q} + x_{1q})\frac{de}{e}$$

$$x_{2y}\frac{dy_2}{y_2} - i_{1y}\frac{dy_1}{y_1} + (x_{2p} - i_{1q})\frac{dp_2}{p_2} + (x_{2q} - i_{1p})\frac{dp_1}{p_1} = (i_{1q} + x_{2q})\frac{de}{e}$$

The following two can be expressed in the following log-differential form:

$$\frac{dy_1}{y_1} = \sigma_1 \frac{dp_1}{p_1}$$

$$\frac{dy_2}{y_2} = \sigma_2 \frac{dp_2}{p_2}$$

where σ_1 is infinite if country 1 is in regime A, equal to zero if it is in regime C, and equal to the partial elasticity of the function $F_1[F_1'^{-1}(w_1/p_1)]$ with respect to p_1 if it is in regime B; σ_2 is determined symmetrically for country 2. We can compute the relative variations of y_1, y_2, p_1, p_2 by rewriting the last four equations in matrix form:

$$\begin{bmatrix} x_{1y} & -i_{2y} & x_{1p} - i_{2q} & x_{1q} - i_{2p} \\ -i_{1y} & x_{2y} & x_{2q} - i_{1p} & x_{2p} - i_{1q} \\ 1 & 0 & -\sigma_1 & 0 \\ 0 & 1 & 0 & -\sigma_2 \end{bmatrix} \begin{bmatrix} dy_1/y_1 \\ dy_2/y_2 \\ dp_1/p_1 \\ dp_2/p_2 \end{bmatrix} = \begin{bmatrix} -(i_{2q} + x_{1q})\,de/e \\ (i_{1q} + x_{2q})\,de/e \\ 0 \\ 0 \end{bmatrix}$$

By matrix inversion, we find these variations, which can be reinserted into the balance-of-payments equation in order to obtain the effect of a devaluation. One sees that the final result depends on eight price elasticities, four income elasticities, plus the two parameters σ_1 and σ_2, which depend on the regime each economy is in.

Bibliography

Alexander, S. (1952). Effects of a devaluation on a trade balance. *IMF Staff Papers* **2**, 263-278.

Alexander, S. (1959). The effects of devaluation: A simplified synthesis of elasticities and absorption approaches. *American Economic Review* **49**, 21-42.

Amemiya, T. (1974). A Note on a Fair and Jaffee Model. *Econometrica* **42**, 759-762.

Arrow, K. J. (1953). Le rôle des valeurs boursières pour la répartition la meilleure des risques. In *Econométrie*. CNRS, Paris.

Arrow, K. J. (1959). Towards a theory of price adjustment. In M. Abramowitz (Ed.), *The Allocation of Economic Resources*. Stanford Univ. Press, Stanford, California.

Arrow, K. J. (1964). The role of securities in the optimal allocation of risk bearing. *Review of Economic Studies* **31**, 91-96.

Arrow, K. J., and Debreu, G. (1954). Existence of an equilibrium for a competitive economy. *Econometrica* **22**, 265-290.

Arrow, K. J., and Hahn, F. H. (1971). *General Competitive Analysis.* Holden-Day, San Francisco, California.

Arrow, K. J., Karlin, S., and Scarf, H. (1958). *Studies in the Mathematical Theory of Inventory and Production.* Stanford Univ. Press, Stanford, California.

Artus, P. (1984a). Le fonctionnement du marché du crédit: diverses approches dans un cadre de déséquilibre. *Revue Économique* **35**, 591-621.

Artus, P. (1984b). Analyse du marché des biens dans les secteurs industriels. *Annales de l'INSEE* **55/56**, 77-106.

Artus, P., and Muet, P. A. (1984). Un panorama des développements récents de l'économétrie de l'investissement. *Revue Économique* **35**, 791-830.

Artus, P., Laroque, G., and Michel, G. (1984). Estimation of a quarterly macrocomomic model with quantity rationing, *Econometrica* **52**, 1387-1414.

Ashenfelter, O. (1980). Unemployment as disequilibrium in a model of aggregate labor supply. *Econometrica* **48**, 547-564.

Autume, A. d' (1985). *Monnaie, Croissance et Déséquilibre*. Economica, Paris.

Azam, J.-P. (1982). L'impact macroéconomique de la politique commerciale en déséquilibre: le rôle des importations de biens intermédiaires. *Revue Économique* **33**, 1089-1114.

Azam, J. P. (1983). Money, growth and disequilibrium. *Economica* **50**, 325-335.

Balasko, Y. (1979). Budget-constrained pareto-efficient allocations. *Journal of Economic Theory* **21**, 359-379.

Barro, R. J., and Grossman, H. I. (1971). A general disequilibrium model of income and employment. *American Economic Review* 61, 82-93.

Barro, R. J., and Grossman, H. I. (1974). Suppressed inflation and the supply multiplier. *Review of Economic Studies* 41, 87-104.

Barro, R. J., and Grossman, H. I. (1976). *Money, Employment and Inflation.* Cambridge Univ. Press, London and New York.

Bellman, R. (1957). *Dynamic Programming.* Princeton Univ. Press, Princeton, New Jersey.

Benassy, J. P. (1973). Disequilibrium theory. Ph.D. Thesis and Working Paper, Univ. of California, Berkeley. Hungarian translation in *Szygma* (1974).

Benassy, J. P. (1975a). Neo-Keynesian disequilibrium theory in a monetary economy. *Review of Economic Studies* 42, 503-523.

Benassy, J. P. (1975b). Disequilibrium exchange in barter and monetary economies. *Economic Inquiry* 13, 131-156.

Benassy, J. P. (1976a). Théorie néokeynésienne du déséquilibre dans une économie monétaire. *Cahiers du Séminaire d'Econométrie* 17, 81-113.

Benassy, J. P. (1976b). The disequilibrium approach to monopolistic price setting and general monopolistic equilibrium. *Review of Economic Studies* 43, 69-81.

Benassy, J. P. (1976c). Théorie du déséquilibre et fondements microéconomiques de la macroéconomie. *Revue Économique* 27, 755-804.

Benassy, J. P. (1976d). Regulation of the wage profits conflict and the unemployment inflation dilemma in a dynamic disequilibrium model. *Économie Appliquée* 29, 409-444.

Benassy, J. P. (1977a). A neokeynesian model of price and quantity determination in disequilibrium. In G. Schwödiauer (Ed.), *Equilibrium and Disequilibrium in Economic Theory.* Reidel Publ., Boston, Massachusetts.

Benassy, J. P. (1977b). On quantity signals and the foundations of effective demand theory. *Scandinavian Journal of Economics* 79, 147-168.

Benassy, J. P. (1978). Cost and demand inflation revisited: A neokeynesian approach. *Économie Appliquée* 31, 113-133.

Benassy, J. P. (1982a). Developments in non-Walrasian economics and the microeconomic foundations of macroeconomics. In W. Hildenbrand (Ed.), *Advances in Economic Theory.* Cambridge Univ. Press, London and New York.

Benassy, J. P. (1982b). *The Economics of Market Disequilibrium.* Academic Press, New York.

Benassy, J. P. (1983). The three regimes of the IS-LM model: A non-Walrasian analysis. *European Economic Review* 23, 1-17.

Benassy, J. P. (1984a). A non-Walrasian model of the business cycle. *Journal of Economic Behavior and Organization* 5, 77-89.

Benassy, J. P. (1984b). *Macroéconomie et théorie du déséquilibre.* Dunod, Paris.

Benassy, J. P. (1984c). Tariffs and pareto optimality in international trade: The case of unemployment. *European Economic Review* 26, 261-276.

Benassy, J. P. (1985). A non-Walrasian model of employment with partial price flexibility and indexation. In G. Feiwel (Ed.), *Trends in Contemporary Macroeconomics and Distribution.* Macmillan, London.

Berthelemy, J. C. (1980). La théorie des transferts, une approche en termes de déséquilibres. *Revue Économique* 32, 31-62.

Berthelemy, J. C., and Gagey, F. (1984). Elasticité-prix de l'offre agricole dans les pays en développement: une note sur la rationalité des agriculteurs dans un contexte non-Walrasien. *Annales de l'INSEE* 55/56, 203-220.

Bickerdike, C. (1920). The instability of foreign exchange. *Economic Journal* 30, 118-122.

Blad, M. C. (1981). Exchange of stability in a disequilibrium model. *Journal of Mathematical Economics* 8, 121-145.

Blad, M. C., and Zeeman, C. (1982). Oscillations between repressed inflation and Keynesian equilibria due to inertia in decision making. *Journal of Economic Theory* 28, 165-182.

Blanchard, O., and Sachs, J. (1982). Anticipations, recessions and policy: An intertemporal disequilibrium model. *Annales de l'INSEE* 47/48, 117-144.

Blinder, S. A. (1981). Inventories and the structure of macro models. *American Economic Review, Papers and Proceedings* 71, 11-16.

Böhm, V. (1978). Disequilibrium dynamics in a simple macroeconomic model. *Journal of Economic Theory* 17, 179-199.

Böhm, V., and Levine, P. (1979). Temporary equilibria with quantity rationing. *Review of Economic Studies* 46, 361-377.

Bourguignon, F., and Leibovich, J. (1984). Offre et demande dans le processus de développement: un modèle agrégé de déséquilibre appliqué à la Colombie. *Annales de l'INSEE* 55/56, 223-243.

Bowden, R. J. (1978a). *The Econometrics of Disequilibrium.* North-Holland Publ., Amsterdam.

Bowden, R. J. (1978b). Specification, estimation and inference for models of markets in disequilibrium. *International Economic Review* 19, 711-726.

Branson, W. H. (1979). *Macroeconomic Theory and Policy,* 2nd ed. Harper, New York.

Branson, W. H., and Rotemberg, J. J. (1980). International adjustment with wage rigidity. *European Economic Review* 13, 309-332.

Bronfenbrenner, M., and Holzman, F. D. (1963). A survey of inflation theory. *American Economic Review* 53, 593-661.

Bruno, M. (1982). Macroeconomic adjustment under wage-price rigidity. In J. N. Bhagwati (Ed.), *Import Competition and Response.* Univ. of Chicago Press, Chicago, Illinois.

Bushaw, D. W., and Clower, R. (1957). *Introduction to Mathematical Economics.* Richard D. Irwin, Homewood, Illinois.

Catinat, M. (1984). Fondement microéconomique par le déséquilibre des équations d'importation et d'exportation. *Annales de l'INSEE* 55/56, 153-180.

Chamberlin, E. H. (1933). *The Theory of Monopolistic Competition.* Harvard Univ. Press, Cambridge, Massachusetts.

Chang, W. W., and Smyth, D. J. (1971). The existence and persistence of cycles in a nonlinear model: Kaldor's 1940 model reexamined. *Review of Economic Studies* 38, 37-44.

Charemza, W., and Quandt, R. E. (1982). Models and estimation of disequilibrium for centrally planned economies. *Review of Economic Studies* 49, 109-116.

Clower, R. W. (1960). Keynes and the classics: A dynamical perspective. *Quarterly Journal of Economics* 74, 318-323.

Clower, R. W. (1965). The Keynesian counterrevolution: A theoretical apraisal. In F. H. Hahn and F. P. R. Brechling (Eds.), *The Theory of Interest Rates.* Macmillan, London.

Clower, R. W. (1967). A reconsideration of the microfoundations of monetary theory. *Western Economic Journal* 6, 1-9.

Coddington, E. A., and Levinson, N. (1955). *Theory of Ordinary Differential Equations.* McGraw-Hill, New York.

Cuddington, J. T. (1980). Fiscal and exchange rate policies in a fix-price trade model with export rationing. *Journal of International Economics* 10, 319-340.

Cuddington, J. T. (1981). Import substitution policies: A two-sector, fix-price model. *Review of Economic Studies* 48, 327-342.

Cuddington, J. T., Johansson, P. O., and Löfgren, K. G. (1984). *Disequilibrium Macroeconomics in Open Economies.* Blackwell, Oxford.

Dana, R. A., and Malgrange, P. (1983). Propriétés dynamiques d'une version discrète d'un modèle de croissance cyclique. *Cahiers du Séminaire d'Econométrie* 25, 109-137.

Dana, R. A., and Malgrange, P. (1984). The dynamics of a discrete version of a growth cycle model. In J. P. Ancot (Ed.), *Analysing the Structure of Econometric Models.* Nijhoff, The Hague.

Danthine, J. P., and Peytrignet, M. (1981). Intégration de l'analyse graphique IS-LM avec la théorie des équilibres à prix fixes: une note pédagogique. In G. Bramoullé and J. P. Giran (Eds.), *Eléments d'analyse du déséquilibre.* Economica, Paris.

Debreu, G. (1952). A social equilibrium existence theorem. *Proceedings of the National Academy of Sciences of the U.S.A.* **38**, 886–893.

Debreu, G. (1956). Market equilibrium. *Proceedings of the National Academy of Sciences of the U.S.A.* **42**, 876–878.

Debreu, G. (1959). *Theory of Value.* Wiley, New York.

Debreu, G. (1982). Existence of competitive equilibrium. In K. J. Arrow and M. D. Intriligator (Eds.), *Handbook of Mathematical Economics.* North-Holland Publ., Amsterdam.

Dehez, P. (1982). Stationary Keynesian equilibria. *European Economic Review* **19**, 245–258.

Dehez, P., and Dreze, J. H. (1984). On supply constrained equilibria. *Journal of Economic Theory* **33**, 172–182.

Dehez, P., and Fitoussi, J. P. (1984). Equilibres de stagflation et indexation des salaires. Working Paper, O.F.C.E., Paris.

Dixit, A. (1976). Public finance in a Keynesian temporary equilibrium. *Journal of Economic Theory* **12**, 242–258.

Dixit, A. (1978). The balance of trade in a model of temporary equilibrium with rationing. *Review of Economic Studies* **45**, 393–404.

Dixit, A., and Norman, V. (1980). *Theory of International Trade.* Cambridge Univ. Press, London and New York.

Dreze, J. H. (1975). Existence of an exchange equilibrium under price rigidities. *International Economic Review* **16**, 301–320.

Dreze, J. H., and Muller, H. (1980). Optimality properties of rationing schemes. *Journal of Economic Theory* **23**, 131–149.

Ducos, G., Green, J., and Laffont, J.-J. (1982). A test of the equilibrium hypothesis based on inventories. *European Economic Review* **18**, 209–219.

Eaton, J., and Quandt, R. E. (1983). A model of rationing and labor supply: Theory and estimation. *Economica* **50**, 221–234.

Fair, R. C. (1972). Disequilibrium in housing models. *Journal of Finance* **27**, 207–221.

Fair, R. C., and Jaffee, D. M. (1972). Methods of estimation for markets in disequilibrium. *Econometrica* **40**, 497–514.

Fair, R. C., and Kelejian, H. H. (1974). Methods of estimation for markets in disequilibrium, a further study. *Econometrica* **42**, 177–190.

Fisher, F. M. (1978). Quantity constraints, spillovers, and the Hahn process. *Review of Economic Studies* **45**, 19–31.

Fisher, F. M. (1983). *Disequilibrium Foundations of Equilibrium Economics.* Cambridge Univ. Press, London and New York.

Fitoussi, J. P., Ed. (1983). *Modern Macroeconomic Theory.* Blackwell, Oxford.

Fourgeaud, C., Lenclud, B., and Michel, P. (1981). A two-sector model with quantity rationing. *Journal of Economic Theory* **24**, 413–436.

Frenkel, J. A., and Johnson, H. G., Eds. (1976). *The Monetary Approach to the Balance of Payments.* Allen & Unwin, London.

Friedman, M. (1968). The role of monetary policy. *American Economic Review* **58**, 1–17.

Futia, C. (1975). A theory of effective demand. Working Paper, Bell Labs., Murray Hill, New Jersey.

Futia, C. (1977). Excess supply equilibria. *Journal of Economic Theory* **14**, 200–220.

Gelpi, R. M., and Younes, Y. (1977). Monnaie et crédit dans une optique d'équilibre non-Walrasien. In *Modèles monétaires de l'économie française*. Documentation Française, Paris.

Gersovitz, M. (1980). On classification probabilities for the disequilibrium model. *Journal of Econometrics* **14**, 239-246.

Ginsburgh, V., Tishler, A., and Zang, I. (1980). Alternative estimation methods for two-regime models. *European Economic Review* **13**, 207-228.

Glustoff, E. (1968). On the existence of a Keynesian equilibrium. *Review of Economic Studies* **35**, 327-334.

Goldfeld, S. M., and Quandt, R. E. (1975). Estimation in a disequilibrium model and the value of information. *Journal of Econometrics* **3**, 325-348.

Goldfeld, S. M., and Quandt, R. E. (1979). Estimation in multimarket disequilibrium models. *Economics Letters* **4**, 341-347.

Goldfeld, S. M., and Quandt, R. E. (1981). Single market disequilibrium models: Estimation and testing. *The Economic Studies Quarterly* **32**, 12-28.

Goldfeld, S. M., Jaffee, D. M., and Quandt, R. E. (1980). A model of FHLBB advances: Rationing or market clearing? *Review of Economics and Statistics* **62**, 339-347.

Goodwin, R. M. (1951). The non-linear accelerator and the persistence of business cycles. *Econometrica* **19**, 1-17.

Gordon, R. A. (1976). Recent developments in the theory of inflation and unemployment. *Journal of Monetary Economics* **2**, 185-219.

Gourieroux, C. (1984). *Econométrie des Variables Qualitatives*. Economica, Paris.

Gourieroux, C., and Monfort, A. (1983). Méthodes d'estimation pour les modèles avec prix planchers. *Annales de l'INSEE* **50**, 49-70.

Gourieroux, C., Laffont, J.-J., and Monfort, A. (1980a). Disequilibrium econometrics in simultaneous equation systems. *Econometrica* **48**, 75-96.

Gourieroux, C., Laffont, J.-J., and Monfort, A. (1980b). Tests of the equilibrium vs. disequilibrium hypotheses: A comment. *International Economic Review* **21**, 245-247.

Gourieroux, C., Laffont, J.-J., and Monfort, A. (1980c). Coherency conditions in simultaneous linear equation models with endogenous switching regimes. *Econometrica* **48**, 675-696.

Gourieroux, C., Laffont, J.-J., and Monfort, A. (1984). Econométrie des modèles d'équilibre avec rationnement: une mise à jour. *Annales de l'INSEE* **55/56**, 5-37.

Grandmont, J. M. (1974). On the short run equilibrium in a monetary economy. In J. Drèze (Ed.), *Allocation Under Uncertainty, Equilibrium and Optimality*. Macmillan, London.

Grandmont, J. M. (1982). Temporary general equilibrium theory. In K. J. Arrow and M. D. Intriligator (Eds.), *Handbook of Mathematical Economics*. North-Holland Publ., Amsterdam.

Grandmont, J. M., and Laroque, G. (1976). On Keynesian temporary equilibria. *Review of Economic Studies* **43**, 53-67.

Grandmont, J. M., Laroque, G., and Younes, Y. (1978). Equilibrium with quantity rationing and recontracting. *Journal of Economic Theory* **19**, 84-102.

Green, J., and Laffont, J.-J. (1981). Disequilibrium dynamics with inventories and anticipatory price-setting. *European Economic Review* **16**, 199-221.

Grossman, H. I. (1971). Money, interest and prices in market disequilibrium. *Journal of Political Economy* **79**, 943-961.

Grossman, H. I. (1972). A choice-theoretic model of an income investment accelerator. *American Economic Review* **62**, 630-641.

Hahn, F. H. (1959). The balance of payments in a monetary economy. *Review of Economic Studies* **26**, 110-125.

Hahn, F. H. (1977). Exercises in conjectural equilibria. *Scandinavian Journal of Economics* **79**, 210-226.

Hahn, F. H. (1978). On non-Walrasian equilibria. *Review of Economic Studies* **45**, 1-17.

Hahn, F. H., and Negishi, T. (1962). A theorem on non-tatonnement stability. *Econometrica* **30**, 463-469.

Hansen, B. (1951). *A Study in the Theory of Inflation*. Allen & Unwin, London.

Hansen, B. (1970). *A Survey of General Equilibrium Systems*. McGraw-Hill, New York.

Harberger, A. C. (1950). Currency depreciation, income and the balance of trade. *Journal of Political Economy* **58**, 47-60.

Hart, O. (1982). A model of imperfect competition with Keynesian features. *Quarterly Journal of Economics* **97**, 109-138.

Hartley, M. J. (1976). The estimation of markets in disequilibrium: The fixed supply case. *International Economic Review* **17**, 687-700.

Hartley, M. J., and Mallela, P. (1977). The asymptotic properties of a maximum likelihood estimator for a model of markets in disequilibrium. *Econometrica* **45**, 1205-1220.

Heller, W. P., and Starr, R. M. (1979). Unemployment equilibrium with myopic complete information. *Review of Economic Studies* **46**, 339-359.

Henin, P. Y. (1981). Equilibres avec rationnement dans un modèle macroéconomique avec décision d'investissement endogène. *Économie Appliquée* **34**, 697-728.

Henin, P. Y. (1983). L'impact macroéconomique d'un choc pétrolier. *Revue Économique* **34**, 865-896.

Henin, P. Y., and Michel, P., Eds. (1982). *Croissance et accumulation en déséquilibre*. Economica, Paris.

Hey, J. D. (1981). *Economics in Disequilibrium*. Martin Robertson, Oxford.

Hicks, J. R. (1937). Mr. Keynes and the classics: A suggested interpretation. *Econometrica* **5**, 147-159.

Hicks, J. R. (1939). *Value and Capital*. Clarendon Press, Oxford. (2nd ed., 1946.)

Hicks, J. R. (1950). *A Contribution to the Theory of the Trade Cycle*. Oxford Univ. Press, Oxford.

Hicks, J. R. (1965). *Capital and Growth*. Oxford Univ. Press, London and New York.

Hildenbrand, K., and Hildenbrand, W. (1978). On Keynesian equilibria with unemployment and quantity rationing. *Journal of Economic Theory* **18**, 255-277.

Hirsch, M. W., and Smale, S. (1974). *Differential Equations, Dynamical Systems and Linear Algebra*. Academic Press, New York.

Honkapohja, S. (1979). On the dynamics of disequilibria in a macro model with flexible wages and prices. In M. Aoki and A. Marzollo (Eds.), *New Trends in Dynamic System Theory and Economics*. Academic Press, New York.

Honkapohja, S., and Ito, T. (1980). Inventory dynamics in a simple disequilibrium macroeconomic model. *Scandinavian Journal of Economics* **82**, 184-198.

Hool, B. (1980). Monetary and fiscal policies in short-run equilibria with rationing. *International Economic Review* **21**, 301-316.

Howard, D. H. (1976). The disequilibrium model in a controlled economy: An empirical test of the Barro-Grossman model. *American Economic Review* **66**, 871-879.

Howard, D. H. (1977). Rationing, quantity constraints and consumption theory. *Econometrica* **45**, 399-412.

Howard, D. H. (1979). *The Disequilibrium Model in a Controlled Economy*. Lexington Books, Heath, New York.

Howitt, P. W. (1974). Stability and the quantity theory. *Journal of Political Economy* **82**, 133-151.

Ito, T. (1980a). Disequilibrium growth theory. *Journal of Economic Theory* **23**, 380-409.

Ito, T. (1980b). Methods of estimation for multi-market disequilibrium models. *Econometrica* **48**, 97-126.

Ito, T., and Ueda, K. (1981). Tests of the equilibrium hypothesis in disequilibrium econometrics: An international comparison of credit rationing. *International Economic Review* **22**, 691-708.

Iwai, K. (1974). The firm in uncertain markets and its price, wage and employment adjustments. *Review of Economic Studies* **41**, 257–276.

Ize, A. (1984). Disequilibrium theories, imperfect competition and income distribution: A fixprice analysis. *Oxford Economic Papers* **36**, 248–258.

Jaffee, D., and Modigliani, F. (1969). A theory and test of credit rationing. *American Economic Review* **59**, 850–872.

Johansson, P.-O. (1981). On regional effects of government policies in a small open economy. *Scandinavian Journal of Economics* **83**, 541–552.

Johansson, P.-O. (1982). Cost-benefit rules in general disequilibrium. *Journal of Public Economics* **18**, 121–137.

Johansson, P. O., and Löfgren, K. G. (1980). The effects of tariffs and real wages on employment in a Barro–Grossman model of an open economy. *Scandinavian Journal of Economics* **82**, 167–183.

Kaldor, N. (1940). A model of the trade cycle. *Economic Journal* **50**, 78–92.

Kalecki, M. (1935). A macrodynamic theory of business cycles. *Econometrica* **3**, 192–226.

Kawasaki, S., McMillan, J., and Zimmerman, K. F. (1982). Disequilibrium dynamics: An empirical study. *American Economic Review* **72**, 992–1004.

Kennally, G. F. (1983). Some consequences of opening a neo-Keynesian model. *Economic Journal* **93**, 390–410.

Keynes, J. M. (1936). *The General Theory of Money, Interest and Employment.* Harcourt, New York.

Keynes, J. M. (1937). Alternative theories of the rate of interest. *Economic Journal* **47**, 241–252.

Kiefer, N. M. (1980). A note on regime classification in disequilibrium models. *Review of Economic Studies* **47**, 637–639.

Kooiman, P., and Kloek, T. (1980). An aggregate two-market disequilibrium model with foreign trade. Working Paper, Erasmus Univ., Rotterdam.

Kooiman, P., and Kloek, T. (1982). An empirical two market disequilibrium model for Dutch manufacturing. Working Paper, Erasmus Univ., Rotterdam.

Kornai, J. (1971). *Anti-Equilibrium.* North-Holland Publ., Amsterdam.

Kornai, J. (1979). Resource-constrained versus demand-constrained systems. *Econometrica* **47**, 801–820.

Kornai, J. (1980). *Economics of Shortage*, North-Holland Publ., Amsterdam.

Kornai, J. (1982). *Growth, Shortage and Efficiency.* Blackwell, Oxford.

Kornai, J., and Weibull, J. W. (1978). The normal state of the market in a shortage economy: A queue model. *Scandinavian Journal of Economics* **80**, 375–398.

Kurz, M. (1982). Unemployment equilibrium in an economy with linked prices. *Journal of Economic Theory* **26**, 100–123.

Laffont, J.-J., and Garcia, R. (1977). Disequilibrium econometrics for business loans. *Econometrica* **45**, 1187–1204.

Laffont, J.-J., and Monfort, A. (1979). Disequilibrium econometrics in dynamic models. *Journal of Econometrics* **11**, 353–361.

Lambert, J. P., Lubrano, M., and Sneessens, H. R. (1984). Emploi et chômage en France de 1955 à 1982: un modèle macroéconomique annuel avec rationnement. *Annales de l'INSEE* **55/56**, 39–75.

Laroque, G. (1978). On the dynamics of disequilibrium: A simple remark. *Review of Economic Studies* **45**, 273–278.

Laroque, G. (1981). On the local uniqueness of the fixed price equilibria. *Review of Economic Studies* **48**, 113–129.

Laussel, D., and Montet, C. (1983). Fixed-price equilibria in a two-country model of trade: Existence and comparative statics. *European Economic Review* **22**, 305–330.

Lee, L.-F. (1984). Regime classification in the disequilibrium market models. *Economics Letters* **14**, 187-193.

Leijonhufvud, A. (1968). *On Keynesian Economics and the Economics of Keynes.* Oxford Univ. Press, London and New York.

Leijonhufvud, A. (1973). Effective demand failures. *Swedish Journal of Economics* **75**, 27-58.

Lerner, A. P. (1944). *The Economics of Control.* Macmillan, New York.

Löfgren, K.-G. (1979). The corridor and local stability of the effective excess demand hypothesis: A result. *Scandinavian Journal of Economics* **81**, 30-47.

Lorie, H. R., and Sheen, J. R. (1982). Supply shocks in a two-country world with wage and price rigidities. *Economic Journal* **92**, 849-867.

Mackinnon, J. G., and Olewiler, N. D. (1980). Disequilibrium estimation of the demand for copper. *The Bell Journal of Economics* **11**, 197-211.

Maddala, G. S. (1983a). Methods of estimation for models of markets with bounded price variation. *International Economic Review* **24**, 361-378.

Maddala, G. S. (1983b). *Limited-Dependent and Qualitative Variables in Econometrics.* Cambridge Univ. Press, London and New York.

Maddala, G. S., and Nelson, F. D. (1974). Maximum likelihood methods for models of markets in disequilibrium. *Econometrica* **42**, 1013-1030.

Malgrange, P., and Villa, P. (1984). Comportement d'investissement avec coûts d'ajustement et contraintes quantitatives. *Annales de l'INSEE* **53**, 31-60.

Malinvaud, E. (1977). *The Theory of Unemployment Reconsidered.* Blackwell, Oxford.

Malinvaud, E. (1978). Nouveaux développements de la théorie macroéconomique du chômage. *Revue Économique* **29**, 9-25.

Malinvaud, E. (1980). *Profitability and Unemployment.* Cambridge Univ. Press, London and New York.

Malinvaud, E., and Younes, Y. (1977). Some new concepts for the microeconomic foundations of macroeconomics. In G. Harcourt (Ed.), *The Microeconomic Foundations of Macroeconomics.* Macmillan, London.

Marshall, A. (1890). *Principles of Economics,* London. (8th ed., 1920.)

Marshall, A. (1924). *Money, Credit and Commerce,* New York.

Meade, J. E. (1951). *The Balance of Payments.* Oxford Univ. Press, London.

Metzler, L. A. (1949). The theory of international trade. In H. Ellis (Ed.), *A Survey of Contemporary Economics.* Philadelphia, Pennsylvania.

Modigliani, F., and Padoa-Schioppa, T. (1978). The management of an open economy with "100% plus" wage indexation. Princeton Essays in International Finance, No. 130. Princeton, New Jersey.

Muellbauer, J., and Portes, R. (1978). Macroeconomic models with quantity rationing. *Economic Journal* **88**, 788-821.

Muellbauer, J., and Winter, D. (1980). Unemployment, employment and exports in British manufacturing: A non-clearing markets approach. *European Economic Review* **13**, 383-409.

Mundell, R. A. (1968). *International Economics.* Macmillan, New York.

Mundell, R. A. (1971). *Monetary Theory.* Goodyear, Pacific Palisades, California.

Neary, J. P. (1980). Nontraded goods and the balance of trade in a neo-Keynesian temporary equilibrium. *Quarterly Journal of Economics* **95**, 403-430.

Neary, J. P., and Roberts, K. W. S. (1980). The theory of household behavior under rationing. *European Economic Review* **13**, 25-42.

Neary, J. P., and Stiglitz, J. E. (1983). Towards a reconstruction of Keynesian economics: Expectations and constrained equilibria. *Quarterly Journal of Economics* **98**, Suppl., 199-228.

Negishi, T. (1961). Monopolistic competition and general equilibrium. *Review of Economic Studies* **28**, 196-201.

Negishi, T. (1972). *General Equilibrium Theory and International Trade.* North-Holland Publ., Amsterdam.

Negishi, T. (1977). Existence of an under employment equilibrium. In G. Schwödiauer (Ed.), *Equilibrium and Disequilibrium in Economic Theory.* Reidel Publ., Boston, Massachusetts.

Negishi, T. (1979). *Microeconomic Foundations of Keynesian Macroeconomics.* North-Holland Publ., Amsterdam.

Nishimizu, M., Quandt, R. E., and Rosen, H. S. (1982). The demand and supply of investment goods: Does the market clear? *Journal of Macroeconomics* **4**, 1-21.

Ostroy, J. (1973). The informational efficiency of monetary exchange. *American Economic Review* **63**, 597-610.

Ostroy, J., and Starr, R. (1974). Money and the decentralization of exchange. *Econometrica* **42**, 1093-1114.

Owen, R. F. (1985). A two country disequilibrium model. *Journal of International Economics* **18**, 339-355.

Patinkin, D. (1956). *Money, Interest and Prices.* Harper, New York. (2nd ed., 1965.)

Persson, T., and Svensson, L. E. O. (1983). Is optimism good in a Keynesian economy? *Economica* **50**, 291-300.

Phelps, E. S. (1967). Phillips curves, inflation expectations and optimal employment over time. *Economica* **34**, 254-281.

Phillips, A. W. (1958). The relation between unemployment and the rate of change of money wage rates in the United Kingdom, 1861-1957. *Economica* **25**, 283-299.

Picard, P. (1983). Inflation and growth in a disequilibrium macroeconomic model. *Journal of Economic Theory* **30**, 266-295.

Portes, R. (1981). Macroeconomic equilibrium and disequilibrium in centrally planned economies. *Economic Inquiry* **19**, 559-578.

Portes, R., and Winter, D. (1977). The supply of consumption goods in centrally planned economies. *Journal of Comparative Economics* **1**, 351-365.

Portes, R., and Winter, D. (1980). Disequilibrium estimates for consumption goods markets in centrally planned economies. *Review of Economic Studies* **47**, 137-159.

Portes, R., Quandt, R. E., Winter, D., and Yeo, S. (1984). Planning the consumption goods market: Preliminary estimates for Poland, 1955-1980. In P. Malgrange and P. A. Muet (Eds.), *Contemporary Macroeconomic Modelling.* Blackwell, Oxford.

Quandt, R. E. (1978). Tests of the equilibrium vs. disequilibrium hypothesis. *International Economic Review* **19**, 435-452.

Quandt, R. E. (1982). Econometric disequilibrium models. *Econometric Review* **1**, 1-63.

Quandt, R. E. (1983). Switching between equilibrium and disequilibrium. *Review of Economics and Statistics* **65**, 684-687.

Reagan, P. B. (1982). Inventory and price behavior. *Review of Economic Studies* **49**, 137-142.

Reagan, P. B., and Weitzman, M. L. (1982). Asymmetries in price and quantity adjustments by the competitive firm. *Journal of Economic Theory* **27**, 410-420.

Robinson, J. (1933). *The Economics of Imperfect Competition.* Macmillan, London.

Robinson, J. (1947). The foreign exchanges. In *Essays in the Theory of Employment.* Blackwell, Oxford.

Rose, H. (1967). On the non-linear theory of the employment cycle. *Review of Economic Studies* **34**, 153-173.

Rose, H. (1969). Real and monetary factors in the business cycle. *Journal of Money, Credit and Banking* **1**, 138-152.

Rosen, H. S., and Quandt, R. E. (1978). Estimation of a disequilibrium aggregate labor market. *Review of Economics and Statistics* **40**, 371-379.

Samueleson, P. A. (1939). Interaction between the Multiplier Analysis and the Principle of Acceleration. *Review of Economic Statistics* **21**, 75-78.

Samuelson, P. A. (1947). *Foundations of Economic Analysis.* Harvard Univ. Press, Cambridge, Massachusetts.

Samuelson, P. A. (1958). An exact consumption loan model of interest with or without the social contrivance of money. *Journal of Political Economy* **66**, 467–482.

Schinasi, G. (1982). Fluctuations in a dynamic intermediate-run IS-LM model: Applications of the Poincaré-Bendixon theorem. *Journal of Economic Theory* **28**, 369–375.

Schittko, U. K., and Eckwert, B. (1983). A two-country temporary equilibrium model with quantity rationing. *Jahrbuecher für Nationalökonomie und Statistik* **198**, 97–121.

Schmid, M. (1982). Devaluation: Keynesian trade models and the monetary approach: The role of nominal and real wage rigidity. *European Economic Review* **17**, 27–50.

Schulz, N. (1983). On the global uniqueness of fixprice equilibria. *Econometrica* **51**, 47–68.

Siebrand, J. C. (1979). *Towards Operational Disequilibrium Macro Models.* Nijhoff, The Hague.

Silvestre, J. (1980a). Continua of Hahn-unsatisfactory equilibria. *Economic Letters* **5**, 201–208.

Silvestre, J. (1980b). Fixprice analysis of exchange economies. *Journal of Economic Theory* **26**, 28–58.

Silvestre, J. (1983). Fixprice analysis in productive economies. *Journal of Economic Theory* **30**, 401–409.

Simonovits, A. (1982). Buffer stocks and naïve expectations in a non-Walrasian dynamic macromodel: Stability, cyclicity and chaos. *The Scandinavian Journal of Economics* **84**, 571–581.

Sneessens, H. R. (1981a). *Theory and Estimation of Macroeconomic Rationing Models.* Springer-Verlag, Berlin and New York.

Sneessens, H. R. (1981b). Rationing macroeconomics, a graphical exposition. Working Paper, CORE, Louvain.

Sneessens, H. (1983). A macroeconomic rationing model of the Belgian economy. *European Economic Review* **20**, 193–215.

Snower, D. J. (1983). Imperfect competition, underemployment and crowding-out. *Oxford Economic Papers* **35**, 569–594.

Solow, R. M., and Stiglitz, J. (1968). Output, employment and wages in the short run. *Quarterly Journal of Economics* **82**, 537–560.

Steigum, E. (1980). Keynesian and classical unemployment in an open economy. *Scandinavian Journal of Economics* **82**, 147–166.

Steigum, E. (1983). Capital shortage and classical unemployment. *International Economic Review* **24**, 461–474.

Stiglitz, J. E., and Weiss, A. (1981). Credit rationing in markets with imperfect information, Part I. *American Economic Review* **71**, 393–410.

Svensson, L. E. O. (1980). Effective demand and stochastic rationing. *Review of Economic Studies* **47**, 339–355.

Svensson, L. G., and Weibull, J. W. (1984). Stability and efficiency from a neo-Keynesian viewpoint. *Journal of Economic Dynamics and Control* **7**, 349–362.

Sweezy, P. M. (1939). Demand under conditions of oligopoly. *Journal of Political Economy* **47**, 568–573.

Tobin, J. (1952). A survey of the theory of rationing. *Econometrica* **20**, 521–553.

Tobin, J. (1980). *Asset Accumulation and Economic Activity.* Blackwell, Oxford.

Tobin, J., and Houthakker, H. S. (1950). The effects of rationing on demand elasticities. *Review of Economic Studies* **18**, 140–153.

Triffin, R. (1940). *Monopolistic Competition and General Equilibrium Theory.* Harvard Univ. Press, Cambridge, Massachusetts.

Tsiang, S. C. (1961). The role of money in trade-balance stability: Synthesis of the elasticity and absorption approaches. *American Economic Review* **51**, 912–936.

Turnovsky, S. J., and Pitchford, J. (1978). Expectations and income claims in wage price determination; an aspect of the inflationary process. In A. R. Bergström, A. J. L. Catt, M. H. Peston, and B. D. J. Silverstone (Eds.), *Stability and Inflation*. Wiley, New York.

Van Wijnbergen, S. (1984). Inflation, employment, and the Dutch disease in oil-exporting countries: A short-run disequilibrium analysis. *Quarterly Journal of Economics* **99**, 233-250.

Veendorp, E. C. H. (1970). General equilibrium theory for a barter economy. *Western Economic Journal* **8**, 1-23.

Veendorp, E. C. H. (1975). Stable spillovers among substitutes. *Review of Economic Studies* **42**, 445-456.

Vilares, M. J. (1981). Macroeconomic model with structural change and disequilibrium. Working Paper, INSEE, Paris and Univ. of Porto.

Vilares, M. J. (1982). A macroeconometric model with structural change and disequilibrium: A study of the economic consequences of the Portuguese revolution of 1974. Working Paper, INSEE, Paris.

Walras, L. (1974). *Eléments d'économie politique pure*. Corbaz, Lausanne. (Definitive edition translated by W. Jaffé, *Elements of Pure Economics*. Allen & Unwin, London, 1954.)

Weddepohl, C. (1982). Equilibria with rationing in an economy with increasing returns. *Journal of Economic Theory* **26**, 143-163.

Weddepohl, C. (1983). Fixed price equilibria in a multifirm model. *Journal of Economic Theory* **29**, 95-108.

Weibull, J. W. (1983). A dynamic model of trade frictions and disequilibrium in the housing market. *Scandinavian Journal of Economics* **85**, 373-392.

Younes, Y. (1970). Sur les notions d'équilibre et de déséquilibre utilisées dans les modèles décrivant l'évolution d'une économie capitaliste. Working Paper, CEPREMAP, Paris.

Younes, Y. (1975). On the role of money in the process of exchange and the existence of a non-Walrasian equilibrium. *Review of Economic Studies* **42**, 489-501.

Younes, Y. (1978). Dévaluation et équilibre avec rationnement. *Economie Appliquée* **31**, 85-112.

Zagame, P. (1977). L'investissement en déséquilibre. In C. de Boissieu, A. Parguez, and P. Zagamé (Eds.), *Economie du déséquilibre*. Economica, Paris.

Index

A

Absorption approach, 136
Asymmetric multipliers, 87
Asymmetric price flexibility, 78

B

Balance of payments, 125, 132, 235
  approaches, 136, 137
Barter economy, 14

C

Classical policies, 61, 79
Classical unemployment, 68, 71
Consumption function, 23
  and expectations, 28, 190, 201
Cost inflation, 145, 152
Cycle, 173, 183

D

Demand inflation, 145, 160
Devaluation, effects, 137, 235

E

Effective demand, 21, 42
  deterministic case, 22, 42
  and manipulation, 226
  and uncertainty, 230

Effective demand function, 44, 219
Efficiency of rationing schemes, 18, 39
Elasticities approach, 137
Elasticities, formula with four, 140
Employment function, 23
Existence of non-Walrasian equilibria, 219
Expectations
  and consumption function, 28, 190, 201
  and dynamics, 209
  effects, 192
  and existence of K-equilibrium, 222
  and indirect utility functions, 27, 50
  and non-Walrasian equilibria, 48
  and perfect foresight, 199, 212
  role, 27, 189

F

Fixprice equilibrium, 45
Frictionless markets, 18, 39

I

Indexation, 91, 118
Indirect utility functions and expectations, 27, 50
Inefficiency and expectations, 214
Inefficiency of non-Walrasian allocations, 48, 75
Inflation, demand and cost, 145
Inflation tax, 152

K

K-equilibria, 35
  with bounded prices, 52
  and expectations, 48
  with fixed prices, 45
  with monopolistic competition, 53
Keynesian policies, 61, 79
Keynesian unemployment, 68

M

Manipulation
  and absence of equilibrium, 227
  and effective demand, 226
  of rationing schemes, 19, 39, 225
Marshall-Lerner conditions, 138
Monetary approach, 136
Monetary economy, 14, 15, 36

N

Non-Walrasian economics, 2
Non-Walrasian equilibria, *see also* K-
  equilibria, 25, 35

P

Perceived constraints, 21, 41
Perceived demand and supply curves, 30,
  54
Perfect foresight
  and dynamics, 212
  and economic policies, 203
  and non-Walrasian equilibria, 199

P

Phillips curves, 163
Price formation, 29, 55
Proportional rationing, 17, 228

Q

Quantity signals, 21, 37, 39
Queueing system, 17, 20

R

Rationing schemes, 16, 37
Real wage rigidity and economic policies,
  99, 118
Repressed inflation, 68, 72

S

Short-side rule, 13, 39
Spillover effects, 21

T

Transactions, 15

V

Voluntary exchange, 17, 38

W

Walrasian economics, 9
Walrasian equilibrium, 10, 37